BREAKING

THROUGH

THE LINE

BREAKING THROUGH THE LINE

Bobby Marshall,

The N.F.L.'s First

African American Player

Terry McConnell

NODIN PRESS

1 2 3 4 5 6 7 8 9

Library of Congress Control Number: 2021945841

ISBN: 978-1-947237-32-2

Photo Credits
Provided by family members: 6, 83, 165, 166
Taken by the author: 5, 12, 88, 160, 161, 163, 164, 165, 171
Hennepin History Museum: 7, 11, 17
Photos in the public domain;: 15, 16, 24, 28, 29, 31, 32, 41, 49, 80, 96, 100, 105, 108, 109, 119, 122, 124, 131, 137, 140, 141, 144, 145, 146, 154, 156
Chicago Historical Society (*Chicago Daily News*): 55, 57
Minnesota Historical Society: 45, 74, 114, 118
Roger and Kathleen Ebert: 67
Brian Larson: 117

Published by
Nodin Press
5114 Cedar Lake Road
Minneapolis, MN, 55416
www.nodinpress.com

*This book is dedicated to my wife,
Carol Pedigree McConnell, who has
totally supported my writing efforts.*

Contents

Foreword

In *Breaking Through the Line* Terry McConnell tells the story of Bobby Marshall, one of the most extraordinary athletes in the history of Minnesota sports. We at the University of Minnesota are proud of his achievements at our institution, where he starred in football, baseball, and track, and also excelled on the ice in a time before the Gophers had a varsity hockey team. We're also proud that Bobby demonstrated academic excellence at the U, earning a law degree in four years, and that in later life he exhibited the qualities we hope to inspire in all our athletes—a strong work ethic, leadership ability, solid moral values, dedication to the community, and love for their fellow humans.

And just as Ohio State has Jesse Owens, and U.C.L.A. has Jackie Robinson, Bobby Marshall also broke barriers, becoming the first African American All American from the Big Ten in football, the first African American to coach in the Big Ten, and the first to play in the nascent NFL.

Breaking Through the Line is rife with stories of Bobby's work ethic—how many athletes can still play football at a high level at the age of 54?—and his leadership abilities. For example, after he graduated from the U of MN in 1907, the Minneapolis Deans pro football team made him coach, captain, and quarterback of the team, and in the same year head Gophers football coach Dr. Henry Williams made him assistant football coach.

The book is rich in tales of the early years of professional sports, but it also devotes ample space to Marshall's contributions to civic life, as a lawyer, a director for the Minnesota State Grain Commission, a deacon of St. Peter's African Methodist Episcopal Church in Minneapolis, and mentoring youth at the Phyliss

Wheatley House, where he coached the youngsters in sports and made inspiring speeches about how to live a successful life.

Compassion and love for his fellow humans radiated from Bobby. He felt that racism was caused by ignorance, and he endeavored to shed enlightenment by showing respect to everyone.

The qualities Bobby Marshall exhibited throughout his life are the qualities we strive to develop in all our student-athletes. I hope many people read about Bobby Marshall, whose little-known but extraordinary story deserves a wide audience.

– Mark Coyle,
Athletic Director, University of Minnesota

BREAKING THROUGH THE LINE

1

The Early Years

The story goes that at the beginning of the 1900 football season a high school team from Minneapolis beat a Big 10 varsity team in a scrimmage. How could that happen? The answer has a lot to do with an African American teenager named Robert Wells "Bobby" Marshall.

Marshall was born on March 12, 1880, in Milwaukee, Wisconsin, at a time when the city had no building taller than four stories and most of the streets were made of dirt. The sound of the hooves of horses set a rhythm for the day and the smell of horse manure permeated the air.[1]

Marshall's father, Richard Marshall, was the son of a slave from Richmond, Virginia. The family got its name from John Marshall, the first chief justice of the United States Supreme Court, who, like Bobby's ancestors, lived much of his life in Richmond. Bobby's mother, Symanthia, was the daughter of Ezekiel and Catherine Gillespie. Ezekiel was a former slave, railway porter, and civil rights leader who helped slaves reach freedom in the Underground Railroad in the 1850s. Working with a Republican leader named Sherman Booth, he attempted to vote in Wisconsin in 1865 and was denied that right. This denial became a court case that went all the way to the Wisconsin Supreme Court. In 1866 the court ruled that Ezekiel had the right to vote in Wisconsin.[2]

Catherine was a light-skinned African American woman

with German-Jewish background who participated in the establishment of the first African Methodist Episcopal (A.M.E.) Church in Wisconsin, where the Gillespie family had assumed a leadership role in the African American community.[3]

Catherine's sister, Jessie Gillespie Herndon, was the second wife of Alonzo Herndon, who founded the highly successful Atlanta Life Insurance Company.

In 1882 Bobby moved with his parents to Minneapolis, which at the time was no more well-developed than Milwaukee. As Bobby walked down the streets with his mother past three- and four-story apartment buildings like the one where his family now lived, he could smell the horse manure wafting up in the air, hear the shouts of fruit vendors proclaiming, "Fresh apples, two for a nickel," and dodge the wheels of the carriages that splattered mud on passersby as they hurried downtown. Passersby may have noticed that his skin was darker than his mother's, but Symanthia Marshall probably didn't mind. Her faith was in God, not in what other people thought.

The wide and fast-flowing Mississippi River cut right through this city, powering the huge mills that ground wheat arriving from farms to the west and south into flour. Minneapolis had only recently surpassed St. Louis as the nation's leading exporter of grain, but it would retain its preeminent position for decades. Though there was no way he could imagine it at the time, Marshall would spend much of his adult life in Minneapolis working as a state grain inspector.[4]

Bobby's religious education was shaped by the African Methodist Episcopal Church his family attended. Bobby's grandson Bill Marshall explains, "Bobby's mother went to the A.M.E. church but she never actually converted to Christianity. She would fall into what would be called Jews for Jesus today. That kind of mind frame. And Jesus was a Jew and she had no problem going to a Christian church. She (Symanthia) looked white and was Jewish. She was well-accepted in her A.M.E church."[5]

In 1885, when Bobby was five years old, there were 673

What Bobby's boyhood neighborhood looks like today.

African Americans living in Minneapolis. Ten years later there were twice that number.[6]

During his childhood Bobby's best friend was a Jewish boy named Sigmund "Sig" Harris who lived in the neighborhood. Their friendship would last a lifetime. Sig's father, Marks Harris, was a partner in the Harris Brothers junk dealership and also a partner in the Harris Machinery Company.[7] Bobby lived between the 1600 and 1700 block of Stevens Avenue South near downtown Minneapolis. The entire block was later demolished to make way for Interstate 94, but there are many buildings similar to the one where the Marshall lived—three- and four-story brick walk-ups— in the Stevens Square neighborhood immediately to the south. At the time the neighborhood was predominantly Jewish, with a few African American and white Christian families, a neighborhood of upper middle-class and middle-class merchants and trades people.[8] Bobby and Sig learned to play baseball at Peavey Park, a sandlot at the nearby intersection of Franklin and Park Avenues. Bobby and Sig got baseball and football teams started at their school, Madison Grade School, and organized boxing tournaments at an old barn on 16th Street.[9]

Bobby's father, Richard, owned his own profitable business repairing boilers for the many apartment buildings in south Minneapolis,[10] at a time when the jobs available to most African American men were limited to work in hotels, railroads, or restaurants as cooks, waiters, custodians, or porters, and African American women worked mainly as domestic servants. Though a smattering of jobs were available in merchants' businesses, there was not a lot of wealth in the Minnesota African American community at the time. For example, about three quarters of African American residents of St. Paul rented the place where they lived.[11] Bobby's family was better off financially than most African American residents of Minnesota.[12]

Bobby as a young adult

Sig and Bobby might have been 15 when they joined the football team at Minneapolis Central High, nicknamed the Pioneers. The school colors were red and blue. Sig played quarterback and Bobby played end. By that time Bobby stood six feet, one inch tall and weighed 180 pounds; Sig was six inches shorter. With his athletic build, milk chocolate skin, and brown eyes, Bobby was a strikingly handsome young man. There was no passing in the game then; each play from scrimmage was either a run or a kick. The rules of football in those days allowed Bobby to run with the ball from scrimmage at the end position. His long arms enabled him to play defense effectively.[13]

Those same long arms made Bobby a great first baseman on the Central High baseball field, and his lanky frame served him well of the school's cycling team.[14]

By all accounts, Bobby adjusted well to being the only African American on his high school teams, but the challenges were probably formidable. One historian observes that in the early

The Central High baseball team; Bobby is at far left.

1900s 'a Negro could never be certain of what awaited him when he entered a store, restaurant, saloon, or hotel outside the black belt.'"[15] an area of Chicago where African American people lived.

The story of Duke Slater can be taken as a case in point. Slater

Bobby (upper left) on the Central High cycling team

was the only African American player on the high school football team in Clinton, Iowa. It was 1914, and after Clinton upset a very strong team from West Aurora, Illinois, the West Aurora fans became unruly. Slater's teammate, Burt Ingwersen, describes the situation. "After the game, the crowd headed for Duke Slater. They were going to be rough. I guess they weren't accustomed to seeing a great Negro athlete." Slater's biographer, Neal Rozendaal, goes on to tell what happened next. "Slater found himself in a very dangerous situation, backed up against a large tree. However, Duke had a way of diffusing such confrontations with incredible charm. He got down in a lineman's stance and invited his hecklers to come at him one at a time. Duke then playfully repelled and tackled each one to the delight of the spectators."[16]

This incident is just one of many faced by talented African American athletes in an era when racist attitudes were blatant and uninhibited. The pioneer African American athletes not only had to be unusually good just to make the team, they also had to have a great understanding of human nature, to defuse incidents that could turn violent in a heartbeat. Steven R. Hoffbeck in *Swinging for the Fences: Black Baseball in Minnesota* calls the ability to defuse racially charged situations "black wisdom."[17] To be able to flourish as an African American in the white world of Minneapolis, Minnesota, Marshall learned "black wisdom" at an early age.

While young Bobby Marshall was busy playing sandlot football and baseball, Frank Crawford was coaching football at the University of Nebraska. In 1891, an African American player, George Flippin, joined the team. Flippin, a hard charging running back at 6'2" and 200 lbs., played under Crawford from 1891 to 1894. In 1892, he beat the University of Illinois with a twenty-five-yard run. The University of Missouri refused to play Nebraska that year because Flippin, an African American player, was on the team. This resulted in a 1-0 forfeit victory for Nebraska. In his senior year the players on the Nebraska team voted Flippin team captain, but Crawford said the team vote was null and void. He told the team that Flippin was not intelligent enough to be captain. Flippin later became a medical doctor and surgeon in Stromburg, Nebraska, where he became famous for making house calls no matter the distance or the family's ability to pay.[18]

Similar stories could be told from throughout the Midwest of athletes, coaches, and fans hostile to the participation of African American participation in organized sports. Only a generation or two previous to Marshall's career, U.S. Supreme Court Justice Roger B. Tawney gave a ruling in the *Dred Scott vs. Sanford* case that stated that African Americans were "so far inferior [to whites] that they had no rights which a white man was bound to respect." In this era when a team had African American players, it was common for them to receive racial epitaphs and violent threats from the fans. One International League umpire blatantly stated that he would always rule against a team that included African Americans. Before a game with Newark in 1887 Cap Anson, one of the top players of the day, called out to the Newark team regarding George Stovey, saying "Get that n____ off the field." Perhaps he was afraid to face Stovey at the plate. Without Stovey pitching, Anson got four hits in four at bats and on the same day the International League owners agreed to not sign African American players. Soon the National League and the American Association did the same. (The American League had not been formed yet.) The owners agreed with Anson, and by the 1890s it was a gentleman's agreement among them that kept African Americans out of baseball until 1947.[19]

And so, as of 1887 African American players were banned from major league baseball. However, in those days, minor league teams were not connected to major league teams as they are today. There was no farm system then, and many towns had their own teams. African American players sometimes formed their own teams, and sometimes a white team would sign an African American player because he was the best player available. Such was the case with Walter Ball, who played with the St. Cloud, Minnesota, team. In 1902, he pitched 17 wins against 7 defeats, struck out 217 batters in 207 innings and batted .307, playing in all but two games. It was common then for players to play another field position when they were not pitching. The next year, 1903, Ball was released from the team because some of the white players objected to his presence. Ball then accepted a contract with the Chicago Union Giants, an all-African American team, and continued to play with all-African American teams after that.[20]

It was during this era that Marshall and his friend Sig Harris were making names for themselves at Minneapolis Central High School. (Other famous graduates of this school were Prince in 1976 and CBS commentator Eric Sevareid in 1930.) At the time, Central High's student body was upper middle class and almost entirely white. Only about forty of one thousand students were African American.[21]

Many African Americans, then as now, lived on Minneapolis's North Side, where people tended to have less money. The success of Bobby's father business made it possible for the family to live on the South Side, in the Central High School district. Years later, Marshall's wife, Irene, described Bobby's father as a "real go getter" who was always looking for new business.[22]

In 1899 and again in 1900 Marshall and Harris led Central to the state football championship. Harris graduated in 1900 and went on to play football at the University of Minnesota, while Marshal led his team to a third championship in 1901.[23]

Bobby also played baseball, tennis, and ice hockey, in high school. Track, basketball, wrestling, boxing and bicycling were sports he played to a lesser extent. Bobby played first base on the Central High baseball team during his sophomore, junior, and senior years, batting and throwing right handed. In his junior and senior years, the team won the Twin Cities baseball championship. His team also won two state baseball championships. In a Central High yearbook a friend describes him as "some pumpkins as a bike racer."[24] Of all the sports he played in high school, Bobby liked ice hockey the most.[25]

In 1900, Bobby's mother, Symanthia, died at the age of 49. She had worked hard as a leader in the St. Peter's A.M.E.

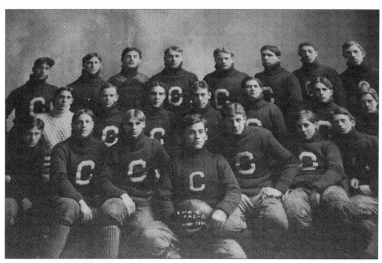

The Central High football team. Bobby Marshall is in the back row, second from the right.

Church, helping improve the situation for African Americans in Minneapolis. She is described in her obituary as "one of the leading race women in the city, taking part in every motion to help the interests of the people."[26] Losing one's mother as a teenager would be a tough blow for just about anybody. Bobby knew, based on the strong religious training his parents had given him, that Symanthia was now in a better place. Richard watched over the children alone after that, raising them to be self-sufficient. Bobby worked in his father's boiler repair business to help support the family that included his sisters Sarah and Alice, and his brother Lewis. For the rest of his high school career Bobby's life consisted of sports, school, and work.[27]

At the beginning of the 1900 season, Central High faced the University of Minnesota varsity football team. The Golden Gophers considerably outweighed the Central High boys. As the game went on, Bobby and his teammates forgot about the Gophers' size and held them to a 0-0 tie.

Bobby must have felt proud to hold a Big 10 varsity team to a tie. But was it really a tie? That score of that game was later disputed by Walter H. Wheeler, an engineer who had played left end on the same Central High School team as Bobby. In 1967, *Minneapolis Star* reporter Abe Altrowitz was interviewing Wheeler in his office and noticed a photograph of that game on Wheeler's wall. There was a football in the foreground of the photo with 0 - 0 painted on it. Wheeler remarked that the score was actually 6 - 0 in favor of Central High. "The 0-0 was painted on," Wheeler said, "because somebody didn't think it appropriate to tell the world that 'a University of Minnesota team had been beaten by mere high schoolers.'"[28]

That game was played on the University of Minnesota field with 700 spectators looking on, most of them Central High rooters. Sig Harris, playing quarterback for Central as usual, made some excellent runs from scrimmage that day. The Central offensive line averaged 160 pounds compared to the University of Minnesota line that averaged 180 pounds. But according to the account in the *Minneapolis Tribune*, the college players were out of sync. "It seemed impossible that [the University of Minnesota] should not defeat the high school team, but ... [Central] outplayed them at nearly every point." The article goes on to say, "There was a slight disposition on the part of the [U of MN] varsity boys to play dirty ball in this [second half] but for the most part they were kept very quiet."[29] The *Minnesota Alumni Weekly*, said the following. "The *Minnesota Daily* [the U of MN newspaper)

All that's left of the Central High's football field, Markley Field, is the ticket booth.

termed this an "exasperating" game in which the varsity was held to a tie. According to the same authority, Minnesota was outplayed in every field of the game, and it was only by the superior weight that she was not defeated. Minnesota was on the defensive all the time and its playing, at times, was ludicrous."[30]

At the end of the 1900 season Central won a championship called the Championship of the West, defeating a team from Elgin, Illinois, 39-0. It was a cold day on a Minnesota home field before a large crowd. Marshall's confident personality shines through in the account of the game in the *Minneapolis Tribune*. "With Marshall smiling in an uplifting fashion the last touchdown was so easy it hardly seemed right to take it."[31] With Bobby playing, Central won its third straight state championship. In his four years at Central High, the football teams Bobby played on only lost one football game. Bobby suited up at the end position.[32]

In 1901 Bobby graduated from Minneapolis Central High School.[33] According to his grandson Bill Marshall, Minneapolis has always had an excellent and racially integrated public-school system, and the years Bobby spent there prepared him well for his college education at the University of Minnesota.[34]

How did University of Minnesota head football coach Henry "Doc" Williams feel about this talented incoming freshman? Williams knew that a lot of Minnesota fans would not like to see an African American on the team. But his team came up against some of the best teams in college football on a yearly basis—teams like the University of Michigan and the University of Chicago—and he also knew these same fans would hate losing to them. To win the Western Conference (Big Ten) championship, he needed to field the best team possible. He certainly remembered how well the team from Minneapolis Central High School, led by Marshall, played against the Minnesota varsity. It turned out that this kid from Central was also a good student: college material.

2

Marshall's First Year at the University of Minnesota

Marshall graduated from high school in 1901. In the fall of 1903, he followed his best friend, Sig Harris, to the University of Minnesota to play football. They were very welcome on the playing field—Harris made All American in 1903 and 1904, and Marshall in 1905 and 1906. Would their religion or skin color affect their on-campus living arrangements?

During the interim before college Bobby played hockey for the Central High ice hockey team, a team described as "plucky" by the *Minneapolis Journal*. On February 22, 1902, Central lost 6-1 with Bobby scoring the only goal.[1] It didn't seem to matter that Bobby had already graduated.

Later that year another African American, Billy Williams, distinguished himself on the playing field. The Minneapolis Millers were at Lexington Park in St. Paul playing a semi-pro team called the Prairie Leaguers that featured Williams at first base. Ned Hanlon, a scout for the Brooklyn Superbas of the National League, was in the stands that day, looking for baseball talent. After the game, he offered, Williams, a slugger and an excellent all-around player, a contract, probably saying something like, "you're a light-skinned guy so we'll pass you off as an American Indian, so sign here, kid." Williams refused, unwilling to go along with the charade. He went on to play twenty-two years with various Minnesota pro baseball teams and served as an important aide to fourteen Minnesota governors.[2] For Williams, life was about integrity, not lying to get ahead.

Marshall enrolled at the University of Minnesota in the fall of 1903, the same year that African American Walter Ball was kicked off the Saint Cloud, Minnesota, baseball team for having the wrong skin color. Bobby made the football team, perhaps aided by a recommendation to Gopher coach Dr. Henry Williams from his friend Sig Harris.

Bobby Marshall

It was a good thing Bobby's family lived in Minneapolis because African Americans weren't allowed to live in University of Minnesota campus dormitories then. At first Marshall lived at home, working for his father's business, which consisted not only of fixing boilers for apartment buildings in south Minneapolis but also plumbing, electrical work, carpentry, and general maintenance in those buildings. Bobby learned all of his father's skills, which enabled him to work his way through college, while also helping to support his family.[3]

In 1903 there was no such thing as a full scholarship for a student athlete in college. Sometimes colleges would offer gifts, part-time jobs, and room and board to entice good players. Alumni and fraternities would offer players "incentives" to choose a given school or improve performance. The NCAA (formed in 1906) wouldn't introduce scholarships until 1952.[4] Bobby took a second job and as a waiter at the Minneapolis Club from 1903 to 1906.[5]

In his junior year Bobby got a room in the Bohemian Flats section of Minneapolis on the west bank of the Mississippi River. (The area is now park land due to the fact that the Mississippi floods too often.) Sig Harris couldn't get campus housing either, because he was Jewish.[6] It was a common problem. Duke Slater, an African American and All-American football star for the University of Iowa Hawkeyes a few years after Bobby, discovered the dorms on the Iowa campus were closed to him as well,[7] and Fritz Pollard, an African American and All American football star, couldn't find a teammate willing to room with him at Brown University in 1915-16.[8]

When Bobby joined the University of Minnesota Golden Gophers football team, he became a part of the most watched sport in the state. There were no NFL, MLB, NHL or NBA franchises in Minnesota then.[9] Bobby's coach, Dr. Henry Williams, in his fourth year coaching the team,

Dr. Henry Williams

was taking a risk having Bobby on his team. Bobby was the first African American football player for the University of Minnesota. And yet, there was a precedent for Williams' decision. In 1890 George Jewett of the University of Michigan (later of Northwestern University) and Preston Eagleson of Indiana University were the first African Americans to play Big Ten football. Fred Patterson of Ohio State followed them in 1891. Jewett was Michigan's leading scorer, rusher, and kicker and the first African American to win a football letter from Michigan.[10] In 1905 Bobby Marshall was the first African American from the Big Ten to make the All-American football team. Marshall was the second African American to win All-American college football honors. The first was William Henry Lewis who played for Harvard University in the early 1890s.[11]

How did Marshall fit in with the largely white Protestant

University of Minnesota football team, Bobby on far left.

culture of the University of Minnesota? Bobby's grandson, Bill Marshall, says, "Bobby was a Christian but he was never ashamed that he was Jewish too. (In Jewish law, if your mother is Jewish, so are you.) When he went to the University most of his friends were Jewish too. He was well accepted because his Jewish friends knew his mother was Jewish."[12]

Another reason Bobby fit in so well at the University of Minnesota was his experience growing up in an integrated neighborhood. Here was a truly multicultural team, with Bobby, an African American at one end, Sig Harris, a Jew, at quarterback, and Ed Rogers, an American Indian, at the other end and team captain.[13]

Training camp for the 1903 season was held near Waconia, Minnesota, thirty miles west of Minneapolis. The team trained for three hours in the morning and three more in the afternoon. "That was some football camp," Marshall told the *Minneapolis Tribune* in 1939. "We had a player named Mumey Weitz, who had quite an appetite. He ate 17 eggs one day and soon came to Doc Williams (the coach) complaining that he was sick. Doc prescribed the egg shells, finely ground, as medicine. Weitz said later that eating the shells made the eggs less restless."[14]

The Gophers football team had a 14-0-1 season in 1903 and was co-champion of the Western Conference (now the Big

Ten) with the University of Michigan. The Gophers repeated as co-Big Ten Champs in 1904 with a 13-0 record. They lost the Big 10 Championship in 1905 with a 10-1 record, losing only to Wisconsin. The Gophers were co-champs again in 1906 with a 4-1 record.[15] Due to concerns regarding the safety of football, the University of Minnesota only played five games in 1906.

Despite his star status, Bobby's presence did not immediately pave the way for other African Americans to join the team. It was not until 1931 that a second African American, Ellsworth Harpole, played and lettered for the Gophers.[16]

The game of college football was quite different in 1903. John Kryk of the *Toronto Sun* writes, "Pre-1906 football in America remains, in all likelihood, the most violent form of sport conceived by man since the Roman Empire. Slugfests, bloodbaths, melees—these were the terms used by witnesses, participants and historians alike to describe the various incarnations of football, from its inception in America in 1869 until its most wanton forms of violence were finally legislated out starting in 1906."[17] Prior to 1906, the forward pass was not allowed and the field was 110 yards long. After a touchdown, the team that was scored upon could elect to kick off or receive. To make a first down the offense had to advance the ball five yards in three downs. The kick-off happened at the 55-yard line in the middle of the field. To make a touchdown it was better to score near the goal post because if the score came near the sideline, the extra point had to be made at a difficult angle from that point. If the angle to kick the extra point was too difficult, a team could use a play called a punt-out, during which an offensive player would kick the ball to a point beyond the 15-yard line where another player would catch it and then drop kick the ball at a better angle for the extra point.[18]

The Michigan game on October 31, 1903, gave Bobby his first chance to be a starter. He has said that being a part of the starting Golden Gophers lineup that day was the number one thrill of his career as an athlete.[19] The Michigan team, coached by Fielding Yost, had won 29 straight games coming into the Minnesota game.[20] They had scored 600 points in 600 minutes of football, thus earning the nickname, "the point-a-minute team."[21]

Marshall later told *Minneapolis Tribune*, "The day before the game, Usher Burdick, (who later became a U.S. Senator from North Dakota) who started at end, had a knee injury and could not play. The night before the Michigan game I went to practice. After practice I joined the crowd at the pepfest, which was being held on the parade ground in front of the Armory. I didn't have any idea I would get a chance to play the next day and I wasn't thinking about much except the excitement of the pepfest and the snake dance and the mob emotion of a pepfest crowd that hoped against hope the Gophers wouldn't be beaten too badly by the ferocious Wolverines. As I was watching the bonfire and listening to the crowd working into a Sky-U-Mah yell, one of the Minnesota substitutes came up to me and said that Dr. Williams wanted me to go home and get some sleep, because I would probably play the next day. The regular right end, Usher Burdick, had developed a charley horse while returning a kickoff in a practice scrimmage a few days before. Because of some home surgery, blood poison had developed, but Dr. Williams didn't find out about it until after Friday's practice. I went home all worked up with excitement. I could hardly sleep. Bobby Marshall, the freshman, might get a chance to play against the great Willie Heston the next day. I could hardly believe it…"[22]

A section from the book, *Football at Minnesota*, sets the stage for game day. "Minnesota's game with Michigan, played on Northrop field (in Minneapolis) October 31, 1903, is generally counted the greatest game of football ever played between two western (Big Ten) elevens. Certain it is that never before, nor since, has football enthusiasm reached such a height. The campus was crowded with a vast throng of students and alumni. By nine o'clock in the morning the trees and telegraph poles overlooking Northrup field began to fill, and by ten o'clock not a point of vantage from which the field could be seen was left unoccupied. In hundreds of cases the boys who took these positions took their lunches with them and camped out in the trees or on telegraph poles, from the early morning until after the game was over. By half past nine, those seeking general admission to the field began to line up, to get first choice of unreserved bleachers or standing room. These persons after waiting patiently for two hours and a half to purchase tickets, waited patiently six hours more before the game was over. The attendance reached fully 20,000."[23]

Marshall described some of the game day events. "I was the first player in the dressing room the next noon. Dr. Williams came in and read off the list of players who were to start the game. Amazed, I heard him read my name for right end. I still couldn't believe it and I thought he meant that I was to be ready to go in if Burdick couldn't hold up. I was still startled and in kind of a daze when I took my position for the opening kickoff. My job—Dr. Williams had said so—was to try to keep Willie Heston from going any place around my end of the line. Dr. Williams was awful worried, I found out afterward, with Heston in the game and a freshman at Minnesota's right end. Captain Ed Rogers was at the other end. I thought it would be wonderful if I could tackle Heston just once and made up my mind to stop him—once—if it was my first and last play of the game."[24]

William J. McNally was just a boy that day, one of the 20,000 people watching the game. In a 1943 article in the *Minneapolis Morning Tribune*, he described his thoughts as this huge event in Big Ten history was about to begin.

YOU WON'T BELIEVE ME, but powerful teams were wont to quit on the field before that fierce and fearful Michigan eleven. In 1902 Michigan had played Stanford at Pasadena in what now would be called a Rose Bowl game. When the score got to be 37 to 0 in favor of Michigan, Stanford insisted on quitting, saying it had used up all its men, and couldn't go on. The only way Yost (Michigan's coach) could get Stanford to go on was to tell it that it could rest for an hour—

right in the middle of the game! The mighty University of Buffalo team, which had beaten a famous Carlisle Indian eleven, and hadn't been scored on all season, met the Michigan team expecting to lick it. When the score reached 128 to 0 in favor of Michigan, the Buffalo team walked off the field, refusing to play any more...

I WAS A LITTLE FELLOW sitting out there in Northrop field and I positively quaked when I saw that fabulous Michigan team come running out upon the gridiron.

My surprise was great—when I noted that the players rather resembled human beings.

I had expected to see orangutans or giants or something. Minnesota was known to have a formidable team that year, but it wasn't seriously accorded a chance.[25]

Minnesota's assistant coach, Pudge Heffelfinger, called out to his players, 'Kill off Heston.' Willie Heston was Michigan's All-American running back who scored 72 touchdowns during his college career. The fans in the stands picked up on Heffelfinger's taunt, yelling 'Kill off Heston.'[26] Minnesota's defense was 'absolutely a stone wall,' allowing Michigan only two first downs in the first half."[27] The Gophers used a seven-man line at a time when most college teams used a nine-man line. This gave the Gopher defense four defensive backs who could tackle Heston for a short gain once Heston got past the line of scrimmage. When Heston played against teams with nine-man lines, once he got past the line of scrimmage he often ran for big gains.[28]

R. S. Westby of Minneapolis recalled, "In the fall of 1903 at the age of 17 years, I was attending a business college in Minneapolis. My older brother secured tickets for the Minnesota-Michigan game. We sat in section 2 of old Northrop field. My most vivid recollection of the game was the remarkable playing of Sig Harris, his great punting and tackling, when on several occasions he stopped the speedy Michigan halfback, Willie Heston, when it appeared he would go all the way. I also remember the other backfield men, Earl Current, Hunky Davis, and Jimmie Irsfield, and the finest and fastest pair of ends that ever played for Minnesota, namely Bobbie Marshall and Ed Rogers..."[29]

There were only 15 minutes left in the second half with the score was still tied, 0-0. Michigan moved the ball on a 65-yard touchdown drive. They also made the extra point, putting the score at Michigan 6, Minnesota 0. (Touchdowns were only 5 points then and extra points were worth 1 point.) With the score close and the clock winding down to the end of the game, what emotions was Bobby experiencing? Was the adrenaline shooting through his blood stream? Bobby made a great play, tackling Willie Heston four yards behind the line of scrimmage. Michigan then had to punt, giving Minnesota the ball back.[30]

Minnesota used an innovative offense devised by the coach, Dr. Henry L. Williams, called the Minnesota Shift. In this offense, only the center and the two ends would line up on the line of scrimmage. The guards and tackles lined up further back with the backfield even further back. Then the guards and tackles would move up to the line of scrimmage with the ends either staying in or heading toward the sidelines. The line would be unbalanced to one side or the other. Once all the players were in their correct positions the play would start, with the offense moving before the defense could get set.[31]

It was getting dark as the Gophers took over on offense. Using the Minnesota Shift, the offensive did some great blocking on lineman Schacht and Minnesota began to move the ball downfield. A few yards from the goal line, Marshall led the blocking on a short run by the fullback, Egil Boeckman, that resulted in a touchdown.[32]

At the June 3, 1953, M Club banquet attended by Bobby Marshall and Sig Harris, Jim Kremer spoke. Kremer had played in the 1903 Little Brown Jug game against Michigan, and he described how the game ended. "We'd just scored the touchdown in 'coffin corner' (where the goal line and the sideline intersect) but we had to have the point (extra point) or we'd be licked 6-5. In those days you could convert from the angle at which you scored or you could try what they called a puntout and then convert. We had a couple of huddles and no one volunteered to punt. I was only 17 and scared but finally when no one said anything I said, 'Gimmme the ball.' I tried to punt to Ed Rogers or Sig. Instead the ball went on a line, a few feet off the ground to Fred Burgan... He wrapped, it seemed like, four arms around it and though Michigan kicked him and slugged him, they couldn't make Freddie drop the ball. If they had we wouldn't have been allowed the place kick." As it happened, Burgan had the ball right in front of the goal posts; he sent the ball to Ed Rogers, who kicked the ball through the uprights easily. So the game ended in a tie.[33]

With only two minutes left in the game, 5,000 deliriously happy Minnesota fans stormed the field. By the time the fans were cleared, it was too dark to resume play so the game was called a tie. This tie meant Minnesota shared the Big Ten title with Michigan and Northwestern. The *Minneapolis Tribune* described Marshall's play as "invincible on defense." Coach Williams commented, "Marshall played a very strong defensive game," and Bobby himself remarked, "Never giving up for an instant during the hardest kind of work was what gave us the touchdown."[34]

After the game, the fans continued the wild celebration as they streamed out of the stadium into downtown Minneapolis, where they drank and sang throughout the night, never tiring of the Minnesota fight song, "Sky U Mah." (Sky is the Sioux word for victory and U Mah means University of Minnesota.)[35]

In "People's Column" in the *Minneapolis Star* from October 24, 1953, H. Leertelotte wrote: "The celebration downtown, after the game will never be forgotten by any of us survivors. Everyone went completely nuts. We headed for the loop. The only streetcar line—the Interurban—was too slow. We walked. We 'snake-danced.' We exulted. There were no strangers. All joined hands in groups of six-eight-ten. We mobbed Schieks—the National Dutch Room—the Nicollet. We visited the theaters. Everywhere we were a 'pain in the neck' to management, but it had to be done. Hadn't our boys just tied…the mighty Michigan?"[36]

The 1903 Golden Gophers football players became a football team of legend. In an interview in the *Minneapolis Tribune* in 1936 Marshall said, "I will always think that the Minnesota team of 1903 would stack up, man for man, with the greatest college teams that have come after it."[37]

When the game was over Oscar Munson, who worked as a custodian, noticed that Fielding Yost, the Michigan coach, had left a water jug on the field. Munson went up to Dr. Louis J. Cooke, of the Minnesota athletic staff, and said in a Swedish accent, "Look, Doc, Jost left his yug." Yost asked for the jug back and Cooke replied, "Well, if he wants it back let him come and win it." This is how the Little Brown Jug rivalry trophy between the University of Michigan and the University of Minnesota began. It's the oldest trophy game in the Football Bowl Subdivision (FBS), college football's top division. As of this writing Michigan leads in this series, 75-25-3.[38]

To get an idea of the popularity of Big 10 football in the early 20th century, keep this in mind. When the University of Minnesota hosted the University of Michigan in 1903 in the Little Brown Jug game, there were 20,000 people in the stands. In the same year the Boston Red Sox hosted the Pittsburg Pirates for the first game of the World Series before 16,242 fans.[39]

3

"This Reception is the Greatest Thing That Ever Happened"

For the 1904 football season Bobby was a starter, playing right end. In the rules of that time, an end could run with the ball from a scrimmage play. Ends couldn't catch passes yet; the forward pass did not become a legitimate football play until the 1906 season.

In a game against Carleton College on October 2, the Gophers won 65 to 0. Bobby ran for two touchdowns, one for 70 yards. He also kicked all the extra points and ran back kick-offs. O'Loughlin, a sportswriter for the *Minneapolis Journal* described Bobby's running with the football as "one of the most slippery men who ever donned football armor."[1]

The next week, *The Appeal* newspaper described Marshall's performance as follows. "Bobby Marshall was very near the whole thing in the football game with St. Thomas' College Wednesday. The way Bobby kicked off, made big gains around the end and kicked goals made Coach Williams smile. He proved himself to be the star of the U. of M. team."[2]

During a practice on October 11 Marshall furnished what the writer referred to as "the fun of the afternoon." On one play he bruised his nose—nothing broken, but quite a bit of blood for a minute. Then the nose began to swell. When Marshall returned to the field, he attempted to wear his nose guard only to find that it would no longer fit! An assistant applied hot and cold water and cold cloths on the sidelines to reduce the swelling and Marshall returned to the field—too late to get into the play.[3]

On October 15 the Gophers football team beat Ames 32-0 before six thousand enthusiastic fans at Northrop Field in Minneapolis. Marshall was involved in many running plays from the end position. "Suddenly Hunter [the Minnesota quarterback] changed his plan of attack, and after trying the Ames left end without a gain, gave Marshall the ball for a dash around the right. The speedy right end broke away from two tacklers who attempted to get him as he was clearing the line, and went off up the field with five of the Ames men almost within touching distance of him. One after another of these fellows dived at him and in fact succeeded in either getting a hold of his legs or falling in his path, but Marshall by some of the most brilliant dodging and twisting that has ever been seen at Northrup Field, managed to elude them all and finally got away down the field for thirty-five yards and a touchdown."[4]

One of the most unforgettable moments in the history of college football took place at Northrop Field two weeks later in Minnesota's game with the Nebraska Cornhuskers. Minnesota and Nebraska were huge rivals at the time and the fans began entering the stadium at noon even though the game would not start until 2:30 pm. With Marshall and Usher Burdick playing the end positions, the Gophers were a very tough team to beat. In the fourth quarter, it was getting dark on the field with the Gophers clinging to a 16-12 lead. After a fumble, Nebraska got the ball deep in Minnesota territory. The Cornhuskers began running plays quickly, marching down the field to the five-yard line. Usher Burdick crashed through the Cornhusker line to try to stop a run. The next play was quickly called but Burdick didn't have time to get back to his side of the line so he stooped down. Due to the darkness, no one noticed him in the Nebraska backfield. The ball was snapped and Burdick grabbed the Cornhuskers quarterback behind the line of scrimmage. The referee didn't blow the whistle to stop the action until Burdick had carried the quarterback 25 yards away from the goal line. The Nebraska scoring threat had been thwarted and the Gophers won. Burdick never told anyone what really happened—how he had been quite a bit offside on the play—until twenty-five years later, when he shared the story with friends. When Coach Doc Williams heard the story, he laughed and said, "Well, that makes up for some of the games Nebraska stole from us."[5]

On November 19, Minnesota played Northwestern in Evanston, Illinois. Earl Current starred at fullback and Marshall starred at left end that day.[6] At the beginning of the second half Marshall broke his collarbone and had to be taken out of the game. An injury for Marshall was a rare occurrence: at the time he wore six jerseys over his shoulder pads as protection. Joe Cutting came in to replace him and played effective defensive end that day. With Marshall out of the lineup, the Gophers still were able to beat Northwestern, 11-0.[7] Cutting considered replacing Bobby Marshall to be the greatest thrill of his football career.

While Bobby was in Chicago for the Minnesota-Northwestern game, he was honored for his heroics on the gridiron at an African American civic club called the Appomattox Club,[8] named after the place where the U.S. Civil War peace treaty was signed in 1865.[9]

In 1904 Bobby was All-Conference for the Western Conference (Big Ten) and Minnesota tied with the University of Michigan for conference champion. The Gophers were unbeaten in thirteen games that season.[10] Their 146-0 win over Grinnell College set a record for most points scored in a college football game. In that game Bobby scored four touchdowns and kicked twelve extra points. Some newspapers named the Gophers National Champions for the 1904 season.[11]

At the end of the last game of the 1904 season, as Sig Harris and Marshall walked off the field, they may have felt sad. For the last ten years—from grade school through high school and two years of college they had been teammates and best friends. They'd still be best friends but they'd no longer be teammates. Sig Harris's playing days for the Gophers were over. Harris, who stood 5 feet and 5½ inches tall and weighed 140 pounds, had started at quarterback from 1902 to 1904 and received All American honors as quarterback in 1903 and 1904. He also played defensive safety and returned punts.[12]

Sig Harris

The 1905 season began, as usual, at the Waconia training camp near the end of summer. Previewing the upcoming season, *Minneapolis Tribune* sportswriter Frank E. Force noted: "The work of Bobby Marshall is of too high quality to need further comment."[13] Force observed that the Gophers' teamwork was not as good as the year before but that, "Bobby Marshall is more reliable than ever...and is doing his work creditably at each scrimmage."[14]

On October 28 the Gophers won over Lawrence University 46-0. Force wrote, "Bobby Marshall played better ball than at any time this season and was especially effective when carrying the ball. He dodged and jumped through the Lawrence players for long runs when coming back for kick-offs and also made good gains from the scrimmage play."[15]

In 1905 the University of Chicago went 11-0 in the Big Ten (Western Conference), seizing the conference championship from the Gophers, whose only loss, 16-12, came against Wisconsin on November 4.[16]

WHAT WAS IT LIKE for Marshall to break the color line at the University of Minnesota? An article published in the Minnesota student newspaper, the *Minnesota Daily*, on December 20, 1905, provides a hint. "Marshall from all appearances was deported from the shadiest part of Africa, but contrary to all expectations his playing in no way resembles his native land. He can get away better than Pat Crowe and when he does he travels like a third class tourist. His lope resembles snow in June and his photograph reminds one of a bad egg in a royal phizz. All western end and takes law as a matter of course."[17] His physical and mental abilities are lauded and clearly no one seems to know about his German Jewish ancestors. Who would like to be called "a bad egg in a royal phizz?"

With football season over and baseball season yet to come,

Walter Eckersall

Bobby stayed in condition during the winter by playing hockey. The *Minneapolis Journal* reported on December 28 that the Central High School alumni ice hockey team defeated Lake Shores 8-1. Bobby was one of the stars of the game.[18]

On November 10, 1906, Bobby boarded the train bound for Chicago with his teammates for the game with the University of Chicago. Was his stomach rumbling as he considered what was at stake? This was Bobby's senior year and if he was going to lead the Gophers to another Western Conference (Big Ten) championship, it was now or never. The game against the University of Chicago Maroons would take place at Marshall Field. Chicago, under legendary coach Alonzo Stagg, had one of the best college teams in the nation—the previous year they'd gone undefeated and they had one of college football's greatest players, Walter Eckersall, at quarterback. Eckersall was a great kicker and runner who had a knack for on-the-field football strategy.[19] "Competition had never before been so keen and rivalry had never attained such as fevered pitch."[20]

It had rained for 24 hours straight before game time, making the gridiron a muddy quagmire, but the conditions didn't seem to stop Marshall. A writer for the *Minneapolis Journal* opined that "Marshall played one of the greatest games at end that has ever been seen in the west or the east either, for that matter. He was down on the field under every punt and had Eckersall stopped repeatedly before the season's greatest quarterback could regain an inch. He divined Chicago's attack on his side and few indeed were the inches made around his end. He ripped holes from the backfield and played with the speed of a racehorse and the power of a traction engine."[21]

John R. Schuknecht, who played halfback on the 1905 and 1906 Gopher teams with Marshall, described the first play from scrimmage as follows: "Bobby was playing right end, and on the first play, Eckersall tried to run around Bobby and me. I managed to break through fast and broke up the interference before it reached the line of scrimmage, so Eckersall was all alone with the ball, whereupon Marshall hit him so hard that he nearly broke Eckie in two and hurled him back for a big loss. I always have believed that play had a great deal to do with our winning the game because it made us confident that we could stop Chicago's backfield."[22]

In the first half, the score was tied 0-0 and in the second half, the Gophers were down 2-0 as a result of a safety. Eckersall punted way down the field, the ball rolling on the wet grass. Art Larkin, the Gopher's quarterback received the punt. He was tackled by a group of Chicago defenders for a safety when he ran back into his own end zone. It was getting dark and the rain had washed off the yard lines so Larkin didn't realize he was in the end zone. This resulted in Minnesota getting the ball back on their own thirty-yard line.

Later in the second half, Larkin asked Bobby if he thought he could make a field goal. Bobby said, "If we can get past the center of the field I think I'll try it."[23] The Gophers advanced to Chicago's 40-yard line. It would have to be a 48-yard kick. The

Gophers had worked so hard and played so well. What a shame to lose now. The center hiked the ball, the Gophers' line held back the hard-charging Maroons, and with one smooth stroke Marshall kicked the winning field goal through the goal posts to give the Gophers a lead that they never relinquished.

Edward Flynn, a long time Gopher fan, witnessed that kick and shared his memories of it with *Minneapolis Star* sports writer Charles Johnson in 1963. "I went to Chicago shortly after 1900 and saw Bobby Marshall kick a field goal—it was from a difficult angle in a snow storm."[24] As the kick sailed through the uprights, Chicago's great quarterback, Walter Eckersall, "threw up his hands in despair."[25] The final score was 4-2. Bobby's heart pumped wildly and elation surged through his veins as his teammates carried him off the field on their shoulders.[26]

Bobby's winning 48-yard field goal in the snow (other sources say rain) got a lot of attention. A  reporter in the *Minneapolis Tribune* stated, "No Minnesota football player ever performed more beautifully for the Gopher institution than did Bob Marshall when he made his place kick."[27] *The Appeal* wrote on November 17, "A movement is on foot to tender Bobby Marshall who stands among the greatest foot ball players that any American college has ever produced, a rousing banquet, at the end of the present foot ball season, which will mark the close of the most brilliant career that any U of M player ever enjoyed."[28]

Alonzo Stagg

During the Chicago game, some Chicago players accused Bobby of playing "rough ball." One of the referees thought that Bobby "should be removed from the field" for "using rough tactics repeatedly." The other referees disagreed with this assessment and Bobby was not removed. Chicago coach Alonzo Stagg said, "It

1906 Minnesota Gophers team picture from the *Minneapolis Star Tribune*, November 11, 1906.

was Minnesota's game fairly and squarely."[29] Stagg was one of the greatest football coaches of all time, with a record of 227-112-26 and seven Big 10 Championships.[30] He had such a commanding presence that if one of his former players was smoking a cigarette and saw Stagg walking down the street, he'd immediately throw it away.

One highlight of the Minnesota Chicago contest was a play where Marshall ran down Chicago star Walter Eckersall to prevent a touchdown that would have won the game for Chicago. The *Chicago Tribune* summed up Bobby's play that day, saying, "without disparagement to the other twenty men in the game, it was Marshall against Eckersall, and the colored lad won."[31] Note that the other players are referred to as men and Bobby is called a "colored lad."

After the game Bobby was quoted in the *Minneapolis Tribune* as saying, "I think we outplayed them at every point, at any rate they did not gain ground at all and were forced to punt at every point." The headlines on the front page of *Minneapolis Sunday Tribune* read "Minnesota Defeats Chicago 4-2; Regains Championship of the West 'Bob' Marshall Saves Day By Place-

Kicking Goal." On the front page there was a team picture of the 1906 Gophers with Bobby second from the left on the first row.[32] Bobby was fast becoming a Minnesota football hero.

TODAY, FOOTBALL IS A GAME of specialists: an offensive team, a defensive team, and a special team for kick offs, field goals, extra points, and punts. In the Minnesota Chicago game of 1906 all eleven Gopher starters played the entire game with no substitutions.[33] One player for the Gophers, team captain and fullback Earl Current, played almost the entire game with two broken ribs and a fractured collarbone.[34]

Football in 1906 was quite different from the 21st Century game. The forward pass had been made legal for the 1906 season but only one pass was completed that day, a four-yard Minnesota completion. If a pass was incomplete in 1906 it was considered a turnover. The pass had to be thrown five yards in back of the line of scrimmage and could not be thrown more than 20 yards beyond the line of scrimmage. A forward pass could not be thrown for a touchdown. In 1906 a new rule was put in place requiring ten yards instead of five yards to be gained in three downs for a first down. This rule made it so hard to score that football became boring to the fans. So, in 1912 new rules were put into effect allowing four downs for a first down, shortening the field to 100 yards, adding ten-yard end zones in back of both goal lines, changing the value of a touchdown from five to six points, allowing touchdown passes, and abolishing the 20-yard rule for forward passes. From 1912 on, there was no limit on the length of a forward pass. These rule changes allowed for more scoring, making football more interesting for the fans.[35] They also opened up the field of play so there were fewer huge pile ups of players, making injuries less likely.

As a result of the win over the University of Chicago the Gophers were tied with the University of Michigan and the University of Wisconsin for the 1906 Western Conference (Big Ten) Championship. Bobby was 23 years old at the time and he was thinking perhaps he should give up strenuous sports like football. After all, he was close to receiving his law degree from the University of Minnesota.[36]

But as the train from Chicago pulled into Minneapolis after the long trip from Chicago, such thoughts were probably far from Marshall's mind. The *Minneapolis Tribune* on November 13 described the celebration when the train arrived. "An immense throng of students lined the platform and cheered the winning eleven as the private car came to a standstill. Then a rush was made to greet the men individually, cheers and Ski-U-Mahs being given for each member of the team and for the coaches.

A tally-ho had been provided and the players were raised on the shoulders of the crowd and carried from the station to the tally-ho. (A tally-ho is a horse and wagon. In 1906 there were not many automobiles in Minneapolis. The first Model T Ford was not produced until two years later.) The horses were removed and a long rope attached to the wagon. Pulling on this rope were more than a hundred female students.

With the girls pulling the tally-ho and the remainder of the rooters following, the procession moved along the downtown streets, singing, shouting, zigzagging all the way up Washington Avenue to Nicollet, up that avenue to Sixth Street, over to Hennepin, down across the river and out University Avenue to the campus.

The second section of the train brought in the university band just in time for them to join the procession and furnish music for the triumphal entry to the university grounds.

The word had been telephoned from downtown that the team had arrived, and when the thousand students escorting the players reached campus they found another two-thousand drawn up to greet the homecoming heroes.

The tally-ho was drawn up on the lawn, and each and every member of the team and many of the substitutes were given a personal welcome. The players were invited to stand on the seats of the bus, one after another, and say a few words to the crowd.

Marshall was the first to be called and he was given a great cheer. He stepped up to the makeshift podium, not knowing that this was the first of many speeches he would make in his life to adoring crowds.

"All I can say," he remarked, "is that this reception is the greatest thing that ever happened. I also want to say that when the place kick was made the team held so well that not a Chicago man came through and there was not the slightest danger of the kick."

Before leaving on the train home Marshall said to a *Chicago Tribune* reporter: "We won the game by hard playing, and we would have won it under any other climatic conditions. Most of the Chicago team think they could have won the game had the ground been dry. Eckerall said in confidence to me: 'You fellows would have won the game no matter what the condition of the ground was. You simply outplayed us.' This was the most gratifying remark I heard made by a Chicago player. It was a clean, gentlemanly, satisfactory game from start to finish."[37]

At the heart of this victory celebration was the first African American to play a prominent role in Minnesota football. This was probably one of the first times in Minnesota that an African American spoke to a large group almost entirely of white people since Frederick Douglass addressed large crowds in Winona and St. Paul in 1867.

I wonder what went through the minds of the University of Minnesota students who were present that day? Here was this well-spoken African American student-athlete speaking to the throng. He was the first African American superstar athlete that Minnesota had ever seen and probably the first African American campus leader ever at the University of Minnesota. He spoke with humility, giving his teammates credit for the victory, and he spoke about a great victory the entire university could share. The rally was certainly was a milestone in the history of race relations in Minnesota.

But, of course, racial prejudice was still a powerful reality.

Many people were not quite sure what to think of Marshall. His daughter, Bette J. Session, said, "They wanted to call Dad an Indian—anything but a Negro."[38]

To understand Bobby's style of football something needs to be told about the style of football in the early 1900s. It was "bone grinding." Teams used a tactic where a group of offensive players would move close together to block the defenders. Bobby was able to perform "flying tackles" to "sail through the air, as though gravity had not been invented...with his heels still in the air as gracefully as an airplane coming to earth." In this way, he could break down the offensive interference. Football experts of the time thought Bobby was the "most gifted Minnesota football player" of that time period in Minnesota football history.[39]

In the game against Carlisle on November 17 at Northrup Field before an "immense crowd" Bobby said his opponents, "went after me several times when I was either out of bounds or down." Bobby described the situation as follows. The opposing player "jumped on me and slugged me and I pushed him away." Sportswriter Murray T. Davenport of the *Minneapolis Sunday Tribune* wrote, "Marshall left the game at the request of the umpire who also threw out Gardner [of Carlisle]. Those men roughed things in several plays and were finally thrown out. Gardner had deliberately held Marshall from going down on a punt a few plays before and bad blood resulted between them." Tom Eagleman, another Carlisle player, recalled in 1965 that he, too, got into a fight with Marshall that day. Eagleman said, "I played less than half the game when I was evicted for scrapping with Bobby Marshall, who was an All American. He kept tripping me, and the third time he did it I took him from behind. I tackled him and then worked him over for a while." The Carlisle teams of this era were made up of American Indian players, the most famous of which was Jim Thorpe. The Gophers lost that day, 17-0 and Bobby's absence was probably a major reason why.[40]

College football during Marshall's college days was such a rough game that the President of the United States, Theodore

Roosevelt, demanded that the game be abolished or changed. In 1905 there were 18 deaths and 137 serious injuries during football games. Eleven of the dead were high school students and three were college students.[41] The rules were changed to make the game safer for the 1906 season. These changes in the rules were put forward by John Heisman who coached at Clemson, Rice, Georgia Tech, Washington and Jefferson, and Auburn. The Heisman Trophy for the best college football player is named after him.[42]

In 1906 Chicago sportswriters unanimously picked Bobby for the All-Western (Big Ten) Team, a distinction he had also earned the previous two years.[43] He was named second team All American by Walter Camp for both the 1905 and 1906 season, a selection that the *Minnesota Daily* called "a farce" and "a travesty."[44] The *Daily* sportswriter felt that first team All American was a must for Marshall. That same year Bobby was also named to the "All Star Football Team of America" winning the vote of every critic making the selection except one.[45] In Bobby's four years of play on the University of Minnesota football team, the Gophers only lost two games, 16-12 against the University of Wisconsin in 1905 and 17-0 against Carlisle Indian Industrial School in 1906.[46] During his college career Marshall scored 10 touchdowns and kicked seven field goals and fifty-four extra points—a total of 134 points. The Gopher football teams Bobby played for between 1904 and 1906 outscored their opponents 1,283 to 63.[47]

Marshall also excelled at other sports in college, earning seven sports letters for the Gophers: four in football (1903-1906), two in baseball (1906-1907), and one in track (1907). He also played first base on the 1907 University of Minnesota baseball team that won the Western Conference (Big Ten) championship.[48]

With football season over, Marshall laced up his skates excitedly and glided on to the ice. The Gophers didn't compete in the Big Ten in ice hockey until 1921 but Bobby played on a University of Minnesota club ice hockey team during college.[49] He also played for the Eagles in the Twin Cities Hockey League, which consisted of six teams in the Twin Cities area. The first game of the 1906-

1907 hockey season was on December 29.[50] On January 6 Bobby skated for the Minneapolis Eagles in a hockey game against the St. Paul Victorias, which the Eagles lost 7-5. The *Minneapolis Tribune* said, "Bobby Marshall, the well known football star, and Jennison of Minneapolis played the best game."[51] Bobby could shoot the puck from the right or left side of his body over the heads of his opponents into the goal.[52] In a winning effort on January 2, 1907 "Bobby Marshall, Jennison and Logerstrom were the stars for the winners, each making a goal."[53] Note the picture of Bobby with the Eagles ice hockey team.

A group of 50 African American men organized a banquet to honor Marshall's achievements at the local Opera Café in mid-January of 1907. At that event Bobby was presented with a silver loving cup by his many friends.[54]

Summing up his college career, it was no small thing to mention that along with his football heroics, Marshall was the first African American to graduate from the University of Minnesota Law School. He was an outstanding student, maintaining a 3.5 academic average on a 4-point scale.[55]

Despite the racism he encountered at the University of Minnesota, Marshall loved going to school there. According to his grandson, Bill Marshall, "Pro sports were all well and good but Bobby Marshall loved University of Minnesota sports more than anything."[56] Bobby received his diploma as a law graduate in the spring of 1907.[57] He'd overcome the odds to become both a lawyer and a football All-American.

4

Marshall Finds His Niche on the Professional Playing Field

Can you name one player in the history of pro football who served as coach, quarterback, and captain at the same time? Hint. He did not play quarterback in college.

After a highly successful college career one would think Bobby Marshall could write his own ticket to success. But in 1907 the African American community in Minneapolis was not large, and there were already several African American lawyers handling its legal needs. A testimonial dinner was held for Bobby in 1907, attended by African American lawyers from the Twin Cities. The founder of the N.A.A.C.P., Fredrick L. McGhee, spoke at this dinner on the topic "What Next?"[1]

That was precisely the question Marshall was pondering. He set up a law office in the Metropolitan Life Building in downtown Minneapolis, but his case load wasn't heavy enough to interfere with continued involvement in the world of sports. Before football season, in the summer of 1907 he played third base and was captain for the LaMoure, North Dakota, baseball team.[2] Many small northern towns included talented African American players in those days, to make them more competitive, but Bobby was probably the only one on the LaMoure roster. The LaMoure newspaper reported on one occasion: "The playing of Bob Mar-

shall has always been a source of great satisfaction to the fans...
(He is) the best third baseman in this section of the country. Surely he has always played consistent ball. He is sure on picking up
grounders, has an easy throw to first, and while not an infallible
batsman, yet he is very dependable with the stick. He should be
warmly welcomed next summer if he sees fit to return."[3]

Bobby also played catcher that year for a newly formed African American team, the St. Paul Colored Gophers.[4] In a game on
May 19, 1907, against the Austin-Westerns, Bobby was behind
the plate with Dude Lytle pitching. As an Austin runner tried to
steal second, Bobby threw the ball over second base into center
field and the runner advanced to third. Lytle's next pitch got by
Bobby, allowing the runner to score. I can imagine Bobby looking
at Lytle and saying, "Sorry, Dude." But Bobby made up for his
mistakes the next inning, hitting a Texas league single into right
field, stealing second base, and then scoring on a throwing error.
The Colored Gophers cruised to a 3-1 victory.[5]

In the fall of 1907 Bobby joined his friend Sig Harris on
the coaching staff for the University of Minnesota's football team,
becoming the university's and the Big Ten's first African American football coach, and one of the first African American football
coaches anywhere in the college ranks. Bobby also coached the
Gophers' freshman team.[6]

That same year Bobby became one of the first (if not the
first) African American high school football coaches, at Central
High School, his alma mater.[7] He walked on to the football field
at Central for the first day of practice, glad to see a group of enthusiastic high schoolers who were eager to be coached by a Minnesota hero.

While the 1907 baseball team Bobby played on, the Colored
Gophers, was an all African American team, the professional foot-
ball team he played on was not. But Bobby was not only the only
African American player on the Minneapolis Deans; he was the
only African American in the entire league, The Sunday Football
League of Minnesota. Maybe this was because Bobby helped or-

The Minneapolis Deans with Bobby in the middle of the back row.

ganize the league and both coached and quarterbacked the Deans. There were five other semi-pro teams were in this league: the St. Paul National Guards, the Stillwater Football Team, the Deephaven Beavers, the Ramblers, and the New Prague Seals. It's likely that Marshall was the first African American quarterback in professional football.[8] He was the second African American player to play any kind of professional football. The first African American to play pro football was Charles W. Follis. He was born in 1879, a year before Bobby, and grew up in Wooster, Ohio, where he played a part in organizing a high school football team at Wooster High School. He continued on to the College of Wooster in the spring of 1901 where he played baseball. In the fall of 1901 he played football for a pro team, the Wooster Athletic Association. A year later he switched to the Shelby Athletic Association's team, where he was a star running back, nicknamed "The Black Cyclone from Wooster." In one game, he gained 150 yards. Another player for Shelby was Branch Rickey, who would later bring Jackie Robinson to Major League Baseball. Follis retired from pro football in 1906 due to injuries but still played baseball for an African American team in Cleveland. He died of pneumonia in 1910, at the age of 31, ten years before the National Football League was formed.[9]

Another African American associated with Branch Rickey was Charles Thomas. In the early 1900s Rickey coached Thomas, a catcher and an African American, on the Ohio Wesleyan University baseball team. On a road trip to play Notre Dame in South Bend, Indiana Thomas was denied a hotel room. Rickey asked if Thomas could stay in his room and the hotel manager agreed. Inside the hotel room Thomas was sobbing and crying, saying "Black skin. Black skin. If only I could make them white."

"Come on Tommy, snap out of it. Buck up," Rickey replied. "We'll lick this one day but we can't if you feel sorry for yourself."

Later, reflecting on this scene, Rickey said, "I vowed that I would always do whatever I could to see that other Americans did not have to face the bitter humiliation that was heaped upon Charles Thomas." During the pregame warm up in 1903 in a baseball game against the University of Kentucky, some fans and Kentucky players directed racial slurs at Thomas and told him to get off the field. Rickey ran over to the Kentucky dugout and yelled, "We won't play without him," so the game was played with Thomas in the lineup.[10]

A similar incident happened in a professional football game between the Minneapolis Deans and the New Prague Seals on November 3, 1907, at Minnehaha Park in Minneapolis. The Seals arrived at 2:45 pm for a 3 pm game, but refused to play unless Marshall was taken out of the game. They argued that Marshall couldn't play because he was the team's coach—a ridiculous claim, considering that "player-coaches" weren't uncommon at the time. The Seals also claimed that certain Deans players were "ringers" brought in for the occasion—another strange claim, considering that in pro sports eligibility is seldom an issue. (The term "ringer" is usually applied to ineligible high school or college players.) "The Dean management claimed they had no one to take Marshall's place, and could not give the spectators a game without him."[11] The New Prague team eventually decided to play the game under protest. That day Marshall realized that the Deans organization stood with him.

The Deans won that game, six to five. Both teams scored touchdowns but the Deans made their extra point and the Seals didn't. (Touchdowns were worth five points then.) "The Deans team had been strengthened by many former high school stars, and these fellows showed the effects of Marshall's coaching by a clever use of the forward pass."[12]

Two weeks later, the Deans beat the Ramblers 52-0 at Minnehaha Park in Minneapolis before a crowd of a 1,000. "Time and again [Marshall] threw the ball to Bresky for forward passes and several times this player got away for a clear field and a touchdown. Marshall punted cleverly and often kicked to one side of the field so that Broderick (of the Deans) could dash along and get the ball."[13] One of the most amazing things about Marshall was how effective he was in all aspects of the game of football: blocking, tackling, running with the ball, catching passes, throwing passes, kicking field goals, running back kick-offs, coaching, and even punting. *The Appeal* newspaper noted, "The Deans, the independent football team of which Bobby Marshall is captain and coach, is one of the best teams in the country. It is made up of former University stars. They would make the U. team go some to beat them."[14]

Marshall, right out of college, is made the captain, coach, and quarterback of a previously all-white team. In the white world of Minneapolis, Minnesota, in 1907, Bobby Marshall was a well-respected man.

Marshall was a busy man in the fall of 1907, coaching high school, college, and pro teams during the same season. The *Minneapolis Sunday Tribune* described Marshall's high school coaching as follows. "When Central started her season, it was thought that the Red and Blue was to have her best team of years. Heavy and fast men were out in numbers and Marshall, the coach, showed that he could teach the game, by getting the team going at a high rate of speed early." Bobby's Central team played North

High for the city championship on Friday September, 15. Central was at a disadvantage because two of its best players, Nichols and Tinkham, were declared ineligible because they had been attending high school for five years. The clash for the city championship was held before the largest crowd ever at the North's field. In the second half North broke away to a 17-0 victory. The star of the game was Fred Chicken, a running back for North.[15] Fred would later play professionally with Marshall on the Minneapolis Marines and Rock Island Independents.

The University of Minnesota freshman players Marshall coached that fall were set to play a scrimmage against the sophomores. A *Minneapolis Tribune* article stated, "Bobby Marshall has been in charge of the first-year men, who are the favorites as a result."[16]

In 1907 Bobby's brother Louis passed the civil service exam to become a mail carrier. Once again, the Marshall family was overcoming racial stereotypes to get jobs usually reserved for whites.[17] Opportunities for African Americans in the U.S. seemed to be increasing nationwide, and President Teddy Roosevelt highlighted the trend by appointing a number of African American statesmen to public office.[18]

From 1907 to 1909 Marshall was busy playing ice hockey in the winter. Stands were set up on Minneapolis outdoor ice rinks where sometimes 300 to 400 people would pay an admission fee and endure temperatures that sometimes dropped below zero to watch a game. Bobby played ice hockey games three days a week, being paid $15 a game. When you consider that the average worker in that era made twenty-five cents an hour, and Henry Ford paid auto workers $5 a day for an eleven-hour day, Bobby was well paid for playing hockey.[19] He started off the new year of 1908 by refereeing the first half of a hockey game between the Minneapolis Lake Shores and the St. Paul Boat Club on Saturday, January 4. In the second half, the referee was Taylor, a St. Paul man. The Lake Shores won 7-5.[20] Who knew that in 1908, ice hockey was played in two halves, not three periods? Bobby played for the local Twin Cities hockey team, the Wanderers, in the winter of 1908. His debut on January 6 is recorded in the *Minneapolis Journal.* "Bobby Marshall made his debut with the Wanderers last night and as a celebration played the game of his life, shooting both goals for the Wanderers and playing a great defensive game."[21] An article from the *Minneapolis Tribune* about another game that season paints a picture of the kind of hockey player Marshall was. "Bobby Marshall, famous in football player, got into the game with a little too much spirit last night and several times played so roughly that he was re-

The Eagles hockey team with Marshall at right.

peatedly put out of the game...Marshall lifted the puck for a nice goal and aside from his rough playing worked his position at cover point with advantage."[22] Cover point is a term for an ice hockey defenseman. Bobby's hockey team, the Wanderers, won the Burton Cup, the city championship of Minneapolis in 1908.[23] According to the *Minneapolis Star Journal* "George LaBatt and Bobby Marshall carried off the high honors for the Wanderers."[24] Bobby was rated one of the best players in the city, and "his sweeping stroke and long reach" made him "very effective in defense work." A severely sprained ankle convinced him to give up pro hockey after the 1909 season. Marshall was the first professional African American ice hockey player.[25] Marshall's friend, A.B. Cassius said the following about Bobby's ice hockey skills. "He was such a tremendous skater and could handle a hockey puck so well that there is always the thought that he could have been the first black to play in the National Hockey League."[26]

In the spring and summer of 1908 Bobby began playing baseball for an all-African American team, the Minneapolis Keystones—also known as the Kellogg Keystones. The team had been organized by Kidd F. Mitchell, who owned the Keystone Hotel and restaurant in Minneapolis. Mitchell recruited many of the top African American baseball players including pitcher Walter Ball, nicknamed the Georgia Rabbit.[27] Bobby played right field, first base, catcher, and won ten games on the mound. Mitchell's teammates included Charles Jessup from the Chicago Leland Giants and William Binga from the Philadelphia Giants. Kidd recognized that Marshall was not only an asset on the field, but also a local hero who would bring fans to the ballpark.[28] The team had a great year, winning 88 games.[29] On April 26 Walter Ball pitched against a team of white players, the Lunds, at Minnehaha Park on a muddy field before 1,500 fans. Ball pitched a four-hit shutout and the Keystones won, 5-0.[30]

At this time, Major League Baseball was entirely white, and its most southern city was St. Louis. Yet in Minnesota an African American team could play a white team and an African American baseball player could play on a white team.

In June and early July of 1908, the Keystones were in a fix. They had lost their best pitcher, Walter Ball, to the Chicago Leland Giants. Marshall, who had a great curve ball, took Ball's place in the starting rotation, posted a 3.29 ERA, and won eight out of nine games.[31]

On August 27 at Downtown Park in St. Paul the Keystones played the first in a five-game playoff with the other local African American team, the Colored Gophers, for the championship of Minnesota. This playoff series could be considered a state championship because these African American teams had both defeated all the white teams in the area. According to African American baseball expert Todd Peterson, this series was of great significance. "Considering the abilities of the combatants involved," he writes, "it was no stretch to say that it was also the first game in Minnesota between two major league clubs."[32] Marshall and the other African American baseball players involved were as good or better than those playing Major League Baseball, and over time, the Major Leaguers found that out. If you saw the movie "42," you may remember the scene where the Brooklyn Dodger players are talking about the effect of having African American players like Jackie Robinson on their team. It wasn't just about racism; it was also about the threat of losing their jobs to African Americans who were better ball players.

This playoff series drew large crowds; 1,800 fans showed up for the first game.[33] The second game was played before 4,000 fans at Minnehaha Driving Park. That day Bobby made an unassisted double play, smacked two hits, scored twice, and a stole a base as his Keystones won 9-2.[34] In the fifth and final game, with the series tied, the Colored Gophers beat Marshall's Keystones, 6-0.[35]

What made this series so popular? Consider that Minnesota didn't have a Major League team at the time and the Negro League hadn't been formed yet. There was no radio coverage and television hadn't been invented. A large number of both African American and white spectators came to see these games—it was the best show in town. Betting was heavy, and the local newspapers provided plenty of coverage in advance of the games.[36] One sportswriter noted that during his time with the Keystones, "Marshall had developed into a good base stealer with some pop in his bat, and he had a long reach at first..."[37]

In the fall of 1908 Bobby helped Dr. Williams coach the University of Minnesota football team again and he also played again for the Minneapolis Deans.[38] On Sunday, October 18, the Deans played the Ascension team at Minnehaha Park in Minneapolis. Marshall kicked a field goal from the 25-yard line, ran the ball effectively from scrimmage, and played the entire game, helping the Deans win 16-0. After the first points were scored, "The next score was a touchdown and Marshall again was the star. The colored boy took the ball on a punt, and dodging half a dozen of the Ascension tacklers, went up the field for a 65-yard run and a touchdown. It was a magnificent run and brought the crowd to its feet."[39]

The *Minneapolis Sunday Tribune* reported on October 25 that the Deans' manager, "not content with a strong lineup, has added several stars to his list ... Bobby Marshall, the former Minnesota end, is captain and coach of the Deans and has had his men hard at practice during the week. The Deans have perfected the forward pass and with Marshall's ability to throw the ball from 30 to 40 yards the game becomes spectacular to the extreme."[40] The Deans were on the cutting edge of pro football. The forward pass had been legalized only two years earlier, and the Deans had already "perfected" this element of the game.

The Deans and the Adams team were scheduled to play at Minnehaha Park on Sunday, October 25, but it was raining and when the Dean's manager saw how muddy the field was he postponed the game until November 1.[41]

On October 30 the *Minneapolis Tribune* reported, "Coach Bobby Marshall of the Deans had 18 players out for practice last night and the men are getting in top condition for the games to come."[42] Marshall had the respect of his all-white team; in no news article I found was there talk of dissension on a Marshall-coached team.

On Sunday, November 1, the Deans beat Adams 16-2 before 1200 fans at Minnehaha Park, and a Minneapolis sports writer wrote that Bobby threw the football "for greater distances and with better precision than any man" in Minnesota in that time period.[43]

The Deans played the St. Paul Quicksteps on November 15 at Minnehaha Park and won easily, 39-0. From the account in the *Minneapolis Tribune*, it seemed that the Deans could have scored a lot more points than that. The *Tribune* writer mentioned that "Bobby Marshall felt that he had won enough honors in the previous games with the Quicksteps and was lying low yesterday, giving his teammates a chance to star."[44]

The Deans' manager. O.C. Olsen, set up a game with the Chicago Eckersalls to be played on Thanksgiving Day. Olsen arranged a financial guarantee for the Eckersalls, making the game possible.[45] "Coach Bobby Marshall and his Deans were out for practice several nights during the week and the big fellows are beginning to carry out their plays with the smoothness of a machine. Marshall who is playing the quarterback position, has never been in better physical condition for football."[46]

Deans' manager O. C. Olsen

The Thanksgiving Day game would be almost a rematch of the encounter, two years earlier, between the University of Minnesota team and the University of Chicago team during which Marshall's last-second field goal won the day, upsetting the favored Chicago team with Eckersall at quarterback. The current Eckersalls team consisted of a group of all-star professionals.

In a *Minneapolis Tribune* article from November 22, W. F. Allen sets the stage for this game. "The one great game of the gridiron season in Minneapolis around which a constantly increasing interest centers is the meeting of the two all-star organizations, the Deans of Minneapolis and the Eckersalls of Chicago. This contest, now less than a week distant, is the talk of football followers and Nicollet field will be jammed as never before when the famous 'Wallie' Eckersall leads his picked warriors onto the field…Eckersall has not lost one whit of his wonderful speed; his kicks are just as long…Eckersall will endeavor to clean up a little score with Bobby Marshall, too. He has not forgotten that day two years ago when the colored boy dimmed the glory of his closing days on the college gridiron with a placekick that gave Minnesota the championship. It was a bitter pill for Eckie and the bad taste still lingers. The two will be opposing generals (quarterbacks) Thursday, and if Eckersall can outwit Marshall he will feel that in a measure he has had revenge. View the game from any angle and it presents possibilities that charge it with an interest seldom equaled...Bobby Marshall will run the team (the Deans.) Bobby will likely shine as a star during the contest. He has development (sic) surprising improvement even over his great form when a varsity player...at Minnesota he was known principally as a defensive player. But in the games this year, he has pulled off some sensational runs through the open field, frequently dodging an entire eleven and once taking the ball at a kick-off for a touchdown...Tickets for the game are already selling like hot cakes. All Twin City football enthusiasts recognize this game as the chance of a lifetime and a situation that may never be repeated. The field will be laid out so a good view of the contest will be had from every stand at Nicollet. Those in the grandstand will face the center of the field."[47]

On the day of the game day, Frank E. Force wrote the following in the *Minneapolis Tribune*. "This game, planned originally as simply a tryout between two strong semi-professional elevens, has developed in interest until it has become one of the greatest games of the season."[48]

In the same article, Force describes Marshall as a coach, writing, "That the Dean team is well coached by Bobby Marshall has been evident to those who have seen the former Minnesota men in the games already played. Marshall has a fine idea of the value of open plays and the pass will be a prominent feature of the Dean repertoire."[49]

Excitement for the game was high, with a University of Minnesota band of fifty members slated to perform before the game and at halftime. University of Minnesota football coach Dr. Henry Williams and his varsity players were going to be admitted into the game free of charge. The Eckersalls team arrived on the overnight Great Western train at 8 am on the day of the game. Kickoff was scheduled for 2:30 pm.[50]

On game day, November 26, the weather was unfavorable for football. The *Minneapolis Tribune* reported, "Instead of being thankful, the weather people dished out a little snow, a mean, chilly wind and a dark, dull sky…The theaters were crowded at both matinee and evening performances and a fair sized crowd saw the football game at Nicollet park (sic)."[51]

The Nicollet Park field was muddy and combined with the cold and strong winds, play on the field was difficult, slippery and treacherous, although the grounds crew did everything possible to make the field playable. At halftime, the score stood at 4-0, on the strength of Marshall's 35-yard field goal. Teammate George Capron drop kicked a ball almost 70 yards that barely missed going through the uprights for a second field goal.

It was a defensive battle with Marshall's 25-yard run from scrimmage being the only offensive highlight. Late in the game the Eckersalls moved the ball deep into Deans territory. Eckersall

DROP KICK AS IN DROP KICK MURPHY?

In a drop kick the kicker lets the ball drop to the ground and then kicks it. The drop kick was commonly used for field goals and extra points up to the early 1930s.[54] In 1934 the football became less round, making a forward pass easier to throw. When the football became less round the bounce of the ball was less predictable making the drop kick less likely to succeed. So, then the place kick (with a player holding the ball on the ground as another player kicks it) replaced the drop kick for extra points and field goals. The drop kick remains a legal kick in N.C.A.A. and N.F.L. football. The last successful drop kick was made on January 2, 2006, when Doug Flutie of the New England Patriots drop kicked an extra point conversion after touchdown in a game against the Miami Dolphins. The Dolphins won, 28-26. The last previous drop kick was made by Ray "Scooter" McLean of the Chicago Bears in the N.F.L. Championship game against the New York Giants on December 21, 1941. The Bears won 37-9.[55]

tried a drop kick. It was blocked, but Eckersall fell on the ball to retain possession and tried another drop kick on the next down. The second kick was also blocked but Eckersall fell on the ball again to retain possession. His third drop kick, from the Deans 20-yard line, tied the score. And that's the way the game ended.[52] I've never heard of or seen a football play where the field goal attempt was blocked and recovered by the offensive team three times in a row. I checked a football rule book and found that that sequence of three recovered field goal attempts was allowed by the rules then and still is.[53] A tradition had now been established to invite teams from other states to play against Minneapolis teams on Thanksgiving.

After the Minneapolis Central High School football team lost the city championship to Minneapolis North High in 1907, Central High hired George "Punk" Webster to replace Marshall as head coach for the 1908 season. Bobby still helped coach the 1908 Central High team.[56] Evidently, he held no grudge about Webster getting the 1908 job. This cooperative aspect of Bobby's character surfaced repeatedly during his career, as Bobby served as an assistant coach at many Minneapolis area high schools.[57]

The year 1908 was a watershed in the history of race relations in American sports. Locally, Marshall had become a Minnesota hero, a head football coach, captain, and quarterback of a previously all-white professional team. But in that same year. on December 26, Jack Johnson, an African American from Galveston, Texas, defeated Tommy Burns for the boxing heavyweight championship. The fight went fourteen rounds and had to be ended by the police. Johnson was declared the winner, and for the first time in history, an African American had reached the pinnacle of professional sport. This sent shock waves across white American. That an African American man could beat a white man at boxing—or anything else—ran against the prevailing attitude of the times.[58] Everything Marshall said and did undercut that kind of thinking. The sports fans of Minnesota and Bobby's white teammates accepted him not only as an equal but as a leader.

A news article in *The Appeal* from October 10, 1908, announced: "If you read this you are invited to the opening of the new Roller Skating Rink in the new and elegant Arcade Hall, 1311 Washington Ave, S. Minneapolis, on Monday evening, October 19th. There will be sessions every Monday and Friday evenings and matinees every Monday and Friday afternoons… Special attention will be given to new beginners. Good music Admission, 25 cents Bobby Marshall, Instructor."[59] Having Bobby involved in any business enterprise must have been a real plus.

By 1909, at 29 years old, Bobby Marshall was a much-loved Minnesota hero with his heroics being reported regularly in the white press.

5

Marshall Plays Pro Baseball for the St. Paul Colored Gophers

On October 31, 1903, and again on November 10, 1906, Bobby Marshall's heroics on the field caused wild celebrations in the Twin Cities. Could he repeat that magic one more time?

In early May of 1909 Bobby left the Minneapolis Keystones and signed with the St. Paul Colored Gophers baseball team.[1] Soon afterward the Colored Gophers went on a 34-game road trip during which they compiled a record of 28 win, 5 losses. and 1 tie. Johnnie Davis of the Gophers was the standout, winning all 14 games he pitched in, but a sportswriter for the *Minneapolis Sunday Tribune* wrote, "Bobby Marshall is a big hit all over the circuit and never fails to get the glad hand for his wonderful fielding stunts around first base."[2] There was a strong rivalry between the Keystones and the Colored Gophers. On Saturday July 24, 1909, the rivalry was renewed at Downtown Park in St. Paul before several hundred fans. Marshall homered and tripled to lead the Colored Gophers to a 5-2 victory.[3] The next day the two teams played again at Downtown Park and the Colored Gophers won again, 8-4, with Bobby hitting safely twice and playing a superb first base.[4]

The rosters of these two teams contain some amazing monikers: Rat Johnson, Peanuts Fuelling, Dizzy Dismukes, Steel Arm

The St. Paul Colored Gophers. Marshall is at the end of the back row on the right side.

Johnny Taylor, Gabbie Milliner, Dude Lytle, Topeka Jack Johnson, Big Bill Gatewood, Slick Jackson, Haywood Kissing Bug Rose, Mule Armstrong, John Big Boy Merida, Lefty Pangburn, Bert Yellow Kid Jones, Louis Spitball Johnson, Frank Bunch Davis, and Cannonball Joe Jackson. The St. Paul Colored Gophers were also known as the Twin Cities Gophers.

On July 26, 1909, the St. Paul Colored Gophers played the first game of a three-out-of-five series against the Chicago Leland Giants. The Colored Gophers and the Leland Giants were widely considered to be the best African American baseball teams in American. A writer for the *Appeal*, an African American newspaper in St. Paul, described the series as "an exhibition of some of the fastest and brainiest playing of the national game ever seen in St. Paul," and called it the "championship of the country,"[5] while the *Minneapolis Sunday Tribune* referred to it as "the world's colored championship."[6] The series began at Downtown Park in St. Paul before a crowd of about a thousand fans. In the first game the

Colored Gophers were down by one run in the eleventh inning. The score was Giants 9, Colored Gophers 8. With one out William Binga singled for the Gophers and then Rat Johnson hit a double, putting two men on base. Marshall approached the plate. Could he again be the hero? With his powerful swing, he hit the first pitch over the center field wall for a homerun and a 10-9 win.[7] The *St. Paul Pioneer Press* noted that the fans went wild after the victory. There was "a frenzied celebration in downtown St. Paul."[8] On July 30, the Colored Gophers won the third game to sweep the series and establish themselves as the champions of African American baseball.[9] African American baseball in the Twin Cities now appealed to white fans as well as African American fans. This was due, in part, to the popularity of Marshall. The white fans were roped off in a segregated seating section.[10]

Love for African American baseball was growing rapidly in the Twin Cities, and Bobby Marshall had fueled that passion, just as he'd fueled the passion for University of Minnesota football in 1903, against the University of Michigan, and in 1906 against the top-rated University of Chicago team. In 1903, 1906 and 1909, the Minnesota team was the underdog. In each instance, Marshall's heroics gave the Minnesota fans the feeling that life's limitations no longer applied—that now, at least for a few hours or days, anything was possible, including their own dreams.

It's important to keep in mind that these games were being played during the "dead ball era," when fields were spacious, home runs were rare, and "small ball" strategies such as bunting, base stealing, and the hit-and-run often decided the outcome of a contest. Considering the times, Bobby displayed great power at bat. During his years with the St. Paul Colored Gophers he racked up a batting average of .266, with 124 hits, 71 runs, and 34 stolen bases, the most on the team for that period. He hit 11 homeruns in spite of the ball's lack of liveliness. The next closest Gopher was George Armstrong with 6 home runs.[11] (Statistics for Marshall's entire professional baseball career are not available.)

Bobby was also a great fielder at first base. One sportswriter

observed that he had "arms like the sweep of a windmill and nothing anywhere near first base gets away from him."[12] Base runners
eager for him to cough up the ball or step off the base found that
"nothing but a locomotive" could move him out of the way. His
long "reach, fielding ability, and fearlessness" made him a great
first baseman. The press called him called "Star of the Diamond,"
and "Pet of the Lady Fans."[13]

The St. Paul Colored Gophers traveled more than five thousand miles by rail in 1909, playing teams in Iowa, Minnesota, and
Wisconsin. With only a twelve-man squad, each player needed to
be an ironman who could play daily with little rest. Many of the
teams the Colored Gophers
played against were made up
of white players, and the Colored Gophers often drew upon
their "black wisdom," sometimes bantering with the fans
but never losing their tempers
or responding negatively to the
racial taunts they received.[14]
According to *The Appeal,* the
Colored Gophers team was
"one of the important Afro-
American enterprises" in St.
Paul, and its success offered an
important counter-argument
to "negative images of black
inferiority."[15] And at the time,

Rube Foster

playing baseball with independent teams like the Colored Gophers gave Bobby his best opportunity[16], since the Negro League
did not come into being until 1920, and Major League Baseball
was already segregated by 1898.

After the Colored Gophers season ended in 1909, Rube
Foster (who later founded the Negro Leagues) recruited Bobby
and teammate Felix Wallace for the Chicago Leland Giants.

a team considered to be one of the greatest African American teams in baseball history. At this point in his career Bobby was one of the best players in African American baseball. Rube Foster organized a series with the Chicago Cubs after their Major League Baseball season was over, the first game taking place on October 18, 1909. The pay was $50 per game, Marshall's highest paycheck ever in baseball.[17]

These games took place at West Side Grounds about two miles west of downtown Chicago where the University of Illinois Medical Center now exists. (Wrigley Field would not be built until 1916.) The field was huge, with the center field wall 560 feet from home plate. The stands, made out of wood, held 16,000 fans.[18]

In the first game, surprisingly, Bobby made two errors at first base and struck out twice with men on base. He had "suddenly became affected with stage fright." He was then benched.[19]

The Cubs had been second in National League that year and had beaten the White Sox for the Windy City Championship. Their infield consisted of the legendary double play combination of Joe Tinker, Johnny Evers, and Frank Chance, and they had won the National League pennant four times between 1906 and 1910 and the World Series in 1908. This was a powerful all-white team that the Leland Giants were facing, and the Cubs won the first game, four to one. In game two the Leland Giants were ahead five to two in the ninth inning with Rube Foster pitching, but Foster tired and gave up three runs. The game was now tied, and there were runners on first and third with two outs. Foster went to the dugout for a relief pitcher and asked the umpire what was the score of the game. The umpire objected to this and the Cubs did too. When the managers of the two teams met to discuss the situation, the runner on third stole home. The umpire ruled that since time had not been called, the run would stand, and gave the Cubs the victory, 6 to 5. The Cubs won the last game 1-0. Foster wanted a rematch, but the Cubs refused.[20]

In the fall of 1909 Bobby accepted the job as head college football coach for Parker College in Winnebago, Minnesota, becoming only the second African American in the U.S. to be a college football head coach. The first had been Matthew Bullock, who coached at Massachusetts Agricultural College, now University of Massachusetts, Amherst, in 1904.[21] Marshall's appointment is described as follows in the *Winnebago City Press-News*. "The football team will get fully organized this week, and be in readiness for the best coaching our boys have ever had. The new coach, who will arrive the first of next week, is Bob Marshall of Minneapolis, a graduate of the law department two years ago, and one of the most famous football players in the history of the University teams...He has a record of a clean life and conduct, and we are assured of the services of a gentleman, as he works here with our boys."[22] Marshall kept on getting good press at Parker College. A November 13, 1909, story in the *Winnebago City Press-News* reads as follows. "Our boys are doing splendid and faithful work every day in football practice. This season far outclasses any other in the response and loyalty of the boys to every day practice work."[23] Marshall coached this all-white team in such a way that "football enthusiasm and loyalty were never better." The biggest game of the season, with St. Thomas College, ended in a 6-6 tie. Marshall chose not to continue coaching at Parker College after 1909.[24]

Dr. Steven R. Hoffbeck states, "There was a time when just about everyone in Minnesota knew the name and fame of Bobby Marshall."[25] He was often referred to in the local press. The following *Minneapolis Tribune* from November 24, 1909 stated, "Bobby Marshall will have to play some game in the Dean-New Prague football contest on Thanksgiving Day if he wishes to hold his prestige, for William Johnson, head waiter at the West Hotel, since he has come out and admitted that he is the brother of Jack Johnson, the 'champ' is the whole show now with the colored population of Minneapolis...The waiters at the West, who used to step lively when Mr. Johnson gave the order, step twice as lively now and no one thinks of talking back.

JACK JOHNSON

Although Bobby Marshall was a Minnesota hero, World Heavyweight Champion of boxing Jack Johnson did not have hero status in Minnesota. In March of 1910 Johnson was in the Twin Cities with his white girl friend, Etta Duryea. Etta was a glamorous woman from Brooklyn, New York, who traveled in the social circles of the elite. They were in a taxi headed for the train station when the taxi broke down. An angry mob surrounded the taxi and the interracial couple needed a police escort to get to the station.[29] Their relationship was no picnic. Johnson was unfaithful, and in December he beat Duryea so badly she had to be hospitalized, yet they were married shortly thereafter. Duryea's mental health was not made any better with Johnson's brutality and America's attitude toward interracial marriage at that time. On September 11, 1912, Duryea died of a self-inflicted gunshot wound.[30]

Two years later, Jim Jefferies, who had given up the heavyweight championship in 1904, came forward to challenge Johnson. They met in the ring on July 4 in Reno Nevada before 22,000 fans. Jefferies was in terrible shape, and made no bones about the fact that he had come out of retirement for the money—the equivalent of more than a million dollars today—and to show the world that a black man couldn't beat a white man. The bout was scheduled for 45 rounds, but Johnson had the upper hand from the beginning and scored a technical knockout in the 15th round. The backlash in parts of white American was strong, with riots and lynchings.

"'Ah always knowed that Mr. Johnson was a distinguished gen'man,' said '13' last night, 'but I never guessed he was a brother of Jack's. Well sah, he is a big man and I don't doubt he has licked Jack, but I bet he couldn't do it now lessen it was a running fight.'"[26]

It's easy to imagine that Bobby was distressed to read articles like that, sitting on the couch in his living room. He felt racial prejudice was a matter of ignorance. Perhaps he pitied the ignorance of a reporter with such a prejudiced view.

Bobby did play in the Dean-New Prague football contest on Thanksgiving Day that year. The next day's *Minneapolis Tribune* said, "In an interesting though rather one-sided game, the Deans beat the 'Seal of Minnesota' eleven of New Prague, at Nicollet Park yesterday by a score of 28-0. The teams were very evenly matched as to weight but the local eleven was much faster and showed a better knowledge of the new game, the first touchdown coming as a result of a well-executed forward pass by Marshall to Hunter...Bobby Marshall played a great game and his handling of punts and dodging runs through a broken field were features. He also used good judgement in directing the play and on the defense was in every play."[27] That season the Deans won the Minnesota Sunday League and became the Champions of Minnesota for a third straight year.[28]

In the spring of 1910 Bobby accompanied the Chicago Giants, a rival of the Chicago Leland Giants, on a two-month road trip to the deep South. The Giants played other African American teams in Houston, Dallas, Mobile, and Pensacola, and won 35 games. Bobby was paid $40 a week along with expenses.[31]

Upon their return, the teams scheduled games in Chicago itself. The *Chicago Broad Ax* newspaper of May 14 mentions plans for a Chicago Giants game early in the season. "Tomorrow will witness a great crowd at Auburn Park at the flag raising of the Chicago Giants, managed by that veteran of base ball, Frank C. Leland. Jim Callahan's Logan Squares will be the attraction for the day and the contest is the best game scheduled for the day. Our own Eight Regiment Band will play a concert from 2 to 3 o'clock p.m. and will render the "Star-Spangled Banner" when the flag is raised by Chicago's favorites…A parade of automobiles, tally hos, carriages and the Chicago Giants Rooter's Club will form at 29th and State street Sunday at one o'clock and all will wear the colors of the club, white and maroon. All are invited to join the parade and assist in making this the banner day in baseball."[32]

In early June of 1910 Bobby returned to Minnesota and re-joined the St. Paul Colored Gophers. He probably wanted to continue his law practice.[33] This was going to be a problem because the legal profession in Minneapolis in 1910 was, pretty much, a white man's game. He hated the Jim Crow laws of the American South that he had to endure while traveling with the Giants.[34] Also, he did not like the fact that some of his teammates on the Giants partied way too much.[35] Bobby knew that in order to stay in top form, you had to train right. He didn't like Chicago one bit and was very happy to be back in Minneapolis,[36] where rac-ism and segregation were somewhat less prevalent than in many of the other places baseball took him. On June 5, before 900 fans at Downtown Park in St. Paul, he hit a single, got a stolen base and made a great catch at first as the Colored Gophers beat the Conrads, 5-3.[37]

That summer, Bobby went on a long stint of road games in North Dakota, South Dakota, and northern Minnesota, for the Colored Gophers, and played the best baseball in his life. He hit .300, stole a lot of bases, and he was considered "one of the fast-est runners in the West." He was loved by the fans, both African American and white, many of whom came to St. Paul Colored Gophers games just to see Bobby play.[39]

In late July of that year he played in an exciting five-game se-ries for the St. Paul Colored Gophers against the Chicago Leland Giants. A rematch of the 1909 series between the two teams, it, too, was considered a "world's championship." As the series began the Colored Gophers had won sixty-two out of sixty-eight games and almost 4,500 fans showed up at Lexington Park to see the first game. The Colored Gophers lost that series, four games to one. They could still beat local teams but not powerhouses like the Chicago Giants. In this series Bobby was the best player on the Colored Gophers, batting .375 (6 for 16) including a home run and a double. His home run was socked to right center field, exactly one year after his game winning home run against the same Giants. In game one he made an interesting double play, fielding a hard-hit ground ball, stepping on first base and then firing the ball to the third baseman Jim Taylor who tagged out the runner coming from second base. But despite Bobby's heroics, "The St. Paul club had been simply overpowered by the Giants."[40]

By playing a huge role in the St. Paul Colored Gophers' triumph over the Chicago Leland Giants in 1909, Bobby was, once again, the hero of the Twin Cities.

6

The Colored Gophers Hit the Road

Later in the summer of 1910 the St. Paul Colored Gophers went on the road again, in Minnesota and Wisconsin, often drawing record-breaking crowds. The local white population found it entertaining to watch an African American team play against a local white team. The local white teams were not entirely local; they'd bring in a few excellent players from elsewhere, some of them Major League veterans. Playing against small town teams with white fans would be quite different from playing in the Twin Cities where many of the fans were African American. How would Bobby Marshall handle that?

On September 18 the Colored Gophers played the Shakopee Rock Springs at the Scott County Fair, which was held in Belle Plaine, 25 miles southwest of Minneapolis. In the top of the ninth, with the score tied 2-2, Marshall whacked a home run to give the Gophers a 3-2 lead. In the bottom of the ninth, Gophers player Harry Brown made an error on a pop fly with two out and two on base. No one scored on that play, but the next Rock Springs hitter knocked the ball over the Gopher left fielder's head, giving Rock Springs a 4-3 walk-off win. But things often went better for Colored Gophers that season; they won 104 games and compiled a .700 winning percentage.[1]

Bobby had given up his law office while on the road, and when he returned to Minneapolis in June he did legal work from his father's home. In September of 1910 Bobby decided not to coach anymore and instead, decided to join the law firm of Franklin, Pitzke, and Marshall. Was the grind of baseball road trips bothering him? Some of the St. Paul Colored Gophers players, Pangburn, Armstrong, Bowman, Brown, and Johnson had quit the team that September. Did that discourage Bobby? Marshall was now a law partner with his college associate, William H. H. Franklin. This firm specialized in the general practice of law along with insurance matters, collection, real estate issues, and personal injury.[2] "Marshall, now 30 years old, again had to decide which road to take. Should he build bridges between the worlds of white and African American Minnesotans through his popularity and athletic prowess or should he be a professional attorney? Either way, in the parlance of his era, he might serve to 'uplift the race.'"[3]

The lure of sports was too strong to resist entirely. Bobby was convinced he was no longer fast enough to play football on the highest level competitively.[4] He became a scout for the University of Minnesota football team. On October 8 Bobby was in Lincoln, Nebraska, scouting the contest between the Cornhuskers and the University of South Dakota. Marshall "brought back from the camp of the enemy tales of hidden (Nebraska) power."[5]

In April, 1911 Bobby organized a team called the Twin Cities Gophers, for which he served as coach, player-captain, and general manager. There had been a power struggle between Bobby and St. Paul Colored Gophers owner, Phil Daddy Reid. Bobby won. He signed some players from the Chicago Leland Giants for his team, and the St. Paul Colored Gophers team folded. The new owners of the Twin Cities Gophers were George Lennon, a clothing dealer, and Glover Shull, a restaurant owner.[6] *The Appeal* states "Bobby Marshall, one time star football player on the University of Minnesota eleven, but almost as well known as a star in the baseball profession, has blossomed out as a magnate in the national pastime this season. Bobby, with Glover Shull of Minneapolis, will direct the Colored Gophers, former world's champion team, and he has gathered under his wing an array of the best talent in the profession."[7] Bobby, as general manager, organized games with white teams. In the April 11 edition of the *Grand Forks Evening Times* it states, "The [Fargo] Athletics have already signed up for two dates with Manager Bobby Marshall of the Twin City Gophers. The colored team will appear in Fargo against the Athletics on Sunday and Monday, May 4 and 5." The same article goes on to report Marshall's view that his team will be a strong one this season and they will be able to give anyone a good game."[8] Bobby was coming into his own, not just as a player but as a leader, an organizer, and an emissary for inter-racial play.

The St. Paul Colored Gophers were now history. Their owner, Phil "Daddy" Reid, gave Bobby one of his first major opportunities in pro baseball by signing him to the Colored Gophers for the 1907, 1909, and 1910 seasons. In April 1909 Reid toured the American South, recruiting star players for his team, and it became one of the greatest in history. Reid married Belle Davis, a world famous African American singer and dancer, in 1910. They took their honeymoon in Europe, leaving the U.S.A. July 27 and thus missing the classic rematch between the Colored Gophers and the Chicago Leland Giants. A flamboyant man, Reid loved cigars, gambling, and fine clothes. As an entrepreneur, he owned a successful saloon that stood at what is now 40 East Kellogg Blvd. in St. Paul. He was a cheerful soul, always happy to do something kind for someone. He died at the age of 58 due to "acute gastritis" and a heart condition.[9]

The Twin Cities Gophers first game of the 1911 season was scheduled for April 16—Easter Sunday—at Lexington Park in St. Paul against Perry Werden's All-Stars, but the game had to be postponed because the field wasn't ready to play on. Werden let it be known that he felt Marshall had postponed the game because he was afraid of facing Werden's team. This riled Marshall, though off the field he didn't get angry often. He suggested to Werden that they reschedule the game for the following Saturday, with the winner talking all the gate receipts.[10] When challenged, Marshall did not back down.

The St. Paul Colored Gophers with Reid, wearing a dark suit and a top hat, in the middle of the front row.

One of the new players on the Twin Cities Gophers was Bert "Yellow Kid" Jones. The nickname referred to his light skin, which resembled that of a comic strip character with the same name. Yellow Kid was playing center field that day. In the first inning, he made a great running catch of a long fly ball, robbing the All-Star's Lefty Davis of a home run. In the fourth inning Marshall hit a triple, knocking in two runs. The Gophers won, 4-1.[11]

In 1911 a racial incident erupted at Lexington Park in St. Paul. Napoleon William "Crawdad" Johnson, an African American waiter at the local Carling restaurant, loved to heckle the players of the white Minneapolis Millers team from the stands. On May 31, the Millers' catcher, Hub Dawson, got fed up with Johnson's heckling, charged into the stands, and attacked Johnson. Then the Millers' manager, Joe Cantillion, grabbed a baseball bat and smashed Johnson on the head. Johnson settled the matter in court, asking for a $10,000 settlement but winning only a $1,400 payment.[12]

The Twin Cities Gophers went on the road, playing in Huron,

South Dakota, on May 16 in a game in which Bobby bashed two triples and a single in an 8-5 win. In Redfield, South Dakota, the Gophers played in a 60-mile-per-hour wind and lost 4-3. On May 25 in Ellendale, North Dakota, before 600 fans, Bobby hit a double in the seventh inning with the Gophers down 2-0. Then the Gophers' Harry Brown hit a towering drive. Ellendale's Bill Eiden, "the Russian Prince," made a great catch, crashing into the right field wall, and then made a great throw to catch Bobby, who had run with the pitch, off second base, giving Ellendale a 2-0 victory. In an early June game against the Bismarck, North Dakota, Marshall, Brown, and Schaffer hit back-to-back home runs in a 7-6 victory.[13] The Gophers' road trip had its ups and downs.

On June 15 the Gophers played against the Devils Lake, North Dakota team. Devils Lake had the lead 7-4 in the seventh inning. With a man on base at the top of the seventh Bobby stepped up to the plate and knocked a home run. Then "Yellow Kid" Jones hit a home run to tie the score. It was getting dark. To preserve the tie, the Gophers needed to shut down Devils Lake in the bottom of the seventh. Zalusky singled. Then the Devils Lake left fielder, Caylor hit a double, which allowed Zalusky to score and gave Devils Lake an 8-7 victory. The next day it was reported in the *Devils Lake World* newspaper that Marshall, "has somewhat overrated himself… the impression (is) that fame has been too much for the cranium under his wooly locks…(and) his continual kicking put him in bad with the local fans and disgusted his former friends." During some of these road trip games Bobby argued a lot with an umpire named Davies.[14] But this article in the *Devils Lake World* is the only piece of negative reporting about Marshall that I've encountered in five years of research.

On the last game of the road trip, played on June 29 the Gophers drew a crowd of more than a thousand fans but lost to the Alexandria, Minnesota, team, 4-1. The Twin Cities Gophers returned to the Twin Cities with more losses than wins.[15] The long and frustrating road trip was finally over. The team had attracted large crowds but had not played as well as the St. Paul Colored

Gophers had in previous years. Bobby's frustration was probably multiplied by the fact that he was both the manager and a player on the team.

Upon returning home in early July the Gophers swept a three-game series with Perry Werden's All-Stars. In the second game Bobby got three hits. The Werdens had a second baseman named Billy Hoke who also wrote a sports column for the *Minneapolis Tribune* called "Texas Leaguers." In his column, Hoke said of Marshall, that he was "unusually fast on his pins for a big man" and "plenty tall enough to grab all the high pegs and dig the low ones out of the mire" like a big leaguer.[16]

A few weeks later the Colored Gophers traveled the four hundred miles back to Devils Lake, North Dakota, for a 4th of July game noteworthy less for its outcome than its banter. The Gophers lost 10-2, but there was a lot of verbal give and take between Marshall and the hometown fans. The *Devils Lake World* commented: "Several pertinent remarks were made during the progress of the game and were it not for this fact all excitement would have been lost. Unable to battle with the sphere [the baseball], the Gophers took to flinging a word battle with the fans, the result being that the fans were not only satisfied with winning the game, but they made the Gophers look as if they were half undressed every time they opened their mouths." On July 6, the Gophers finally beat Devils Lake 7-1 after five straight losses. The *Minneapolis Journal* reported that for that game, "the umpire had an off day" [and therefore was] "unable to stop the Gophers."[17]

On July 11 Bobby's team arrived in Hibbing, Minnesota, for a seven-game series with the Hibbing Colts. They beat the Hibbing Colts 4-3 in a 10-inning game on July 13. The game was marred by Hibbing third baseman Dick Brookins, who intentionally spiked a Twin Cities Colored Gophers base runner. On July 18 Bobby was in the midst of an 0-17 hitting slump when he bashed a home run off the same Dick Brookins, who had taken the mound for the Colts. Bobby was nursing a bad ankle at the time and "the range fans gave the lanky first baseman a warm ovation as he limped around the bases." The Colts won that day, 8-4. In their final contest the Colored Gophers won 9-2, with Bobby hitting three singles, bringing their overall record against the Colts to 6-2.[18]

But the Colored Gophers were running out of steam. In early August the Alexandria, Minnesota, team swept them in a three-game series. Some of the players became disgruntled, and William Binga left the team, claiming that "on account of bad management, they have had a disastrous season—and the players are much dissatisfied. Baseball is a business and needs good management."[19] One thing was obvious: the Twin Cities Gophers of 1911 were not anywhere near as good as the St. Paul Colored Gophers teams of earlier years. The team folded after the season.[20]

With the Colored Gophers' season over, Marshall no doubt breathed a sigh of relief. Being a coach can be a tough business, even for a superstar.

On August 22 Bobby played tennis at the Minneapolis Racquet Club, and on Labor Day weekend he played first base for Perry Werden's All-Stars, a team he's played against at the beginning of the season.[21]

In September, weighing his options, Marshall decided to give up his law practice. It wasn't panning out. It's likely that in 1911 Bobby was doing legal work with well-known white attorneys in the firm of Nash and Armstrong, yet by September it was clear that his law career was foundering.[22] He couldn't find enough clients in either the white or African American community. Most of his clients were Jewish.[23] Though Bobby was well-known as a sports hero, H. H. Franklin had become the African American lawyer of choice for the Twin Cities.[24]

The Appeal newspaper remarked in one report that the "call of the pigskin and the lure of the diamond" was foremost for Marshall. Bobby agreed. "I love games of all kinds from tennis to football. Anything to be fighting to win a game. It's what I live on."[25] By playing pro baseball in the spring and summer and pro football in the fall, Marshall could make between fifteen and eighteen thousand dollars a year—more money than he was making as a lawyer.[26] But would that be enough money for Bobby Marshall? Should he look for another job?

7

Will Minnesota's Hero
Gain National Recognition?

By now Marshall was well-established as a Minnesota hero. But to gain national recognition, it would help a lot to play against the greatest football player in America, Jim Thorpe. Could a game against Thorpe's Canton Bulldogs be arranged?

In September 1911, to supplement his income, Bobby accepted a position as crew chief grain inspector, a civil service position, for the Minnesota State Grain Inspection Department. He was now in the 'hum drum world of business.'[1] How would this affect his career as a professional athlete?

In an era when most African Americans worked jobs like railway porter, barber, or janitor, this was an excellent position. Bobby would travel around Minnesota to check the scales at the grain elevators where farmers brought their crops, to make sure they weren't being cheated by the grain dealers. Marshall would show up without notice, check the scales and also check for mold in the grain, and he wouldn't hesitate to write up a citation for unacceptable business activities. A granary executive might occasionally try to bribe him, but Marshall was well-known for his honesty and diligence in protecting the rights of the farmers. Bill Marshall, Bobby's grandson, says of Bobby's work for the Grain Commission, "It was more than a vocation. It was a calling."[2]

Marshall worked out of the office of the State Weighmaster as an employee of the state of Minnesota. An article in *The Appeal*, attempts to find parallels between this position and Marshall's prowess on the gridiron: "Even here the aggressive methods which won renown upon the athletic fields are making themselves felt. Assigned to duty…with a crew of men to command, Bobby is still vigorously forcing the pigskin called 'business' to the 'goal' of success." His job title was State Weigher.[3]

But his position with the State Grain Commission naturally limited Marshall's options to continue his sporting career. Long-distance travel was out. Aside from the weekend, the sporting events he participated in would have to take place locally.

But while Marshall was working to break down racial barriers, theories of racial difference were gaining credence in highly respectable places. In 1910 the Eugenics Records Office was established in Cold Spring Harbor, New York, with the support of world-renowned scientists, inventors, and writers such as David Star Jordan, biologist and chancellor of Stanford University, Vernon Kellog, famous Stanford biologist, William B. Castle, Harvard geneticist, Charles R. Henderson of the University of Chicago, Luther Burbank, "the plant wizard," George Bernard Shaw, H.G. Wells, Alexander Graham Bell, and Margaret Sanger, founder of Planned Parenthood.[4] The complete list of those active in the movement reads like a "Who's Who in Biological Science."

This was not a wild and unruly bunch of rednecks, looking to lynch African Americans or burn crosses. It was a group of some of the most prominent scientists of the age, and yet they held a very violent idea as a tool to further their ends: sterilization. They took it as their role to identify the traits that were harmful to human evolution and eliminate them by sterilizing people who exhibited them. The leaders of the eugenics movement were mostly white Anglo-Saxon Protestants, so it is not entirely surprising that the groups they targeted as inferior were Jews, African Americans, American Indians, Slovaks, Turks, and Russians, to name a few. Ben Westhoff, an award-winning journalist and grandson of University of Minnesota Eugenicist Sheldon Reed, points out that, "The perfect human, in the eyes of most eugenicists, tended to be white Northern European." According to some eugenicists, people of lower intelligence and other undesirable traits should be sterilized.[5] What would these eugenicists think of Bobby Marshall?

Undaunted by what anyone thought of him, scientist or not, in the spring of 1912 Marshall organized another African American baseball team, the Minneapolis Hennepins. He commented that there was "no reason why

Bobby Marshall (left) and Joe Davis in Minneapolis Hennepins uniforms.

the team cannot be one of the fastest in the country." Louis Marshall, Bobby's younger brother, was a member of the team. They were not as good as the St. Paul Colored Gophers had been, but they had sharp looking uniforms, due to the fact that the team was funded by the Hennepin Clothing Company. The *Titanic*, in route from Ireland to the United States, crashed into an iceberg and sank on April 15, 1912, at 2:30 am. The Minneapolis Hennepins were not doing much better, losing all eight of the games they played in the Twin Cities. For example, on Sunday June 9 Marshall's all African American Hennepin Clothing baseball team lost 12-4 to Perry Werden's All-Stars, a team of white players, at Nicollet Park. Bobby batted clean up, went one for four at the bat, played catcher and had 11 put outs. The Hennepins' biggest weakness was fielding; they made 35 errors during those seven games. The team folded in early August.[6]

By late July Marshall was already playing for another local team, the St. Joe-Deckerts. On the afternoon of July 28 Bobby was playing left field for St. Joes in a game against the Athletics of the North Minneapolis Athletic Association. The Athletic won 15-9. Bobby went 2-5 at the plate and hit a home run in the sixth inning with a man on.[7]

A Minneapolis baseball fan in the summer of 1912 could take a trolley ride to Nicollet Park to see a baseball game. If a man took a woman to the game, the woman would get in free. On Sunday, August 4, Perry Werden's All Stars were set to play the St. Joseph Saints at Nicollet at 3:30 pm. The game could be played at Nicollet that day because the Minneapolis Millers American Association (Double A) minor league team didn't have a game scheduled. That day the *Minneapolis Sunday Tribune* reported that, "Bobby Marshall, the colored boy who made a great reputation at the University of Minnesota in baseball and football will be in uniform for the Saints…"[8] Werden's All-Stars defeated the St. Joseph Saints 12-2 that day. Marshall played left field and went one for three at the plate, hitting a double.[9]

On November 7, 1912, boxer Jack Johnson, the reigning heavyweight champion, was arrested by Chicago police for bringing a white woman across state lines "for the purpose of prostitution and debauchery," a violation of the Mann Act. The woman in question, Belle Schreiber, had been severely beaten by Johnson more than once, and she provided essential testimony so a case against Johnson could be made. The judge who set Johnson's bail at $30,000, was Kennesaw Mountain Landis who would later, as commissioner of Major League Baseball, enforce a policy of no admittance of African American players. Johnson was in Chicago to marry another white woman, Lucille Cameron, and the couple were married on December 4.[10] At that time, marriage between whites and African Americans was frowned upon by many people in white society. This practice, called miscegenation, was illegal in many states. Though Johnson was a sports hero, he was also considered an unsavory character due to his generally shameless behavior and violence toward women. Marshall cut an entirely different image, and it helped pave the for the time when an African American man could marry a white woman or play on a Major League baseball team, without social stigma.

The results of the 1912 baseball season were a mixed bag. Bobby had played well but his team, the Hennepins, had lost a lot of games. That fall he played football for the All-Star team in Minneapolis. On Thanksgiving Day, November 28, an almost capacity crowd of nearly 7,000 filled the stands at Nicollet Park to watch the All-Stars play the Minneapolis Beavers, who, two weeks earlier, had defeated the Minneapolis Marines, 7-3, to qualify for the game. In the second half, the Beavers had just scored a touch-down and the All-Stars next drive stalled around midfield. Pickering of the All-Stars stood back in the backfield, ready to punt the ball. But just as the ball was hiked, Marshall raced down the field and Pickering, instead of punting, threw a perfect forty-yard pass. Marshall pulled in the ball while running at full speed and scored easily. *The Minneapolis Morning Tribune* gave the play a sub-headline, calling it the "Most Sensational Forward Pass of the Year." The All-Stars won that day, 34-7. Pudge Heffelfinger, an All-American interior lineman from Yale and assistant coach for the University of Minnesota football team, played a great game for the All-Stars. Heffelfinger was in his forties at the time.[11]

Bobby started the 1913 baseball season with a reorganized version of the Minneapolis Hennepins. They played white teams in rural Minnesota and South Dakota. Around June 22 they headed for St. Cloud, Minnesota to play the Pretzels. Bobby hit a double to give the Hennepins a 3-0 lead. But the Hennepin's pitching collapsed in the later innings and they lost 11-3. The team headed for South Dakota in late June where they won eight straight games before falling into a slump. Bobby's last game for the Hennepins was on July 13 against the Watertown, South Dakota, team. He was playing catcher as the Hennepins lost 9-2.[12]

On June 29 Bobby was in the lineup in the Twin Cities as catcher for the West Side Athletics. It was probably not much fun for Bobby that day because the Athletics lost to the Camerons,

22-3.[13] Bobby certainly didn't have a problem playing for two teams at the same time.

It was probably just as well that Bobby left the Hennepins after the July 13 game. A week later, after a 15-0 loss to the Sioux Falls squad, an article in the *Sioux Falls Daily Press* stated, "A more merciless grounding was never before given a team in Sioux Falls…[The Hennepins] were absolutely at a loss. Sioux Falls had them buffaloed so that half of them could not have held on to an ice cream cone if it had a handle to it." By late July the Hennepins folded and that was not surprising because Bobby Marshall was no longer with the team.[14]

Bobby had begun playing for a white team, the St. Cloud Pretzels. Bobby played second base, right field, and shortstop for the Pretzels and hit .495 in his last four games. These four games were against the French Lick Creek, Indiana, Plutos, an African American team, with a 79-7 record that season.[15] When he played for teams such as the Pretzels he was paid $20 to $30 per game.[16]

Fortunately, Bobby could travel to athletic events on weekends, making it possible to continue playing football in the fall. He played for the Minneapolis Marines from the 1913 season through the 1917 season. Bobby was now 6'2" and he weighed 195 pounds. He played halfback for the 1913 season.[17] The *Minneapolis Tribune* described his 1913 season as follows. "Marshall is one of the mainstays of the Marine team…He has been playing great football all season and is a hard man to stop."[18]

On Sunday, October 26, the Marines defeated the Adams team from Duluth, 14-0, in front of three thousand Duluth fans, scoring touchdowns twice on passing plays. The Adams team had not been defeated in four years and, as the *Minneapolis Morning Tribune* noted, "Bob Marshall played a conspicuous part in the game. He was a tower of strength on the defensive, and his powerful line smashing and end skirting made one think of the days when the colored boy was the star of the Gophers. He still retains his old time dash and there was seldom a play in which the dusky athlete did not figure…The playing of Marshall was really the deciding factor in the game."[19] An article in the *The Appeal,* stated, "Bobby was smashed up a little but he says that's all in the game." This article describes Marshall as "our football star."[20] Bobby was breaking the color line again, playing for the Marines. The Marines were an awesome team in 1913, winning the Minnesota pro football title.[21]

Thanksgiving Day football was a tradition in the Twin Cities and 1913 was no exception. The weather was cold that afternoon but not too cold for the overflow crowd of 3,000 fans. Although the Marines had Bobby at right halfback, the Marines couldn't generate enough offense to score any points and lost to the University All-Stars16-0. Jack Marks of Dartmouth College scored both touchdowns for the All-Stars and George Capron drop kicked a field goal.[22]

Bobby started the 1914 baseball season with a new African American team named the Colored Gophers, but after the Colored Gophers were shellacked 15-4 by the St. Joe Deckerts on May 14, he returned to the St. Cloud Pretzels. It was understandable that he wanted to leave the Gophers, of whom a local newspaper wrote: "They could neither hit, field, nor throw the ball." But it was not a great season for Bobby and a sportswriter wrote that, "his fielding has not been up to standard nor has his work with the big stick been what is expected of him." On August 24, the Pretzels played against the Plutos before a standing-room-only crowd of almost 2,000. Bobby "scored a run, stole two bases and saved the day for St. Cloud with a running, jumping catch in right field of long drive off the bat of the Plutos shortstop Johnnie Cunningham."[23]

Bobby showed great ability in just about any sport he chose to pursue, including motorcycle racing. An article in the *Virginia Enterprise* from St. Louis County, Minnesota, from July 3, 1914 said, "The colored athlete is said by friends to be a motorcyclist of more than average ability. He possesses plenty of nerve, uses his head and has excellent control over his machine."[24]At the Minnesota state motorcycle championship in July Bobby got his cycle up to a speed of 80 miles an hour.[25]

While still playing for the Minneapolis Marines in the 1914 football season, Marshall also organized his own football team, "Bobby Marshall's All-Stars" to play a game against the Indians on October 4 at Nicollet Park. Marshall was at quarterback, but the All-Stars lost 6-0-before a small crowd. "Bobby Marshall did good individual work for the defeated team, making several long gains, but the rest of the team showed lack of practice in team play." The game was played in four ten-minute quarters. There was only one substitution and that was for the Indians.[26]

Marshall had another good game on November 1 when the Minneapolis Marines faced the St. Paul Laurels before 3,000 fans at North Side Park, and the outcome was much better. The *Minneapolis Morning Tribune* described his contribution as follows: "Bobby Marshall …played left end for the Marines yesterday and was the star of the game. The former Minnesota player kicked five goals from touchdowns, and scored a touchdown after a run of 40 yards. He also played a fine defensive game…Marshall at left end was the real star of the game." The Marines, playing in their red and white uniforms, won, 43-0.[27]

The St. Paul Banholzers offered stiffer resistance against the Marines a week later at North Side Park, but still lost 20-0. Marshall was among the three Marines singled out for praise; he kicked three extra points but missed the fourth, which was at a tough angle.[28]

On Thanksgiving Day, November 26, a record crowd of 7,200 attended the Marines game against Johnny McGovern's All-Stars at Nicollet Park. The promoters for the game donated $100 to the American Red Cross. The All-Stars had the upper hand until the final minutes, when the Marines scored a touchdown to pull within one point, at 14-13. But Marshall's extra point attempt went wide and the All-Stars preserved the win.[29] Reflecting on such incidents, Bobby would later say to his grandson, Bill Marshall, "Even heroes fail sometimes. You have to accept defeat and move on. You have to accept it, as long as you tried your best."[30]

While Marshall was making the case by example, week after week, for an integrated society of equals on the playing field, and off, others were determined to move society in the opposite direction. In 1914, for example, Dr. Charles Dight was elected as a Minneapolis alderman. Dight considered himself a socialist and held passionate views about the nature of mankind. He must have been well-received as a city politician because in 1915 the Minneapolis City Council named a nine-block stretch of road east of Hiawatha Avenue "Dight Avenue." Born in 1856 in Mercer, Pennsylvania, Dight, grew up on a farm, and as a thirteen-year-old he decided he wanted to become a doctor. At twenty-two he graduated from the University of Michigan School of Medicine. After two years of private practice he joined the University of Michigan medical faculty. Two years later he presided over the American Medical School in Beirut, Lebanon. Upon returning to the United States he was resident physician and teacher of physiology at the Shattuck School in Fairbault, Minnesota. After that he taught at the Medical School at Hamline University that became part of the University of Minnesota in 1907. As a medical doctor, he would become an opinion leader of great influence, and he would also become the leader in Minnesota of the eugenics movement.[31]

Dr. Charles Dight

Another opinion leader eager to promote a racist agenda was Thomas Dixon, Jr. Dixon was born in Shelby, North Carolina, in 1864, and one of his earliest memories was the lynching of an African American man accused of raping the widow of a Confederate soldier. His mother told him the lynching, done by the Ku Klux Klan, was an act of justice. He was educated at Wake

Forest and Johns Hopkins and left college to become an actor, but was not successful on the stage. After failing in a second career as a lawyer, Dixon followed in his father's footsteps and became a Baptist minister, preaching in New York City. He finally made a name for himself as a writer, publishing three books that glorified the Ku Klux Klan: *The Leopard's Spots* (1902), *The Clansman* (1905), and *The Traitor* (1907). These books were instrumental in spreading the doctrines of the Klan all across American—even to Minnesota.[32] They vilified the behavior of African Americans following the Civil War and glorified the KKK members who, in response, murdered hundreds of African Americans throughout the South.

As the KKK grew in strength in many states, Dixon's novel, *The Clansman*, was made into a movie called *Birth of a Nation*. Long, highly melodramatic, and technically innovative, it transformed a bigoted view of American history into popular entertainment. After watching the film in the White House, then-President Woodrow Wilson, a Virginian who looked favorably on the activities of the KKK, is reported to have said: "It is like writing history with lightning, and my only regret is that it is all so terribly true."[33]

This revived version of the KKK didn't target only African Americans, but also Catholics and Jews. The Klan's 1916 rule book expressed the view that only 'good Christian white people' who believe in racial purity and Protestant morality could save the country from destruction.[34] On his motorcycle trips on Minnesota roads, Bobby, part German, part African, might have laughed out loud at the absurdity of such theories of racial purity. But the growing popularity of the Klan was no laughing matter.

In the baseball season of 1915, Bobby rode his motorcycle to Cokato, Minnesota, about fifty miles west of Minneapolis, to play catcher for a white team. He was joined by Minneapolis Marines football player Rube Ursella. The pay per game would be up to $20 for a pitcher, $12.50 for a catcher, $10 for an infielder, and $5 for an outfielder.[35] Bobby was still working for the grain commission during the week, but he found competitive sports irresistible, and he enjoyed playing for teams like Cokato on the weekend.

That fall Marshall agreed to play for the Minneapolis Marines again. Jim Quirk, pro football historian, describes him at this point in his career as, "a big, tough end who was almost indestructible."[36] The Marines won the Twin City Championship that year, defeating the St. Paul Laurels 3-0 on October 31 with Bobby at left end. Four thousand fans thrilled to this tight match at Nicollet Park.[37]

The Thanksgiving Day game between the Minneapolis Marines and the local All-Stars was also widely anticipated, and lots of money was being bet. Marine supporters were giving two to one odds while All-Star supporters were giving 10-7 or 10-6 odds. The *Minneapolis Morning Tribune* ran an article before the game in which it was pointed out that "no more noted Gopher ever played than Bobby Marshall, the Negro end, who will again be on the left extremity of the Marine line...Members of the rival teams prophesized that the game would be the most desperately contested football struggle Minneapolis has seen."[38]

Although the Marines lost to the All-Stars 7-0 on Thanksgiving Day, sportswriter Fred Coburn of the *Minneapolis Morning Tribune* called the event "the best independent football game ever played in the city." The crowd of 6,000 fans that showed up for the game was comparable to what the University of Minnesota team would sometimes draw.[39] A film of the game was made and shown in the Grand Theater in Bemidji, Minnesota.[40]

WEDDING BELLS

Marshall's life took on a new dimension in October 1916 when, at the age of thirty-six, he married a pretty eighteen-year-old African American woman named Irene B. Knott.[41] Her family was from the South, and Bobby met her while touring in Montana. Like Bobby, Irene was of mixed race, a light skinned African American.

Bette, Irene, and Kathy

Her mother, Katie Knott, lived in Great Falls.[42] The November 11 issue of *The Appeal* mentions a party held "in honor of the following persons, our two new brides, Mrs. Donald Brady and Mrs. Bobby Marshall." The party was held at the home of Mrs. J.H. Redd on Aldrich Avenue in Minneapolis.[43] Bobby and Irene had five children together, Robert Jr., William, Donald, David and Bette. David and Donald were twins, and David had a birth defect that caused his death at the age of one. Bette was originally named Cecile Lavern but she changed her name to Bette as an adult.[44] Irene is described as "charming" in *The Appeal* newspaper.[45] Irene is in the middle of the picture on this page with her daughter, Bette Session, to her right. To Irene's left is Kathy Washington, Bobby's granddaughter.

Evidently Bobby and Irene didn't get much of a honeymoon because three days later Bobby was at Nicollet Park playing left end for the Minneapolis Marines against the East Ends team. The 2,000 fans in attendance saw a tough battle. Sampson threw a pass to Bobby that set up a touchdown, and the Marines won, 7-0.[46] The Marines had a much easier time of it on Sunday, November 12, 1916, when they defeated the St. Paul Laurels 38-0 at

Nicollet Park. Bobby caught a 30-yard pass and was singled out by the *Minneapolis Tribune* for his excellent play on the line.[47]

The Marines had attempted to schedule a game with Jim Thorpe's Canton Bulldogs that year, to show the world that Marshall and his Minneapolis Marines were as good as any team in America, but Thorpe turned down the offer.[48] At the time, Marshall had no idea if the opportunity to face the great Jim Thorpe would ever present itself again.

Local contests weren't hard to come by. On Thanksgiving Day—a beautiful afternoon—the Marines took on the Minnesota All-Stars at Nicollet Park. The Minnesota All-Stars were made up of 1916 University of Minnesota football players. Sportswriter Walter Camp called the 1916 Gophers team the "most perfect in history."[49] Betting was heavy and Marine fans were giving two to one odds that the Marines would win. It was a see-saw battle, highlighted by Rube Ursella's excellent punting for the Marines. (His punts were frequently 70 yards long.) Neither team could pass the ball effectively and the 7,500 fans in attendance had to content themselves with a 0-0 tie.[50]

On December 3 the Marines defeated the Davenport, Iowa, Athletic Club 20-7, thanks in large part, to Marshall's defensive play at left end. Bobby also scored a touchdown on a five-yard pass from Sampson. The touchdown Davenport scored was the first one the Marines had given up in three years.[51] Traveling all the way to Iowa was something new for Marshall and the Marines. Most of their games were played much closer to home. They arrived for their game with Davenport at 7 am, stayed at the Hotel Dempsey, received an auto tour of the area from the home team, played the game before 3,000 fans, received 60% of the gate receipts and left town at 8:30 pm.[52]

Now Marshall had a full-time job during the week, a wife who would give birth to five children, and weekends full of athletic events year-round. Would there be enough hours in the day for Marshall to take care of all his responsibilities?

8

The Minneapolis Marines, World War I,

the Influenza Epidemic, and Race Riots

On April 2, 1917, U.S. President Woodrow Wilson declared war on Germany, initiating American involvement in World War I, which had already been raging for three years. On May 18th of that year Congress passed the Selective Service Act requiring men aged 21-30 to register for military service. That didn't affect Marshall because he was thirty-seven.

Most African Americans favored American involvement in the war, and more than 370,000 African Americans joined the war effort, working mainly in non-combat roles such as dock workers, ditch diggers, and other support tasks. However, 40,000 black soldiers did see combat action. Many African Americans viewed this war as an opportunity to prove that they were worthy of becoming citizens with equal rights.[1]

With the onset of war in Europe the flow of immigrants to the United States had dwindled, and as young American servicemen were sent overseas to fight demand for labor in northern cities became acute, especially in the North. Recruiters went south to encourage African Americans to move north, where industrial jobs would afford them a better standard of living. As a result, one million African Americans moved from the rural South to the urban North between 1916 and 1919.[2] African American men took advantage of job opportunities often found in factories. African American women also moved in great numbers, finding jobs in northern cities as domestic workers. The effect of this migration was not as significant in Minneapolis as it was in cities like Chicago and Detroit. In Detroit, the increase in African Americans after World War I was 611.3% while in Minneapolis it was only 51.5%. But wherever they relocated, these new arrivals faced unfavorable treatment from the locals, both African Americans and white.[3]

But in most cases, they were leaving behind a social environment that was even worse for citizens of African descent. In the South, most African Americans had lost the right to vote. Jim Crow laws, in effect from 1881 to 1964, denied African Americans equal rights in 26 states, including all the Southern states that seceded from the U.S. in the Civil War. Segregation was a legal fact of life. African Americans were not allowed to play against white people in sporting events, or even use the same bathrooms, water fountains, or hotels.

The term Jim Crow came from a song and dance routine from minstrel shows that toured America from the 1820s to 1870s. In one show, a white actor named Thomas Dartmouth "Daddy" Rice mocked an old African American slave called Jim Crow. Rice made his face look dark with burnt cork, danced in bare feet carrying a banjo and sang,

> *Come listen all you gals and boys*
> *I's jist from Tuckyhoe*
> *I'm goin sing a little song*
> *My name's Jim Crow*
> *Weel about and turn about and do jis so*
> *Eb'ry time I weel about and jump Jim Crow*[4]

In Plessy v. Ferguson (1896) the Supreme Court had sanctioned segregation, forcing African American Southerners into separate and unequal facilities, including schools. Most African

American Southerners worked on farms as sharecroppers, living in poverty.

On July 2, 1917, in East St. Louis, Illinois a four-day riot broke out. The Illinois National Guard failed to act as rioting whites killed more than a hundred African Americans and burned down a large portion of the African American community. A protest was staged in late July of the same year in New York City. Five thousand African Americans marched to protest the violence in East St. Louis. Another 20,000 applauded the marchers from the sidewalks.[5]

In August the Third Battalion of the 24th Infantry Regiment, an African American unit, was stationed in Houston, Texas, where the Jim Crow laws were strictly enforced. On August 23 more than a hundred of these soldiers attacked the city, killing 17 white people. Thirteen of the soldiers were executed and 53 received a sentence of life imprisonment.[6]

In October the first known Ku Klux Klan attack took place in Minnesota in a town called Lester Prairie. The victim was a German man, Hugo Klatt, who was viciously attacked and beaten while his sisters were struck with rotten eggs and stones.[7]

That same year Bobby received the news that his father had just died.[8] Richard Marshall had taught his son Bobby about the value of hard work and the effort and determination it would take to reach any worthwhile goal. Bobby was grieved by the loss, but shouldered his responsibility as the new head of the Marshall family along with his work as Minnesota state grain inspector, and his leadership role with the Minneapolis Marines.[9]

Bobby and the other players for the Minneapolis Marines continued to solicit donations for the war effort and for the benefit of American war veterans and their families. During halftime at football games they would encourage the fans to donate money in jugs with the players' names on them.[10]

In 1916 and 1917 the Marines scored 455 points compared to their opponents 48 points. They went 15-0-1 during this period and "were considered one of the top ten professional clubs in the country."[11] Historian Steven Hoffbeck describes Marshall's play with the Marines as follows. "He played with a rare combination of strength and craftiness, depending on leverage and experience to handle his opponents across the line."[12]

Once the Marines' had finished their 1917 season, Bobby and three of his teammates—Fred Chicken, Rube Ursella, and Walt "Big Boy" Buland—left for Rock Island, Illinois, for a game on Sunday Dec. 2 between two teams straddling the Mississippi River, the Independents of Rock Island, Illinois, and the Athletics of Davenport, Iowa. Chicken, a halfback, Rube Ursella, a quarterback, and Buland, a tackle, played for Rock Island, while Bobby played end for Davenport. At that time, the Independents and Athletics were pro football rivals, and this game was of much interest among local fans. The teams were considered to be evenly matched and the betting was heavy among local sports fans. Tickets for the game at Douglas Park in Rock Island cost 50 cents plus a five-cent war tax. Johnny Walker, sportswriter for the *Davenport Daily Times*, wrote the following on the Saturday before the game. "With the stage all set and the advance sale indicating the largest crowd that ever witnessed a tri-city gridiron combat, the Athletics

Ticket booth at Douglas Park

of Davenport and the Independents of Rock Island will get together in mortal combat Sunday afternoon at Douglas park, Rock Island, to settle definitely the professional championship of the tri-cities. Both teams are on edge and ready to uncork a great exhibition of football. Both have strengthened for the crucial game of the season and the contest that is on tap should be without doubt the grandest grid mill of local pigskin history."[13]

Rock Island won 23-7 with Chicken and Ursella running the ball effectively. Bobby caught two passes, one for 17 yards, and another for 8 yards, had a five-yard gain on a run, and ran back a punt. During this time period, pro players were able to easily move from one pro team to another during the same football season. After the game, Johnny Walker wrote, "If the so-called football contest between the Rock Island Independents and the Davenport Athletic Club staged at Douglas Park Sunday afternoon did not kill professional football in the tri-cities, then there are a lot more chumps in the tri-cities than the writer believes at this time." Walker was disappointed in his team's loss and it bothered him that so many good players from the Minneapolis Marines were added to the Rock Island roster. It also bothered him that some of the Davenport players had played a football game in Omaha, Nebraska, the day before and were probably too tired to play well. The Rock Island team double-teamed Marshall throughout the game.[14]

Prospects looked bright for the Minneapolis Marines as the 1918 football season approached. But a catastrophe of momentous proportions struck Minnesota, and the entire world, that year, and it upset the plans of the Minneapolis Marines and millions of other people. A flu epidemic, widely—but erroneously—referred to at the time as the Spanish Flu, broke out and reappeared in several waves throughout the year, eventually claiming fifty to one hundred million lives world-wide over an 18-month period.[15] Football schedules were curtailed and games were cancelled due to the possible spread of disease in big crowds. The Minneapolis Marines cancelled their entire season.[16] In the fall of 1918 the University of Iowa, in Iowa City, cancelled all large group events to prevent the spread of the deadly flu. For the Iowa Hawkeyes game with Coe College the fans were banned from the stands. This ban was enforced by the S.A.T.C., Student Army Training Corps., a 1918 version of the R.O.T.C.[17] In Rock Island all public events, including those of schools, churches and theaters were cancelled for almost a month from October 18 to November 13, 1918, for the same reason.[18]

It's a safe bet to say Bobby enjoyed his time playing football in Rock Island. It would not be the last chance he got to play there.

9

Bobby Joins the
Rock Island Independents

J im Thorpe, one of the greatest athletes of all time, had already turned down one football game against a Bobby Marshall led team. Would he do it again?

By 1919 Thorpe, an American Indian, was witnessing a great change in the demographics of the North. It now was becoming apparent that more African Americans were moving into Midwestern cities like the Twin Cities. "As increasing numbers of southern blacks migrated to the northern states, racial attitudes began to harden in the Twin Cities. All pretense of a delicate balance of racial harmony in Minneapolis evaporated. Fear of Reds [communists], foreigners, and migrating African Americans brought a different climate to the Upper Midwest, increasing discrimination in employment and housing."[1] In 1920, although less than one percent of Minnesota's population was African American, the presence of just one African American in a Minnesota town made many long-time residents nervous.[2] The riots in East St. Louis and Houston in 1917 may have played a role in arousing such feelings in a population with little exposure to ethnic diversity.

To prepare for the 1919 football season, Bobby decided he needed more protection against injury. He took a metal washboard and carefully positioned it around his abdomen. He did this before every game and it took an hour of careful preparation. It was probably a quite difficult taping job.[3]

At about the same time, another African American N.F.L. football star, Duke Slater, started stuffing magazines in his socks for protection against getting kicked in the shins—a common practice on the field. Another problem Slater faced was getting spiked on his hands during a pile-up on the field.[4]

In 1919 and 1920 Marshall wore the green and white uniform of the Rock Island Independents.[5] He took the train from Minneapolis to Rock Island on weekends during football season. Bobby considered these two seasons as his most challenging "because of the travel and partly because of the quality of the opponents."[6]

When the Independents started practice on September 9, Marshall was still playing for the Minneapolis Marines. Walter Flanigan, the manager of the Independents, was quoted in the *Rock Island Argus* newspaper as encouraging anyone from Rock Island who wanted to try out for the team to do so.[7]

Rock Island's fans were already excited by the prospect of seeing Jim Thorpe play. Thorpe had offered to bring his Canton Bulldogs to town if he got a $5000 guarantee for the game.[8]

On September 3, 1919, it was reported in the *Argus* that former Minneapolis Marine quarterback Rube Ursella would coach and play quarterback for the Independents. The *Argus* called Ursella "one of the greatest professional football players in the country." It reported the next day that, "When it was announced in last night's *Argus* exclusively that Ursella had arrived in Rock Island and had agreed to assume the role of coach, the grid fans of the city went into estacies of delight... there was a general handshaking and patting on the back with a few impromptu dances..." Excitement for the new football season was at a fever pitch. More than nine thousand fans showed up just to see a 45-minute evening practice under the lights at Douglas Park. Ursella laid out firm discipline, requiring that all players report to practice unless they had a good excuse not to be there. He could punt a football so far that the Rock Island City Commission considered a proposal to move back the fence surrounding the field. Ursella had decided to leave the Minneapolis Marines because the Rock Island team could draw larger crowds resulting in better pay for him. However, he agreed to a contract allocating an equal share of the money the team took in to each player.[9] What N.F.L. superstar would agree to such a financial arrangement today?

Walter Flanagan, manager of the Independents, met with representatives from the Moline and Davenport teams on September 11, and they agreed that men would be charged $1.00 for admission while women would be charged $.50. It was an increase in price, but they felt it could be justified by the improved quality of play.[10]

Billy Sunday, the Christian evangelist, gave three sermons in Rock Island on Sunday, September 14, at a tabernacle erected just for this event on Fifth Avenue and 24th Street at a cost of $16,000. All local churches affiliated with the event were closed so parishioners could attend, and twenty thousand people heard Billy Sunday preach that day.[11]

Meanwhile, on the same day, Coach Ursella held a tough practice. The players were working on conditioning; pads and uniforms had not been given out yet. The *Argus* reported, "The candidates are fast rounding into shape. Superfluous flesh can be seen dwindling from all of 'em."[12] So many fans showed up to watch the practice that they got in Coach Ursella's way, and he began to order "secret practices" open only to those associated with the team.[13]

For the 1919 season Ursella implemented the same Minnesota Shift offense that Coach Williams had used at the University of Minnesota years earlier.[14]

It was reported on Tuesday September 23 in the *Argus* that another former Minneapolis Marine, Walt Buland, had joined the team. Buland, a very large man, played tackle and definitely strengthened the front line.[15] Also on September 23 former Minneapolis Marines star halfback Fred Chicken announced he would play for the Independents in the 1919 season. The *Argus* on September 24 said, "Chicken's arrival will mean the strongest and fastest backfield in the middlewest."[16] It was announced in the *Argus* on September 26 that Dewey Lyle, a former star guard for the Marines, would also join the Independents for the 1919 season. The *Argus* reported that "Lyle is said to be a ponderous sort of fellow, tipping the scales around 185 or 190. But for all this heft he is rated as an exceptionally fast man on his feet, and both Buland and Ursella say he is a wonder in providing interference for the Minneota shift formation. They also say that he could get down the field on a punt faster than any Marine player."[17] A guard who weighed 185 or 190 wouldn't last long in today's pro football environment.

In the first game of the season, on Sunday September 28, the Independents bested the Rockford A.A.C. 20-0 before a crowd of 2,000 at Douglas Park. The Independents' line averaged 189 pounds and backfield players averaged 176.[18] Fred Chicken averaged between seven and eight yards per carry while Buland and Lyle were impressive in line play.[19]

In a practice on Tuesday night after the Rockford game, Ursella stressed conditioning, and required that every man run several times around the field both before and after the signal drill to improve his wind.[20]

On Sunday October 5, the Cincinnati Reds won a World Series game against the Chicago Black Sox (now the White Sox) 5-0, largely on the pitching of "Hod" Eller, who struck out nine. That same day, the Independents defeated the Chicago Hamburgs 21-0 before a crowd of 2,500 at Douglas Park. Among the highlights: Ursella returned a punt for 40 yards, and Lyle and Buland sparked the defense, making most of the tackles and hustling downfield on punts.[21]

That same day Marshall and the Minneapolis Marines crushed the St. Paul Ideals 36-0 at Nicollet Park. Marshall had a good day, scoring one touchdown and kicking four field goals."[22] It would be his last game for the Marines for some time. An end for the Independents, Dempsey, was injured that day in the game against the Hamburgs, and Bobby was needed in Rock Island to play the position.[23]

The next game on the Independents schedule, Hammond, Indiana, featured some phenomenal players, including center Des Jardien of the University of Chicago and end George Halas of the University of Illinois—later the long-time coach of the Chicago Bears. These and other Hammond stars commanded high salaries and practiced every day like the college teams did. The Independents knew they were going to have their hands full for this one. Local interest for the Independents was growing by the day, betting was heavy, and Tony and His 20th Century Jazz Band was scheduled to play. The day before the contest an enthusiastic *Argus* sportswriter wrote, "Tomorrow's game, it is predicted, will eclipse any grid battle ever staged in the tri-cities."[24]

After finishing his week's work as a Minnesota state grain inspector, Bobby boarded the train at the Minneapolis train station for Rock Island. The conductor yelled, "All Aboard" and the train rolled south, roughly following the path of the Mississippi River. As he looked out the train window, Bobby might have been wondering if his Rock Island fans and teammates would accept him as readily as they had in Minneapolis? After all, Rock Island was 363 miles south of Minneapolis.

The Independents lost to the Hammond team, 12-7. The *Argus* reported that "Marshall, playing his first game for Rock Island at end, did stellar duty in staving off defeat until the last. It is difficult to estimate the defensive strength he added to the Independents. The big Negro smashed well planned end runs time and again." Other defensive standouts were Dewey Lyle at guard and Walt Buland at tackle. Fred Chicken, who made a forty-yard touchdown scamper in the first quarter, was deemed the most brilliant performer for Rock Island on offense.[25]

When he signed with the Independents, Marshall broke the color line again. We can give credit to Walter Flanigan, Independents general manager, for signing him, and we can give

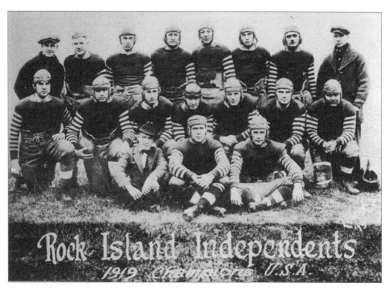

Marshall is pictured in the middle of the back row of this photo of the
1919 Rock Island Independents

credit to the *Rock Island Argus* for not objecting to the signing.
Minnesota is a lot farther north than northwest Illinois, and the
Independents had a Southerner on the team, Tom Henry. Henry,
a halfback, had played two years at Louisiana University in 1915
and 1916. The *Rock Island Argus* describes him as "a player of
the rangy, speedy type," and predicted his presence on the team
would give the Independents a backfield "unsurpassed in the
middle west."[26] Would Henry be able to play on the same team
as Marshall without friction or ill will? To judge from the reports
filed by sportswriters for the *Rock Island Argus* throughout the
season, the answer is yes. Combing through those records, I found
no reports of racial tension concerning Henry, Marshall or any
Rock Island football player.

Of course, Bobby faced racism both on and off the field, but
there is no evidence that he was not well-received by the Rock
Island community. In one article an *Argus* sportswriter speaks of
"Young Bobby Marshall," though Marshall was thirty-nine years
old at the time—an age when most pro football players have long
since retired. At this point in his life Bobby was also known as

"Rube" Marshall. "Rube" was a name casually applied to people of Jewish heritage, and Bobby was a Christian with Jewish heritage.[27]

He had long since learned to weather such thoughtless jibes as the joke that appeared on the sports page of the *Argus* for October 18, 1919, about a "darkey" arrested for stealing chickens. "The jury returned a verdict of not-guilty and as the lawyer for the defense congratulated the Senegambian, he said: 'Well Moe your (sic) free and my fee for the case is $10.' To which Moe replied 'Well judge, Ah Lack (sic) finances, but you can sure have them chickens.'"[28]

The 1919 match-up between Rock Island and Davenport was a huge event in northern Illinois and eastern Iowa. A large crowd was expected and the ever-popular Tony's 20th Century Jazz Band had once again been scheduled to provide entertainment. The *Argus* reported that if the Rock Island Islanders won "…there will be no limit of rejoicing in the town Sunday night, because a victory over Davenport, no matter how easily or hard earned, always makes the world brighter in Rock Island."[29]

The Independents trounced Davenport, 33-0 that day with another ex-Minneapolis Marine, Eddie Novak, at halfback. The sportswriter for the *Argus* was impressed with Marshall's football skills that day, but he also noticed something else. "Young Bobby Marshall was just like a father to both teams. He never missed a chance to help a prostate player to his feet." Though he refers to the 39-year old Marshall as a "colored boy," he also describes him as "like a father to both teams."[30] Marshall was doing something on the football field that Sunday afternoon more important than playing well; he was demonstrating through his actions the high quality of his character. And such behavior was slowly changing America's perception of African Americans.

Meanwhile, Coach Ursella's training methods were beginning to pay off for the Independents. An *Argus* sportswriter reported that "the pace increased in the last quarter, rather than slowed up. The Islanders (Independents) were clearly in better condition than the Iowans."[31]

A week later the Independents faced a Cincinnati Celts team that featured Greasy Neal at halfback: a good name for a running back. Neal was also an outfielder for the Cincinnati Reds National League baseball team. Bobby played the entire game at right end, and the Independents beat the Cincinnati Celts 33-0 before a crowd of 3,000. A drizzling day held down the size of the crowd and made the field slippery, but Coach Ursella's Minnesota Shift offense worked well just the same. The Independents would have scored more points but the quarters were shortened to 10 minutes so the Celts could catch a train home. One reporter enthused: "Marshall enjoyed his pastiming at end as much as if it had been a barbecue. Also, he added to the total count by catching his usual forward pass over the goal line." He added light-heartedly, in reference to Bobby's commitment to his day job in Minneapolis during the week, "Marshall always leaves his 15-year old shoes in Rock Island between Sundays and he simply couldn't play without wearing 'em." By in large, the Cincinnati team was made up of southern players who were probably playing against an African American for the first time.[32]

The following Sunday the Independents faced another team—Pine Village, Indiana—of similar makeup. A number of the Pine Village players had been stars at Georgia Tech. Team manager Claire Rhode—farmer, sportsman, millionaire—paid his players well for good performance, and scoured the country to find the best he could. As a result, the team played 14 years without a defeat and had lost only six games in the previous two decades. Before a crowd of more than four thousand people at Douglas Park, the Independents held Pine Village to a scoreless tie. Ursella missed on four drop kick field goal attempts, the last one missing by only a foot. Marshall recovered a fumble and caught a pass from Ursella for 10 yards. There were no substitutions, with the starters on both teams playing the entire game.[33]

On November 9 the Independents, also known as the Islanders, creamed Moline, 57-0, in a rain filled game, with Marshall catching a long pass from quarterback Rube Ursella and returning a punt thirty-five yards.[34] A week later they defeated Hammond A.A. 55-0.[35]

But their next foe would present a greater challenge. The Columbus Panhandles had won the world title as best pro team seven times. It had never been easy for Independents manager Walter Flanigan to secure games for the Independents. He had to negotiate with each opponent how the gate receipts would be split, and to get the Columbus Panhandles to come to Rock Island Flanigan had to agree that there would be no free tickets given out. Panhandles manager Joe F. Carr claimed that on one occasion his team had played in a city "where there were more free admissions than paid ones." One Cleveland sportswriter had nicknamed the Panhandles the "Manhandlers" because of their tough yet sportsmanlike play. In the *Rock Island Argus* on Saturday Nov. 22 the sportswriter referred to the Independents as "Ursella's trained pigs." (The epithet was revived in the 1980s and early 1990s when the offensive linemen of the Washington Redskins, "the Hogs," led the Redskins to three Super Bowl championships.) The sportswriter went on to describe Marshall as "a youngster of some 42 years who can still outplay 99 percent of those 20 years his junior," then added: "but even he has to take off his hat to age in the person of John Nesser, quarterback (of the Panhandles), who is in his 46th year." (Bobby was actually 39 years old at the time.) The Independents handed the Panhandles a 40-0 loss that Sunday. Their defense was so strong the Panhandles threw at least six interceptions and failed to make even a single first down.[36]

On Thanksgiving Day that year—a snowy, cold, muddy, day—the Davenport Athletic Club played in a rematch against the Independents, losing 26-0 at Douglas Park before 1,500 shivering fans. Marshall ran a punt back for 20 yards.[37]

The following Sunday the Independents were set to play the Akron Indians at Douglas Park with only two days rest. The Indians featured the shifty and effective running back Fritz Pollard, an African American who, a year later, would break the color line in the N.F.L. a week after Marshall. It was the coldest weather of the season, and the field at Douglas Park was covered with areas of hard-frozen water and mud. The Indians got only one first down that day, and neither Marshall or Pollard had a good day offensively. Pollard threw an interception and both of them fumbled twice in the sloppy weather. But the Independents' defense was staunch and they emerged with a 17-0 victory.[38]

Jim Thorpe

The Canton Bulldogs had agreed to come to Rock Island on December 7 for the World Championship of professional football, encouraged, no doubt, by the attractive terms: Ticket prices were set at $2 each; each team would receive $5000 if all 5,000 tickets were sold. If not, the Independents agreed to pony up $2,000 to the Bulldogs to guarantee they received the maximum sum. On the Tuesday before the game, half of the tickets had already been sold, and a Super Bowl-type atmosphere descended on Rock Island, largely due to the mystique of the legendary Jim Thorpe, who would be on the field for the Bulldogs. The *Rock Island Argus* described him as follows: "The head of the Canton Bulldogs is the best known athlete in the world. He starred in the 1912 Olympic games in Stockholm, Sweden, and has since been mixed up in various athletic enterprises where he has never failed to make good ... He is a fine sportsman, a wonderful luminary in all athletic, and a good fellow to boot." The *Argus* sportswriter assured fans that the Independents would be at full strength, and went on to report "Chicken is coming out of his slight Thanksgiving hangover and will be able to alternate with Henry in the backfield." But it was much ado about nothing. The next day it was reported in the *Argus* that the Bulldogs had pulled out of the event after learning that the Independents had recently beaten the Akron Indians 17-0. Independents Manager Walter Flanigan traveled to Canton, hoping to convince Thorpe and his team to reconsider, and even offering a one-sided $7,000 guarantee, but to no avail.[39] It was the second time that Thorpe had avoided a contest in which Marshall was also involved. He had also cancelled an encounter when Bobby played for the Minneapolis Marines in 1916. Perhaps, he was less that eager to tarnish his reputation by coming off "second-best" to Marshall on the playing field. In any case, football fans in Rock Island were devastated by the abrupt cancellation, and to this day, anyone who takes an interest in the early years of professional football has got to rue that missed opportunity, and to wonder how that match-up might have gone down.

In 1919, at the age of 39, Marshall made the All-American Professional Team—the equivalent of N.F.L. All Pro today[40]—and the 1919 Rock Island Independents ended the season with a 9-1-1 record. They scored 309 points and gave up only 12 during that span, and when it was over they declared themselves Champions of the U.S.A. Then again, so did the Canton Bulldogs.[41]

The year-end players' meeting was held on December 12, and each player received a share of the $8,100 profit. An *Argus* reporter, looking forward to the coming year, saw only good things ahead: "One thing was sure, in the rather indefinite plans for next year. And that was that football here next year is to be on the highest plane the game has ever attained."[42]

10

Bobby Marshall Becomes the First African American in the N.F.L.

In Rock Island, the 1920 football season began on September 13 with a meeting attended by both players and fans where it was announced that ticket prices for the year would be $1.65. Manager Walter Flanigan announced that Jim Thorpe had invited the Independents to join a new professional football league along with the other top professional teams.[1] The new league was officially formed in Canton, Ohio, on September 17 under the name the American Professional Football Association (A.P.F.A.). Two years later the name was changed to the National Football League (N.F.L.).[2]

Thorpe was elected president of the league,[3] and Flanigan was invited to join the board of directors. At the league's first meeting, representatives from Rock Island and Decatur, Illinois; Canton, Cleveland, Akron, and Dayton, Ohio; Hammond and Muncie, Indiana; Rochester, N.Y.; and Racine, Wisconsin were present. It was formed with the guidance of Ralph Hay, owner of a Hupmobile auto dealership in Canton—the city which is now the home of the N.F.L. Hall of Fame.[4] Bobby made his debut in the new league on September 26 with the Rock Island Independents, and Fritz Pollard, another African American, made his debut with the Akron Pros a week later.[5] Pollard, a quarterback, led his team in 1920 to the first N.F.L. championship.

In the early years of the N.F.L. a few other African Americans also saw game time, notably Paul Robeson, a tackle for the Akron Pros (Robeson graduated Phi Beta Kappa from Rutgers University); Duke Slater, a great lineman for the Rock Island Independents and Chicago Cardinals who later became a judge in Chicago, Ill.; Harold Bradley for the Chicago Cardinals; Sol Butler, quarterback for the Akron Indians; and Dick Hudson and Ink Williams, receivers for the Hammond Pros.[6]

The first game ever to feature an N.F.L. team took place on Sunday, September 26, 1920, at Douglas Park in Rock Island, when Marshall's Independents took on the St. Paul Ideals—a team that had not been asked to join the new league—and that day they made it clear why, losing 48-0.[7] (The park now features a regulation-size baseball field, a softball field, a little league field, and a kids' playground, but the only thing left of the football stadium is the ticket booth.)

When the Independents took the field in their brand-new green and white uniforms on that rainy afternoon, Bobby Marshall, number 14, arguably became the first African American ever to play in the N.F.L. He was 40 years old at the time; the average age of the other starters on the Independents was 27.5 years old.[8]

It's important to remember that in those days, each team scheduled its own games, many of which were with teams that weren't members of the A.P.F.A. (N.F.L.). With teams playing opponents of widely varying strength, and also scheduling more or fewer games as opportunities presented themselves, it was impossible to maintain meaningful league standings. Therefore, every game was not crucial in determining a league "champion." Some opponents were official members of the A.P.F.A., some were not. The league championship was, in 1920, not determined by standings alone. Instead the official league champion was determined by a vote of representatives from each member team.[9]

Bruce Copeland, sportswriter for the *Rock Island Argus*, described the contest between the St. Paul Ideals and the Rock Island Independents as follows. "Kuehl's 82-yard run through a broken field for a touchdown in the third quarter was as flashy a spring as was ever witnessed on the grounds. Waddy [Kuehl] picked his way with unerring accuracy through a huge gap opened up by Buland and Marshall, shook off four secondary defenders and headed for the northwest corner of the field with all the speed of a greyhound." In the third quarter, "Wyland kicked off to Mikesh, who was thrown for no gain by Fitzgerald and Marshall ...the fans howled their pleasure over the splendid playing of Mansfield, Novak, Chicken, Buland, Fitzgerald, Wyland, Marshall, Smith, Lyle, Cook and Ursella."[10]

On October 3 the Independents played the Muncie Flyers, before 3100 fans at Douglas Park, and the results were similarly one-sided. Marshall was spectacular, with an interception, kick-off return, and several extra-point kicks, as the Independents won, 45-0.[11] The Muncie Flyers may be the only team in N.F.L. history to play only one N.F.L. game in a season.[12]

On October 10, a team from Hammond, Indiana, came to Douglas Park to play before 2,544 paying customers. Perhaps aware that they were "out of their league," the Hammond team resorted to the foulest tactics a football team could impose." A reporter tallied up the injuries after the game: "Ursella's knee suffered a severe wrench that necessitated his removal to Iowa City today for special treatment by Dr. Watson, noted trainer of the University of Iowa college squad. Duey Lyle was deliberately kicked in the face, sustaining a cut on his upper lip that penetrated to his teeth and necessitated seven stitches to close. Eddie Healey, the former Dartmouth star linesman, making his ostentatious debut with the Islanders (Independents), was 'cleated' on the right cheek clear to the bone, and he, too, had to have the wound sewed with five stiches. Fred Chicken left the game in the last quarter, battered and bruised. Jerry Mansfield, carries three facial bruises as the result of frequent pummeling. Walter Buland stood his half of the opposing line on its ear most of the time, but took many vicious wallops and kicks with a triumphant smile that characterizes a winner." But the Rock Island defense held

Walt Buland, Fred Chicken, and Rube Ursella

firm, allowing Hammond only three first downs, and the Independents won, 26-0.[13]

On October 17 the Independents were set to take on the Decatur Staleys, the team that would later become the Chicago Bears. Playing end for the Staleys was George Halas, who became a legend as the Bears' head coach. Leading up to the game the Independents held secret practices. 'Rube' Ursella returned from Iowa City limping noticeably, but stated that his injury would not keep him out of the Staley game.[14] In the picture on this page Rube Ursella is seen in a kicking motion next to two teammates, running back Fred Chicken and lineman Walt Buland.

In an article in the *Rock Island Argus* a few days before the game a sportswriter wrote, "There should also be a brilliant forward passing duel between Wyman, Mansfield and Marshall for the Independents and Koehler, Halas and Chamberlain of the Staleys."[15] In this era, the passer had to be five yards behind the line of scrimmage to throw a pass. This rule was not changed to the modern rule of passing anywhere behind the line of scrimmage until 1933.[16]

The Independents used the Minnesota Shift offense, a predecessor of the man-in-motion offenses since then.[17] A crowd of seven-thousand fans showed up on October 17. Rube Ursella did play, as promised, despite knee trouble earlier in the week. The Staleys scored the game's only touchdown in the second quarter due to a mental lapse by Fred Chicken in the defensive secondary that opened a lane for a 43-yard touchdown run. The final score was Staleys 7, Independents 0. Hardly a passing duel.[18]

The loss to the Staleys was cause for introspection. Copeland suggested in the *Argus* on October 19 that players like Marshall, Chicken, and Wyman, who came in from out of town on weekends, should give up more time from their work-week jobs and come to Rock Island for daily practices. Waxing philosophical, Copeland added, "If we know ourselves aright, we discern that the soul of defeat is OURSELVES; none other."[19]

In a different article in the *Argus* of the same day, Copeland handed out some compliments. "Oke Smith's grand defensive playing in the second half literally set the Staleys on their ears, for it was his brilliant running-in dashes that shattered the same interference and spilled runners for behind-the-line losses. Oke is now at the top of his form and makes an admirable running mate for the cagey veteran, Bob Marshall."[20]

At practice on October 19, manager Walter Flanagan read the riot act, saying, "Henceforth, Missouri tactics will be employed by those affiliated with the club management. The 'show me' policy shall rule. The moment any player betrays lack of first class physical condition, he will incur his release automatically. No alibis will be tolerated. It will be, 'Give us your best or get out.'"[21]

So, the question was, would the Independents give it their best against the Racine Cardinals the following Sunday afternoon? As the 4,000 fans filed into Douglas Park many of them were probably wondering which Independent team would show up, the lax one or the fired up one. Many feared that Paddy Driscoll, the star runner for the Cardinals, would run roughshod over the

Independent's defense. But the defense stood their ground and the game ended with a slim 7-0 victory for Rock Island.[22] (Incidentally, that same team became the Chicago Cardinals two years later. It moved to St. Louis in 1960, and on to Arizona in 1988, where it's been ever since.)

On October 26 Copeland wrote the following in the *Argus*. "Cagey old Bob Marshall, who seems to have beat Ponce d Leon to the 'fountain of youth' is in better physical condition than ever before, despite his 42 years- (really only 40) 22 of which have been devoted chiefly to almost every branch of athletics. Bob's head work pulls the team out of many near-disasters. His regard for the tri-cities (Rock Island, Moline, and Davenport) is akin to affection."[23] A story is told by Minnesota sports historian, Kwame McDonald, how once "cagey" Bobby had a bad ankle. He knew that in the next game, if he taped that ankle, players from the other team would attack it mercilessly. So, he taped his *other* ankle, played very effectively, and got through the game without further injury to his vulnerable joint.[24]

The following Sunday afternoon, the Independents faced the Chicago Tigers with Sid Nichols at quarterback for the Independents in place of an injured Ursella. In the fourth quarter, Nichols completed a pass to Marshall that put the ball on the Tigers' 30-yard-line. A few plays later Wyman ran the ball in for a touchdown from the four-yard-line, giving the Independents a 20-7 victory.[25]

A week later, the Independents were scheduled to play the Decatur Staleys for a second time. A special train had been chartered to take a thousand fans from Decatur to Rock Island for the game. On November 2 Copeland reported that Decatur coach and end George Halas had suavely predicted that his team would defeat the Independents by at least three touchdowns "without having his own goal line even so much as threatened."[26]

On the afternoon of Sunday November 7 rain threatened but did not materialize. Despite the threatening weather 4,991 fans turned out at Douglas Park for the game. A number of the

Independents players were injured, and their offense could only muster five first downs. The Staleys got only six. As the afternoon wore on the game got rough in the third quarter play was briefly suspended while Captain Ursella and Bob Marshall pressed a claim against their opponent for flagrant unsportsmanlike conduct. The game ended in a scoreless tie. Halas's prediction had been half right. The Independents hadn't crossed his goal. The next day Copeland added details about the Sta-

George Halas

leys' unsportsmanlike play, which he could easily spot from the vantage point of the press box above the field. He noted that on the most egregious offense "the ball had been dead three or four seconds when Trafton came crashing in and deliberately slid over Gunderson's face. Flagrant is too mild a word to describe such utter lack of sportsmanship. A cave dweller could have done no better."[27]

Marshall considered his seasons with the Rock Island Independents as his toughest.[28] After a game like this one, he probably asked himself why was he traveling all the way to Rock Island every weekend to face this kind of injustice?

But the grueling season continued. The Independent's next game was scheduled for Thursday, November 11—Armistice Day, a holiday only recently established to commemorate the end of World War I. The team would be traveling on three day's rest to Monmouth, Illinois, to face the Original Thorn-Tornadoes of Chicago. Gunderson, Wyman, Nichols, Smith, and Chicken were injured, and Marshall was switched from end to right tackle. It was the coldest day of the season, with a hard-driving northwest wind and frozen ground. The game ended in a 7-7 tie.[29]

A mere two days later, the Independent took on the Dayton

Triangles at Douglas Park. Unable to rise above the numerous injuries and widespread fatigue, they were shut out, 21-0.[30]

The last game of the season was held on November 28 at Douglas Park, against a ragtag team of collegians and newly recruited players. So few members of the opposing team showed up that the coach had to recruit fans from the stadium to field a viable squad. The Independents won 48-7, but Marshall didn't play. His days as a Rock Island Independent were over.[31]

The Independents finished the 1920 season at 6-2-2.[32] The Akron Pros claimed to win the league title with an 8-0-2 record.[33]

But if Marshall and his team fell short of championship status that year, he achieved something arguably greater by becoming the first African American to play in the N.F.L. At the end of the season he was named to the "Third Team All-Star Professional Team" while another African American, quarterback Fritz

Fritz Pollard

Pollard of the Akron Pros, was named to the First Team. Bruce Copeland, sporting editor for the *Rock Island Argus*, made the selections.[34]

What was it like back then for African American players? Pollard summed it up very nicely. "You had to be tough as nails to play in that league. And that went double if you were black, because they really came after us."[35] Pollard faced verbal and physical abuse at games from other players. Pollard recalled, "'The white players were always trying to hurt me and I had to be able to protect myself if I was going to stay in the game." If a white player abused Pollard on the field Pollard added, "I'd pay them no mind, but I would notice who the player was, and at the first opportunity that presented itself I'd kick them right in the guts or hit my knee up against their knee, knocking it out of joint. And then I'd let them know, quietly, why I did it." Pollard faced tremendous animosity from some of the fans in the Pennsylvania Coal League in 1923. On occasion he was greeted with rocks and bottles from the fans when he entered the playing field.[36]

One can only wonder why Pollard seems to have faced more racism on the football field than Marshall. Historian Peter Gorton tells the story of the great left-handed African American baseball pitcher in this first half of the 20th Century, John Wesley Donaldson. Donaldson pitched many games for small town Minnesota teams and followed a general rule of always waiting for all the white people to enter a building before he entered. To survive as an African American, one needed to always be aware of the possibility of a racist attack and do everything possible to avoid it.[37] Marshall, a man who traveled all over the Midwest, must have developed a keen awareness of how to avoid trouble in white society.

11

The 1920s Roar in

More Ways Than One

The 1920s brought many changes to the lives of Americans, including Bobby Marshall. Some were good; others not. Marshall was a Republican, and he loved Teddy Roosevelt, who served as a Republican U.S. President from 1901 to 1909. (Roosevelt later formed his own party and ran for President again, unsuccessfully.) Perhaps Marshall loved Roosevelt because of his passion for social justice. Roosevelt invited African American leader Booker T. Washington for dinner at the White House in 1901, a bold move for that time. When Roosevelt died in 1919, Marshall may have seen it as a bad omen for racial equality. Among the changes he witnessed during that era were the passing of the 18th Amendment prohibiting the production, importation, transportation, and sale of alcoholic beverages, and the 19th Amendment giving women the right to vote.

One constant in Marshall's life was his insatiable appetite for football. No longer a member of the Rock Island Independents, he was back in Minnesota, breathing the brisk Minneapolis air and looking forward to the 1920 Thanksgiving Day game. He was set to play in an afternoon game for Frank Mayer's College All-Stars against his former team, the Minneapolis Marines. That week, the weather had been a mix of heavy rain, snow, and cold, and the two teams agreed it would be better to play the game indoors at a local ice hockey rink called the Hippodrome. The weather must have improved because the game was played outdoors at Nicollet Park. It ended in a scoreless tie,[1] but the All-Stars almost scored when Parker Anderson intercepted a pass and was about to go all the way for a score when he slipped and fell. The Marines' Melly Nelson attempted a 20-yard drop kick for a field goal that missed by inches. And Marshall, now forty years old, distinguished himself on both sides of the ball. One sportswriter summed it up as follows: "Bob Marshall played in his college days' form. He was down on punts fast, stopped many passes and always eluded the clever Marine interference on the wide end runs to get the man with the ball." Two of the athletes who were scheduled to perform for the All-Stars, Con Eklund and Joe Sprafka, withdrew at the last minute because they were dentists and were afraid of injuring their hands.[2]

By the 1920s the game of football was changing. Forward passes were used more often and the formations were less bone grinding. A sports writer for the *Minneapolis Journal* wrote on December 19, 1920 that, "we have the forward pass and Bob (Marshall) receives these with the best of them, and intercepts them too."[3]

During this period Bobby also remained active in pro baseball. In 1919, he played on North Dakota's Mott and Regent team and in 1921, he played 57 games for a team in Estevan, Saskatchewan, batting .450.[4]

In 1920 Lotus Coffman became the president of the University of Minnesota. He continued a policy whereby African Americans were not allowed to live in white University of Minnesota dorms. (University of Minnesota housing was not fully integrated until 1954.)[5] Coffman also had an unwritten policy against allowing African Americans to participate in sports at the University of Minnesota.[6] In fact, no African American were on the Gophers' football teams in the 1920s.

An incident took place in Duluth on June 15, 1920, that

offers chilling evidence of the state of race relations at that time. Elias Clayton, Elmer Jackson, and Isaac McGhie, three African American men with a traveling circus, were accused of raping a white woman and incarcerated in the town jail. A mob broke into the jail, seized the suspects, and lynched them from lampposts nearby. Two Catholic priests pleaded with the mob to stop what they were doing but to no avail.[7]

Marshall and other African American athletes were facing more racism, not less, as the 1920s unfolded. A 1922 study by the Illinois Commission on Race Relations reported that "There seems to be no feeling between white and Negro members of a school team, but the Negro members are sometimes roughly handled when the team plays other schools." In discussing this study author John Carroll notes, "The best evidence indicates that the few African-American athletes who participated in Chicago interscholastic sports in 1908 and before were better accepted than those who competed after World War I, but that they too usually encountered trouble when playing against all-white teams."[8] What was true about racism in Chicago was also likely true in Minnesota.

That sense of hostility and panic boiled over in Tulsa, Oklahoma, on May 31 and June 1, 1921, when white rioters set fire to more than a thousand houses, a hospital, a school, a library, and several churches and businesses in the Greenwood section of town, which was largely African American. The "official" death count of 36 is now considered too low by historians.[9]

Yet by this time in his career, Marshall had long since become a local stalwart on the sporting scene. He seemed oblivious to both the racial undercurrents of the time and the well-known antipathy of Coffman to African American athletes. Bobby accepted an offer to join the Gophers' coaching staff to work with the ends, especially Blumer and Wallace.[10] When Marshall walked on the Gophers' practice field on September 26, 1921, he continued his Big Ten coaching career that began in 1907. Bobby Marshall is the first African American coach in Big Ten history.

In 1921 Marshall joined the Minneapolis Liberties football team. He was now forty-one but still considered by his opponents to be playing "a heap of classy football".[11] A Michigan football man, Vic Turosky, played against Marshall in the 1920s. Turosky spoke of a game during which Marshall grabbed him by his ankle, lifted him into the air, and "slammed" him to the ground. "'That's when I knew what real power was,' Turosky marveled."[12]

The Liberties traveled to Duluth, Minnesota, for a game with the Duluth Kaysees on October .16, 1921. In the first half, the Liberties failed to score but held Duluth to only seven points. They weakened in the second half, however, and Duluth won, 35-0.[13]

The following week they took on the Knights of Columbus team, aided by center Paul "Shorty" Des Jardien, who had been an All-American center for the University of Chicago. A large Sunday afternoon crowd at Nicollet Park witnessed the Knights of Columbus nip the Liberties 7-6 in a "hard and clean game … Bobby Marshall played a good game at left end for the losers."[14]

Over the years Marshall played many football games at Nicollet Park, which was located at the corner of Chicago

Nicollet Field

Avenue and 17th Street in Minneapolis. The park had 4,000 seats and was home to the minor league Minneapolis Millers baseball team. It also hosted many high school football games. Among its many distinctions a few stand out. General Mills unveiled its first Wheaties "The Breakfast of Champions" sign on a wall of Nicollet Park, and the park was also the site of the shortest home run in baseball history. On August 2, 1904, Andy Oyler hit a ball deep into the mud two feet in front of home plate. It was a rainy day and no one could find the ball in the mud, enabling Oyler to score.[15]

The Liberties defeated St. Louis Park 13 to 6 on October 30 at South High field. "Substantial gains by Crawford, Larson, and Carlson through the Park line brought the ball in the shadow of the St. Louis goal where Marshall wriggled his way through for a touchdown." Bobby played right end that day and also kicked an extra point.[16] A reporter for the *Minneapolis Star* wrote the next day, "Bobby Marshall needs no introduction... He has played in this city for many years and is regarded as the wonder of professional football."[17]

In 1921, Bobby played for the Liberties, Frank Mayer's College All-Star, and also for the Ironwood Legion team in Michigan's Upper Peninsula. Two years later a sportswriter for the *Ironwood Daily Globe* was still reminiscing about Marshall's skill on the gridiron. "Since the memorable game with Bessemer two years ago when Marshall first appeared here at end he has been a fixture and was counted one of the stars of the game."[18] And the game was still a topic of conversation twenty years later. In the *Ironwood Times* of November 12, 1941 it states, "Ironwood defeated the Bessemer city team, 13 to 0 (20 years ago on the same date). Although both Bessemer and Ironwood had announced only home players would be used, Ironwood had Bobby Marshall and Bessemer imported Wilson and Wheeler from the Green Bay Packers."[19]

Ironwood was not an N.F.L. team, just a local pro team. Located about 300 miles from Minneapolis, in would have been a very long weekend drive for Marshall, which suggests how deeply he loved the game of football—and perhaps how good the money was.

In early November of 1921 Bobby continued his coaching duties for the University of Minnesota football team. Bobby's long-time friend Sig Harris was also on the coaching staff.[20]

Bobby played in an afternoon game with the All-Stars team against the Minneapolis Marines at Nicollet Park on Thanksgiving Day, November 24. Nicollet Park field had to be cleared of snow before the game. One thousand five hundred people braved the cold to witness another episode in this enduring rivalry. Even after the snow was removed, the field was covered with a sheet of slippery, frozen turf that was almost impossible to run across, and neither team could mount a touchdown drive. The only touchdown came late in the third quarter when one of the All-Stars fumbled a punt. The ball was picked up by Christianson of the Marines who ran 32 yards for the game's only score.[21]

In 1922 and again in 1925 Marshall negotiated with Rube Foster, founder of the Negro League, to bring a Negro League baseball team to Minnesota. The negotiations failed, in part because Minneapolis was too far away from other Negro League Cities, making transportations costs too high. Another problem was that Bobby's team was supported by W. R. McKinnon who owned the Askin and Marine Clothing Company. McKinnon, a white businessman, may not have wanted to be involved in the Negro League.[22]

Bobby played on many baseball teams in the 1920s, one being the Minneapolis Bufaloes in 1922. The Buffaloes lost 9-4 to the Minneapolis Pantages and lost again on the 4th of July, 12-0 to Little Falls. The Buffaloes' hundreds of fans were disappointed because they felt they were not watching "some real baseball."[23] It is likely that Bobby was also disappointed because he then joined the Askin and Marine Colored Red Sox in Minneapolis where he played third base and became the captain of the team. The team won their final 11 games and finished the season 30-9. The

In this photo of the Colored Red Sox, Bobby is third from the right in the back row.

maroon-and-gray-clad squad was owned by McKinnon and managed by right fielder/utility man Will Brooks."[24]

During the 1922 football season, Bobby played football again for both the Ironwood Legion and the Twin Cities All-Stars. The *Ironwood Daily Globe* noted on November 9 that, "Alongside of Tezak (on the Ironwood line) will be Bobby Marshall, colored Minnesota end who has starred here throughout the season."[25] Marshall also played quarterback for that 1922 Ironwood team.[26]

During the 1923 baseball season, Bobby played first base, second base, and catcher for the St. Paul Uptown Sanitary Shop, a semi-pro team. "The team would get together at (teammate Lee) Davis' house in Minneapolis and carpool to games in outlying towns." That car must have been crammed full of players. No seat belt laws then. Bobby once remarked about playing sports during weekends in this era, "We didn't make a lot of money but we sure had a lot of fun."[27]

One day in late spring of 1923 four members of the Sanitary Shop team missed the bus for Hibbing, where they were scheduled to play the Colts the next day. It was an all-night bus ride to Hibbing and the next day the tired Sanitary Shop team got shellacked by the Colts, 22-1. Bobby did get two hits that day, a double and a single in four at bats. The four Sanitary Shop players who missed the bus showed up for the next game but the results were even worse, a walloping 37 to 1 loss.[28]

Between 1921 to 1925, Marshall played pro football on the Ironwood Red Devils, the Minneapolis Liberties, the Twin Cities All-Stars, Hibbing Miners and Duluth Kelleys. At times he played for three different teams in the same year. It isn't surprising, therefore, that contract disputes would arise. On November 27, 1922, Johnny Dunn, recently deposed coach of the Marines, claimed that Marshall had signed a contract with his team. Marshall denied it.[29] If he had signed a contract, where was it?

One of the most interesting games of this era was a clash between the Hibbing Miners and the Green Bay Packers on September 23, 1923. Many of the former Rock Island players had joined the Hibbing team including quarterback Rube Ursella, tackle Walter Buland, and Marshall, now nick-named "Ink" and playing left end. Buland was the coach of the Miners. A Green Bay crowd of 2,760 watched the Packers beat the Miners that day, 10-0. Curly "Captain Lambeau hurled the pigskin into the waiting arms of Wheeler, Mathys and Lyle for considerable yardage" for the Pack-

In this photo of the Uptown Sanitary Shop team, Bobby is in the middle of the back row.

ers. There were no hard feelings after the game. Coach Buland said, "We bit the dust for the first time in two years and from now on, up our way, we'll be thinking that the Packers are just as good as they are cracked up to be…You have a splendid field for your games and your organization treated us like 'kings.' No wonder they call Green Bay the best 'little' football country in the country." Bobby "Ink" Marshall played well that day. According to the *Green Bay Press Gazette*, "Hibbing's line was of the stonewall variety with Walter Buland, the veteran Rock Island players, and "Ink" Marshall cutting quite a figure."[30] The *Hibbing Daily News* later reported that "Bobby Marshall and Underwood, ends, were into every play and caused no little trouble for the Packers."[31] Bobby, now weighing in at 205 pounds, was the heaviest lineman on the Miners.[32] According to the *Hibbing Daily News* Marshall was "…undoubtedly the greatest colored player of all times."[33] Another undoubtedly great player involved in this game was Curly Lambeau of the Packers. As you can see in the picture, Curly's hair really was quite curly. He coached the Packers for many years and was also head coach of the Chicago Cardinals and Washington Redskins, compiling a total N.F.L. coaching record of 226 wins, 132 loses and 22 ties. Lambeau Field, built in 1957 in Green Bay is named after him.[34] Lambeau Field is the second oldest N.F.L. stadium; the oldest is Soldier Field in Chicago.[35]

Curly Lambeau

In his early 40s Bobby Marshall remained a Minnesota hero who seemed to be living a charmed life. Could that continue?

12

The Roaring 20s Continue to Roar

As the 1920s unfolded, would things get better for Bobby Marshall, other African Americans, and other minorities? Or worse?

In 1923 Dr. Charles Dight, a local medical man and enthusiastic proponent of eugenics, founded the Minnesota Eugenics Society.[1] An eccentric man, Dight worked for many different causes and lived in a tree house.[2] Selective breeding had been a commonplace of livestock managers for millennia, but in the early twentieth century, in light of Darwin's theories and the rediscovery of Mendel's work on the influence of heredity, politicians and medical professionals had begun to seriously consider whether the same techniques might be applied to humans. Dr. Dight was among them. He published a pamphlet in 1922 titled "Human Thoroughbreds, Why Not?" The problem with such theories is that they required a standard of perfection, and ideal, and it was usually a white Northern European. The eugenics movement encouraged the passage of laws to restrict "inferior types" (people who were not white Anglo-Saxon Protestants) from coming to the U.S. One result was the passage in Congress of the Emergency Immigration Restriction Act of 1921.[3] We tend to think of intellectuals, college professors, medical doctors, public servants, and scientists as keepers of the best ideals in society, but in the 1920s, this was sometimes not the case.

Nor were such attitudes and theories the exclusive property of intellectuals. By 1923, when Dight founded his institute, the Ku Klux Klan had grown to 30,000 members in Minnesota.[4] A conflict arose between the Klan and Colonel George Leach, the mayor of Minneapolis, because he wouldn't allow Minneapolis police officers to join the organization. The mayor started an investigation into Klan doings at the University of Minnesota, and the Klan accused him of drunkenness and lechery, and endorsed William Campbell, a Klan member, for mayor. But the Klan, however powerful, could not win over a majority of Minneapolis voters, and Mayor Leach defeated Campbell easily.[5]

Cross burnings and Klan parades were occurring all over Minnesota at the time.[6] Elizabeth Dorsey Hale notes in her book *The Ku Klux Klan in Minnesota* that, "In many towns there was little distinction between membership in the Klan and membership in a conservative Protestant church." A Minnesota woman recalled a time in the 1920s when Klansmen marched into the middle of Protestant church service with their white hooded uniforms, pledging "allegiance to the flag."[7]

Oct. 6, 1923, three-hundred Klansmen attended the first state Klan convention in St. Paul. That day happened to be the University of Minnesota's homecoming, and the Klan, popular on campus, had a float in the homecoming parade. That afternoon the Iowa State football team took on the Gophers at Northrup Field in front of eleven thousand fans, four hundred of which had driven up from Ames, Iowa, to root for the Cyclones. One of the Cyclone stars was an African American, Jack Trice, a great defensive tackle and offensive line blocker known for his flying tackles. He stood six feet tall and weighed 200 pounds, big for that time. At Iowa State Trice had to live off campus at an upstairs room in the Masonic Temple because African Americans were banned from Iowa State dormitories. He had gained admission to the school only after taking extra courses to qualify. He worked two custodial jobs to pay for room, board, and tuition, while his mother mortgaged her house to cover additional expenses. Jack's father, a Buffalo Soldier in the 10th Calvary of the United States Army, died when Jack was seven. Life for Trice on the Iowa State campus was lonely. A fellow classmate later recalled that "he sat next to us in the classrooms, strolled through the south side, attended convocation, worked out in the gym, rubbed elbows with us, but never stepped over the invisible barrier into our intimate confidences. It is only the truth that he lived alone and apart."[8]

Jack Trice

During the homecoming game on October 6, Trice broke through the line on a reverse and several Minnesota players hit him extremely hard in the abdomen. Louis Gross, a tackle who played opposite Trice on the Gophers team that day, recalled, "It was an accident, of course. It could have been three players who ran over him or half a dozen. We didn't realize he was hurt seriously at the time." Minnesota fans were reported to be chanting, "We're sorry, Ames (where Iowa State is located). We're sorry." But Trice suffered severe abdominal injuries, internal bleeding, and hemorrhaging of the lungs. Two days later he died.[9]

On October 5th, the night before the game, Trice wrote a note at his desk in his room at the Curtis Hotel in Minneapolis on Curtis Hotel stationary. Trice had not been allowed to play in games in St. Louis and Nebraska but was allowed to play in Minneapolis. "My thoughts just before the first real college game of my life: The honor of my race, family + self are at stake. Everyone is expecting me to do big things. I will! My whole body + soul are to be thrown recklessly about the field tomorrow. Every time the ball is snapped I will be trying to do more than my part. On all defensive plays, I must break through the opponents line at (sic) stop the play in their territory. Beware of mass interference, fight low with your eyes open and toward the play. Roll block the interference. Watch out for cross bucks and reverse end runs. Be on your toes every minute if you expect to make good." These words are written on a plaque on the outside wall of an Iowa State gym. In 1997 the football stadium at Iowa State was officially named "Jack Trice Stadium."[10]

The death of Jack Trice helps me understand about the courage it took for all the African American athletes who dared to break through the color line, from Bobby Marshall to Jackie Robinson.

Unlike Jack Trice, Marshall never suffered a life-threatening injury playing football or any other sport. Marshall, a devout Christian, may have considered this a real blessing.

On Sunday, October 7, 1923 the Hibbing All-Stars played the Ironwood Legion at Ironwood Ballpark in Michigan's Upper Peninsula. The game is notable less for the score—Hibbing defeated Ironwood 13-0—than for an incident that occurred on the field. Once Hibbing jumped out to an early lead, the fans started to insult the Hibbing players. Things really got ugly when two of the Ironwood players attacked Marshall. According the local newspaper, he had been "the idol of Northern Michigan" during the previous two seasons when he played for Ironwood, but was now, having signed with another team, an object of derision. Marshall held his own in the fight, and his assailants were eventually ejected from the game and escorted from the field.[11] Being a man of strong Christian faith, he may have considered what a blessing it was that he could defend himself so well.

On October 21 Marshall, Rube Ursella, and Walter Buland played for the Hibbing Miners against their former team, the Rock Island Independents. Directly across the line from Marshall was Duke Slater, the first African American interior lineman to play in the N.F.L. The Hibbing team wasn't an official N.F.L.

team; the Independents were. Not surprisingly, the Independents won the game, 27-7.[12] It is surprising that Marshall, at the age of 43, was still running back kick-off returns. Even more surprising is the reaction of almost 3,000 Rock Island fans to the return of Marshall, Ursella, and Buland. "The Hibbing outfit was given a great cheer when it dashed on the field with Rube Ursella, Walt Buland and Bob Marshall, all former Independents, in the line up… They were popular with the local fans when they performed under

Duke Slater

the Green and White colors and have many friends in this city."[13] Bobby Marshall was good at making friends, wherever he went.

The Thanksgiving Day game between the Minneapolis All-Stars and the best local team in Minneapolis had been a tradition since 1907. In 1923 that team was the Minneapolis Marines. The two teams agreed prior to the game that the winners would take 65 percent of the gate receipts, the losers 35 percent.[14] Bobby played the entire game at left end for the All-Stars. The All-Stars were not a team of has-beens. Their coach, Russell Tollefson, only selected players who had been playing football regularly that year.[15] Bobby played the entire game at left end for the All-Stars but the Marines won, 7-0, making it their third straight Thanksgiving Day victory over the All-Stars.[16]

Marshall may have been the oldest player on the field that day, but he felt he still had something to contribute. A few weeks later, in an article published anonymously in the *Minneapolis Journal*, he took a look back at where he'd come from: "When I am reminded of the fact that I started playing on the varsity 20 years ago, I can't believe it. I don't feel any different. I love the game as much and get as much fun playing it. They say I am slowing up. I don't know in what way. I am as tough as I ever was. My legs don't bother me. My arms are good and my eyes were never better. Maybe I can't run as fast as I could, but I know where I am going better and I get to the same places I used to."

The author of the article offers a similarly glowing account of Bobby's excellent physical condition. "For Bobby, at 43 years, is one of the most astonishing specimens of the Fountain of Youth embodied in Man that Minneapolis scientists know. For 25 years he played football, the most grueling of physical tests, and this year he played 12 full games of professional football in the national association, finishing with the All-Star-Marine game on Thanksgiving when he celebrated his quarter century as a football player by playing one of the best games of his life and then dancing until 2 a.m."

Bobby then offers readers a few tips for staying in condition: get enough sleep, take a hot bath when you're tired, and make use of your long experience to play smart. "There is no reason why I should not go on playing for seven or eight years."

The journalist goes on to ask Marshall whether he considers himself "a throwback to the jungleman who prospered or died by the weight of his warclub, the skill of his spear, and the strength with which he opposed his foemen?"

"I don't know," Bobby replied, kindly ignoring the racist tinge of the question. "I don't know what part of Africa my relatives came from. But whatever it was, they grew big strong men, for my father's family were all big fellows and he told me about his father and grandfather in Richmond, Virginia, years ago. In those days my folks were all fine athletes, he said, and I guess love of athletics in my people must go way back to Africa when they ran wild. I surely have been running wild all my life. I love games of all kinds from tennis to football. Anything to be fighting to win in a game. It's what I live on...."

The writer goes on to describe Marshall's features. "He is as straight as an Indian and has the thin narrow head of the Nilotic (an African tribe of Uganda) and the same straight nose and high cheek bones." (The writer evidently was not aware that Bobby's ancestry dated not only from Africa but from Jewish people in Germany.)

At this point Bobby goes into more detail about his possible ancestry. "While I don't know anything about where my ancestors came from in Africa, I am sure it was not from any of the Congo tribes…All of my family have been built as I am. Maybe we came from one of the interior tribes in Uganda which have the straight nose and high cheek bones and which are believed to have come from Egypt centuries ago."

The writer ends the article as follows, "Is Bobby Marshall the gentlemanly polished athlete, a descendant of one of the chieftains who led those terrible fighters into battle? He (Bobby Marshall) smiles at the thought. He doesn't seem so, for Bobby- out of a football game- is one of the gentlest of men. His eyes twinkle with humor. 'But I don't know,' he laughs. 'We came from there originally, and something must have happened to my great-great-great grandpappies. Life in the jungle couldn't have been er soft.'"[17]

When baseball season came around in 1924 Bobby joined the Motor Company team in the Twin Cities. This team featured Dick Hudson, who also played in the backfield for the Minneapolis Marines, a short-lived local N.F.L. football team. Hudson was also a sports promoter who handled an African American basketball team in Chicago called the Savoy Big Five. Later Abe Saperstein took over the team and it became the Harlem Globetrotters.[18]

It was reported in the *Minneapolis Sunday Tribune* on September 21, 1924, that Marshall had once again joined the Ironwood American Legion professional football team.[19] When one considers the horrible treatment he had received on the field in Ironwood a year earlier while playing for the rival Hibbing Miners, it's amazing Marshall would agree to sign with Ironwood again, but he didn't hold grudges.

In 1924 Marshall was still considered a Minnesota hero and the historic Little Brown Jug game of 1903 with Michigan, which ended in a 6-6 tie, was well remembered. In a newspaper article in the *Minneapolis Star* on Oct. 31, a day before the Minnesota-Michigan homecoming game, a reporter wrote, "Who is the greatest Negro who ever lived?" The answer, "Bobby Marshall."[20]

But 1924 was not a year of great happiness for Marshall. On August 5, his twenty-five-year-old wife, Irene, filed for divorce, on grounds of cruelty, nagging, and stinginess. She also alleged that on two occasions he gave her a black eye.[21] At a distance of several generations, it isn't easy to determine how much of this is true. Marshall's grandson Bill offers perhaps a more likely explanation. "The reason for the divorce was that Bobby did a great deal of traveling, leaving Irene alone. Violence toward Irene was a dubious charge because Bobby was never known to act out in a violent way to anyone, especially his family members." Getting a divorce was difficult in 1924, so the charge of physical violence may well have been an expedient to convince a judge. Whatever the case may have been, the judge agreed to grant the divorce.[22]

The St. Paul Colored Gophers reorganized in 1925 with Marshall on board. On April 26 they played the team from Bertha, Minnesota, 150 miles northwest of Minneapolis. Bobby had a ground rule double that day, one of only three hits the Colored Gophers could manage as they lost to Bertha, 16-1. This loss is not surprising, considering the Gophers' opponents had the African American, John Wesley Donaldson, on the mound, one of the greatest pitchers of all time.[23] In his career Donaldson pitched 690 games, winning 413 and striking out opposing batters 5,081 times.[24]

In 1925 Bobby played left end for the Duluth Kelleys of the N.F.L. The name came from Kelleys sporting goods store in Duluth, which supplied the team with uniforms and equipment.[25] Duluth won the professional championship of Minnesota that year but didn't play well against the rest of the league.[26] On October 11 the Kelleys played the Rock Island Independents before a packed house of 4,000 fans at Athletic Park in Duluth. The field was small and a fence prevented regular play near the goal line. When Rock Island advanced the ball to the Duluth two-yard line, the decision was made to make the goal line the ten-yard line so the defense and offense would not be inhibited by the fence. Once again, at the age of forty-five, Marshall faced Duke Slater across the line. On one kick-off Bobby fielded the ball at the 20-yard line and ran back it back for a 12- or 20-yard gain (sources vary). Unlike the 45-year-old Marshall, other players on the Duluth Kelleys were in their twenties since N.F.L. careers in the 1920s—and also today—are usually quite short.[27] The 1925 season would be Marshall's last in the N.F.L., but his pro football career was by no means over.

Ed Shave, a sportswriter who officiated at many of Marshall's games, described these games as "rugged physical battles." Marshall "had to take a great deal of physical punishment" and gave back twice as much. Shave states the following about Marshall. "Never once in any of those games did he ever protest, never complained, never retaliated." He was "one of the great gentleman athletes of all time."[28]

The Minneapolis Liberties played the All-Stars, also a Minneapolis-based team, on November 29, 1925, at Nicollet Park. The previous day the *Minneapolis Star* had reported that Marshall was still in "good football trim" despite twenty years as a professional, and Marshall proved them right by playing the entire game for the All-Stars. Both teams failed to convert drop kicks for points after touchdowns, and the game ended in a 6-6 tie. The Liberties were undefeated at that point and had won the northwest semi-pro championship a year earlier. "[29]

Meanwhile, eugenicist Dr. Charles Dight, after finishing his term on the Minneapolis City Council, devoted most of his time lobbying for a state law that would allow sterilization for those who, in the opinion of experts, were feeble-minded or insane. Written consent for such sterilization had to be obtained from a spouse or nearest relative. In 1925, Minnesota was the seventeenth state to pass such a law. Between 1928 and 1960, more than 2,300 people were sterilized in Minnesota and over 60,000 Americans were sterilized nationwide. Dight and many of his fellow eugenicists worked to have the law extended to criminals but no such legislation was ever passed in Minnesota. Laws allowing sterilization were passed in thirty-three states with these laws targeting people who were promiscuous, feebleminded, epileptic, criminal, or unfit in some other way. The Nazis in Germany were paying close attention to American sterilization laws, and when they came to power they extended them many-fold, implementing the forced sterilization of hundreds of thousands of "undesireables."[30]

In an article in the *Minneapolis Tribune* on December 13, 1925, sportswriter George A. Barton offers some insights into Marshall's life. He mentions how Red Grange became very wealthy playing pro football but had to work his way through college as a chauffeur for an ice-wagon. Then he mentions that Marshall "was one of the greatest ends that ever donned a cleated shoe." Barton describes Marshall's heroics in defeating the University of Chicago football team in 1906, and adds:

> *"Wealthy followers of the Minnesota team stated after the game at the hotel where the Gophers were stopping and on the train coming home that there would be nothing too good for Bobby Marshall when he finished school. Many of them patted Bobby on the back and invited him to call on them when he graduated in the spring of 1907. Bobby learned that all the hand-patting didn't mean a thing for when he completed his university course he obtained employment in a Minneapolis grain elevator and has played professional football for the past 20 years to help swell his earnings."*[31]

Barton compares Red Grange to Marshall, both of whom were great football players, and raises the question why was it that Grange cashed in heavily from pro football while Marshall did not? Barton's unstated conclusion is that Marshall wasn't able to make the kind of money Red Grange did from pro football because he was an African American.

In May, 1926, an all-African American baseball team that

Marshall played on, the Minneapolis Colored White Sox, went to Winona, Minnesota, to play the local team. Winona is on the Mississippi River 130 miles south and east of Minneapolis. When the Colored White Sox arrived in Winona the night before the game, they were denied access to all the hotels in town, so the team had to sleep in the bus. The *Winona Republican Herald* noted, "The colored boys played poorly, probably as a result of their lack of sleep the night before." Playing second base that day, several ground balls got by Marshall and he was taken out of the game. The Colored White Sox lost, 17-3.[32] -

In the fall of 1926 Bobby played football briefly for the Rochester, Minnesota, Aces (formerly the Minneapolis Liberties),[33] but he left the team in late September to sign with the Twin Cities All-Stars, becoming the oldest active football player in the United States at the age of 46.[34] On September 26 he suited up at right end with the All-Stars for a game against Ernie Nevers' Duluth Eskimos. The *Minneapolis Daily Star*, in a preview of the game, observed that "although dangerously close to the half century mark, Bob is in the best of condition because of his athletic activities."[35] But Nevers, who had played his college football at Stanford, was the star of the day, making yardage effectively on-line plunges and off-tackle runs, passing with accuracy, and also kicking effectively. The Eskimos won, 7-0.[36] (A few years later Nevers set an NFL record that still stands, scoring 40 points in one game when playing for the Chicago Cardinals. The Eskimo franchise later became the Orange, New Jersey, Tornadoes, then the Newark Tornadoes, the Boston Braves, the Boston Redskins, and finally the Washington Redskins.)[37]

Marshall continued to play for the All Stars of Minneapolis that season. In a hard-fought battle against a team from Eau Claire, Wisconsin on October 24, the All Stars eked out a 7-0 win with a long touchdown pass in the fourth quarter. One sportswriter reported the next morning that "Bobby Marshall, at right end for the All Stars, had one of his best days."[38]

But Marshall's busy life was more than just grain inspections interspersed with weekend sporting events. He also got involved with the Phyllis Wheatley House, an African American social institution that had been created in Minneapolis in 1924 to provide recreation, education, and day care for the city's African American citizens. "The Wheatley," as it was affectionately called, was also the only place in Minneapolis where non-whites from out of town could find lodging. In 1926 Bobby gave a speech to the track club at the Phyllis Wheatley House on good sportsmanship and clean living.[39]

In later October Louis Larson, coach and captain of the All-Stars, left the club, and coaching duties fell to Bobby, by now widely considered the grand old man of football, and Elnar Cleve.[40] Here is another example of no matter how strong racism was in Minnesota in the 1920s, Marshall always had the respect of his teammates.

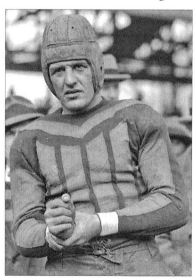

Red Grange

On September 25, 1927, Red Grange, the Galloping Ghost from the University of Illinois, came to Nicollet Park with the New York Yankees, a short-lived N.F.L. team, to play the Minneapolis Marines. After a long absence, Marshall was back with the Marines, a team that was no longer in the N.F.L. It was drizzling and the field was muddy, which prevented Grange from making any spectacular runs. The wet weather also led to a number of fumbles, and the game became a defensive battle. Bo Molenda of the University of Michigan scored the game's only touchdown on a three-yard run to give the Yankees the win. Marshall played left tackle that day for the Marines. Regarding this game, the sportswriter for the *Minneapolis Morning Tribune* wrote, "The veteran Bobby Marshall and Herb Swanbeck played the strongest game for the Marines on the line."[41] Dick Cullum, a Minneapolis sportswriter said, Bobby was still "one of the most respected ends" in pro football in his late forties.[42]

Fritz Pollard, the other pioneering African American in the first year of the N.F.L., was cut by the N.F.L.'s Akron Indians after the 1926 season because he had "failed to play up to the form expected of him." Three other African American players were also let go at the end of that season—Inky Williams, Sol Butler, and Dick Hudson—and it's worth speculating whether a rising tide of racial prejudice was actually the underlying cause. Also relevant is the fact that in 1926 the American Football League (A.F.L.) folded and many players from that league went to the N.F.L., making it easier to release African American players. The demand for talented players diminished further the next year when the N.F.L. contracted from twenty-two teams to twelve.[43] Many N.F.L. owners wanted to institute a ban on African American players similar to the ban that Major League Baseball had put in place.[44]

Under a bright sun at Memorial Stadium the Gophers varsity football team played an alumni team before 20,000 fans at University Appreciation Day on May 5, 1928. A 48-year-old Bobby Marshall was on the field and he played "manfully," though the varsity left the field with a 7-0 victory over the alumni.[45]

The next year Marshall played with the Rafert football team that defeated the W.B. Foshay team 8-0 on Oct. 20. The game took place in the Twin Cities Park League.[46]

Bobby Marshall's Minnesota a century ago can be described as follows. By 1928 there were 100,000 Minnesotans enrolled in the Ku Klux Klan.[47] The Minneapolis African American community did not fit the stereotype of a ghetto. Between 1923 and 1925 the crime rate in the Minneapolis African American community was little different from other parts of the city. Its illiteracy rate was only 1.7% compared to 16.3 % for the United States as a whole. After World War I there were no race riots in Minneapolis as there had been in Chicago, Omaha, and Detroit. This was perhaps due to the fact that African American and white leaders in Minneapolis worked together to prevent unrest. But during that era there were no federal, state, or city agencies to help African Americans find jobs and housing. Instead African American churches, social clubs, and barbers lent a helping hand. Housing for African Americans was restricted to certain neighborhoods in Minneapolis, something that would remain true throughout Bobby's life.[48]

As the 1920s ended, Bobby Marshall approached 50 years old. Could this aging star athlete maintain his hero status and influence in the civic affairs of Minnesota in his 50s?

13

Hard Times, Hard Hearts,

but No Hard Feelings

On January 1, 1930, the United States was in the middle of the Great Depression, and the cost of the daily *Minneapolis Tribune* was three cents. By 1933 there were 15 million Americans out of work, and half of the banks in the U.S. had failed. With the Great Depression raging and racism in America getting worse, would the N.F.L. turn its back on African Americans just as Major League Baseball had?

At the time Marshall was still playing pro football and baseball regularly, while also continuing to work for the Minnesota Grain Commission. In 1930, he played football for a Chippewa Falls, Wisconsin, team. His longtime friend A. B. Cassius recalls that the Chippewa team had players half of Bobby's age, "players like Buckets Goldenberg of Pittsburg and Johnny Blood of professional football fame."[1]

On June 2, 1931, Bobby played with a Gopher alumni team against the current Gopher baseball team. The alumni players were rusty, and Marshall had to dive for a lot of wild throws at first base. Pitching for the alumni that day was Fritz Crisler, who coached the Gophers football team in 1930 and 1931.[2] Crisler would coach the 1947 University of Michigan football team to an undefeated 10-0 season, a national championship, and a 49-0 victory over the USC Trojans in the Rose Bowl. Crisler finished coaching college football with a remarkable 116-32-9 record.[3]

In October of 1931 Bobby agreed to coach the linemen for the Ace Box Lunch team in the Senior Football League for the Minneapolis area. This league, which played on Sundays, had more than 80 teams formed by the employees of various businesses, government agencies, and fraternal organizations in the area. For example, the Naval Reserve, the American Legion, 9 Minute Auto Wash, and Ewald Creamery had teams.[4]-

On November 11 Bobby played in a Minneapolis high school alumni game for the Red and Blue Central High graduates vs. the South High graduates before 5,000 fans.[5] It was Armistice Day, the day marking the end of World War I, now called Veterans Day. The players had only two weeks to prepare for the game, which ended in a 7-7 tie. Both touchdowns came as a result of forward passes. The *Minneapolis Star Tribune* reported the next day that "such former Gopher line greats as Ray Eklund, Mark Matthews and Roger Wheeler for South, and the aged Bobby Marshall and Duke Johnson for Central, performed brilliantly."[6] Something seemed to go deep in the hearts of the adult Minnesota men who spent a holiday on the gridiron for the love of the game and their old school. It's also striking that so many Minneapolis high school players went on to play at the University of Minnesota, in contrast to today's Big Ten athletes who come from all over the U.S.A. and the world. Of course, high speed commercial airline travel wasn't yet a reality. And to its credit, the University of Minnesota football still draws local talent, perhaps the best recent example being star end Tyler Johnson from Minneapolis North High School.

In the spring of 1932, at the age of 52, Marshall joined a new African American baseball team, the St. Paul Monarchs, that scheduled mostly out-of-town games against small town teams. Bobby played first base for this team. In July they were on a ten-game win streak when they faced the St. Paul Milk Men at Lexington Park in St. Paul. That Sunday two thousand fans came out to the ballpark, but were disappointed to watch the Monarchs lose 9-3. One bright spot was Marshall's pinch hit single in the eighth inning. Bobby was considered the "grand old man" of that team.[7]

On September 6, Marshall was scheduled to be in the line-up in the All Nations Diamondball tournament on the African American team. In this tournament, teams made up of twelve ethnic groups competed against each other. The players involved had to be from Minneapolis or St. Paul and their ethnicity was determined by the father. If the father's ethnicity didn't fit into one of the twelve ethnic groups involved, the mother's ethnicity would come into play. The twelve teams were: Polish, Russian, Scotish, Swedish, Italian, Slavic, Irish, French, German, Norwegian, Jewish, and African American. The German team shut out the African American team on September 7. On September 13, the Irish team edged out the Scotmen, 2-1 to win the tournament on Gil Harrington's 2 run home run in the second inning. The All Nations Diamondball tournament was held annually from 1930 to 1940.[8]

In December the Minnesota All Stars took on the Carlsons, winner of the Twin Cities Park League. A *Minneapolis Star* article described Marshall, who was playing for the All Stars, as someone who "can still show the opposition plenty of football despite his 49 years."[9] (Marshall was actually 52.) The All Stars won 12-6 on a snow-covered South High field with Bobby coming in to play as a substitute.[9]

To judge from the frequency of his appearances on the field, Marshall was slowing down as an athlete. He played less often, and was sometimes used as a substitute rather than a starter. But he kept his hand in. On May 31, 1933, he played first base on an alumni baseball team that lost to the University of Minnesota varsity, 6-2.[10] And in a game on October 5, in front of 2,000 fans, Bobby played left tackle for the Minnesota All Stars as they defeated the Northern Giants 39 to 0 under the new floodlights at Nicollet Park.[11] A week later the Minnesota All-Stars defeated the

Marshall, Hefflefinger, and Munn

Eveleth-Virginia Miners, 40-0 with Bobby at left tackle.[12]

Marshall, Pudge Hefflefinger, and Clarence "Biggie" Munn are pictured together in their football gear in a photograph that appeared in the *Minneapolis Sunday Tribune* on November 12, 1933. They had all played in a game the day before between the alumni of the University of Minnesota Gophers and the St. Thomas Tommies at Nicollet Park. The Gopher All Stars won 6-0 with Marshall playing almost three quarters at left tackle and Hefflefinger, at age 66, playing six minutes at right guard for the Gophers. The game was played on Armistice Day as a fund raiser for the Disabled American Veterans Relief Fund.[13] At 53-years-old, Bobby looked trim, tall, and ready to play, towering over Heffelfinger and Munn. Munn later went on to coach the Michigan State Spartans to a national collegiate championship in 1952 with a 9-0 record. During his years at Michigan State Munn maintained the highest winning percentage of any Michigan State football coach, .846.[14] Heffelfinger was a three-time All American guard at Yale, ending his college career in 1891 and then coaching football at the University of Minnesota, the University of California, and Lehigh University.[15]

In the 1930s things had gotten worse for African American football players in the N.F.L. According to Robert W. Peterson, author of *Pigskin: The Early Years of Pro Football,* there was "plenty of testimony from black pros that they tended to absorb a lot more blows, both before and after the whistle, than their white colleagues." Then, in 1934, the N.F.L. banned all African Americans from playing in the N.F.L.[16] This meant that the Chicago Cardinals' Joe Lillard could no longer play. The *Chicago Defender* newspaper described him as "easily the best halfback in football." Why the ban on African Americans now? In the 1930s the Great Depression intensified tensions between minorities and white America, in part because whites and African Americans were often in competition for the same jobs.[17]

The career of George Preston Marshall is a case in point. He took over as owner of the Boston Redskins N.F.L. franchise in 1933, naming the team the Redskins because a few of the players were American Indians. In the 1930s he spearheaded the move to ban African Americans from the N.F.L. In 1937 he moved the team to Washington, D.C. and renamed the team the Washington Redskins. Marshall made his money from a group of laundries his dad had started in Washington, D.C. and he was the final N.F.L. owner to add an African American player to his roster, doing so only after U.S. President John F. Kennedy pressured him to do so in 1962.[18]

As racism in America got worse, Marshall continued to set an example that people could look up to. And he continued to participate in the local sports scene. One day during the 1934 baseball season, he teamed up with pitcher Johnny Davis, with whom he'd often played in the past, as the battery for the Minneapolis White Sox. With Johnny at 51 and Bobby 54, it was one of the oldest batteries ever to appear in organized baseball ever. The White Sox beat the Leslie Lawrence post team that day, 15-0.[19]

In an afternoon baseball game on June 5 the University of

Minnesota Gophers baseball team played an alumni team to a 6-6 tie. The *Minneapolis Star* reported the next day that "Bobby Marshall laughed in the face of creaking muscles and caught the whole game for the alumni."[20] Marshall was always happy to be involved in Gopher alumni activities. Regarding this game, *Minneapolis Star* columnist Charles Johnson said, "Pudge Heffelfinger had better look out for his honors as athletic's iron man. Bobby Marshall is well past the 50 mark, and he's still playing baseball, football and other sports."[21]

On Sunday, October 28, Bobby was set to play in a football game with the Minnesota All Stars against the Ironwood Panthers. The day before the game the *Ironwood Daily Globe* wrote: "Welcome home, Bobby Marshall. We're glad to see you back on the Gogebic Range. No player has ever performed here who was more popular. You have always been a clean sportsman, and that's why we have sort of adopted you here as our own." Five thousand Ironwood fans showed up—roughly the total population of the town today but the fans didn't have much-to cheer about because the All Stars won, 41-0. "Pleasing to old time fans was the appearance of Bobby Marshall who went in for tackle. Bobby looked the same as when he left here." Marshall didn't play the entire season for the All Stars in 1934 but joined the team for the Ironwood game because of his strong affection for the town, thinking of it as "his old home."[22] Here as elsewhere, Marshall had won the respect of thousands of people by his play, his sportsmanship, and his strength of character.

On January 23, 1935, Bobby was a guest at the Old Guards of the Diamond annual event at the Dyckman Hotel in Minneapolis. He gave a speech that night, summed up by *Minneapolis Star* sports writer Charles Johnson as follows: "The other night at the annual session of the Old Guards of the Diamond, Bobby Marshall admitted three high spots of his football career. They were: HAPPIEST MOMENT- When he made the Minnesota team in 1903; GREATEST THRILL- Kicking the winning field goal in the 4-2 win over Chicago in 1904; MOST EMBARRASSING MOMENT- When a silver bread plate slipped from underneath his sweater as he was leaving the dining room of the Edgewater Beach Hotel in Chicago." Who would admit a silver bread plate slipping out of one's sweater at a hotel? There was a transparency and

Marshall and Cy Olson at the Old Guards dinner, 24 January 1935

openness to Marshall that must have made him a very appealing after-dinner speaker. It must have also made him a wonderful friend to have. The *Minneapolis Tribune* writer who reported on this Old Guards of the Diamond event said, "Bobby Marshall, guest of honor…stole the show Wednesday night with sparkling reminiscences of feats on the gridiron and diamond by men whose names still live in memory."[23]

Bobby quit playing pro football in 1934 with his last game a victory over Ironwood. Regarding his play at age 56 Bobby said to Martin Quinn, sportswriter for the *Minneapolis Tribune*, "Sure, I could go out and hold down a job in the line next fall. I could take care of a tackle (position), even if I couldn't play the end (position) I used to. I could run with most of the pro tackles today, and after 35 years I should know how to handle the job… Yup, I can still run with the tackles…In the early days the guards stayed on the line on offense. The old guards would have a hard time in the modern game learning to pull out of the line on offensive plays. Now the guards lead practically every running play, and they are often used in forward-lateral drives…The physical abuse the early football player took was terrific. And he had to take it, for substitutes rarely were sent in for anything less than a broken leg. Many of the early squads numbered only 13 or 14 men, so most of the starters looked forward to a full afternoon of it." At 56 years of age Bobby was 6 feet and a quarter inch tall and weighed 196

Bobby in 4 shots, *Minneapolis Tribune*, June 14, 1936

pounds, only nine pounds heavier than his college playing weight. The trophy Bobby is holding was given to him by the African American citizens of the Twin Cities. "The trophy cites his selection as a member of Walter Camp's second all-American team in 1906." The middle bottom picture is from Bobby's high school graduation and the middle top picture is from Bobby's 1925 pro football season.[24]

Looking back on Marshall's long football career, lasting friendships were made. Former football teammates Sig Harris and Fred Chicken would sometimes come over to Marshall's home to sing old songs and play poker.[25]

In the 1930s Marshall often gave speeches to African American youth in various churches and community centers. In 1933 and 1935 he gave inspiring speeches to Twin Cites high school football players at an African American organization called the Sterling Club. He continued to speak on the themes of clean living and sportsmanship and coached youth in boxing and football at the Phyllis Wheatley House. He also helped with Golden Gloves boxing and officiated youth football. In 1936, he was honored at a Big Brothers Banquet for his work with youth. Bill Henegan, a Twin Cities sportswriter, said Marshall was a "great man because he spent so much of his time sharing his knowledge with younger people." James S. Griffin, Deputy St. Paul Police Chief, said Bobby was "the outstanding man of the Minneapolis African American community." Civil rights pioneer and president of the Minneapolis public school board Harry Davis called Marshall the "'image, the mentor, and the star' of the Minneapolis African American community."[26] Davis credits Bobby as one of his main inspirations. Bobby's grandson, Bill Marshall, says of Bobby, "He tried to energize youth in sports to lead a better life."[27]

Bobby played in the annual alumni Minnesota varsity baseball game on June 4, 1936. Sportswriter Bob Beebe of the *Minneapolis Tribune* wrote, "Bobby Marshall who is past 50 was out there playing first base like he was 20 years younger ..."[28]

Bobby's role in community work in the 1930s takes on even greater significance when one considers that in the 1930s poverty and crime were increasing, and housing stock was deteriorating in the African American community of Minneapolis. The Depression hit the African American community extremely hard. Unemployment for African Americans in St. Paul and Minneapolis rose to 60 percent, while the rate for whites hovered around 25 percent. The eleven railroads that came through the Twin Cities laid off many African Americans and many small businesses owned by African Americans folded due to lack of capital. One of the few jobs that was safe was with the postal service. Many African Americans were on government welfare programs or government work projects, and there was a great deal of discrimination against African Americans in these programs.[29]

In the late 1930s, Bobby was playing sports less often, and turning his attention more often to the athletic activities of his sons.

14

Bobby and his Sons

On October 4, 1937 Bobby Marshall attended an American Legion dinner at the Dyckman Hotel in Minneapolis to honor captains of Minneapolis high school football teams. A number of former University of Minnesota football stars were there including Sig Harris, Earl Pickering, and George MacKinnon. In the photograph related to this event from the *Minneapolis Tribune*, Marshall is second from the left in the back row and Sig Harris is first from the left in the front row.[1] In so many Minnesota social events related to sports Marshall's presence was a way of saying, "Hey America, don't forget about the value and dignity of the African American athlete. It's time to give us an equal chance."

That time was long overdue, in fact. Yet it had not yet come, and when Marshall's three sons were considering athletics as a career, they took that fact into account. Bob Beebe of the *Minneapolis Tribune* interviewed Marshall in his column of October 8, 1936. Beebe wrote, "Bobby said his son, Bobby Jr., age 18, has the makings of a football player but he can't seem to get the boy interested in the gridiron sport. 'It's airplanes with him.'"[2] World War II was five years ahead, and Marshall was busy raising three sons and a daughter while also holding his day job at the grain commission and participating in athletic events on nights and weekends. His three sons, Bobby Jr., Billy, and Donald, were all excellent athletes, but what professional sports could they aspire to? Major League Baseball and the N.F.L. were closed to them and the N.B.A. would not be a reality until 1946. The first African American in the National Hockey League, Willie O'Ree, didn't make his debut until 1958, playing left wing for the Boston Bruins.[3] So instead of contemplating a career in baseball, football, basketball, or hockey, the three Marshall brothers focused on boxing.

On February 14, 1939, Bobby Marshall Jr. won his light heavyweight bout against George Rodgerson by knockout in the Northwest Golden Gloves tournament at the Minneapolis Auditorium, with Marshall Jr. boxing prettily and punching hard.[4] The next evening, he won a decision over John Stevens with many punches to the midriff. But he lost to Sam Stupar in the semifinals, and Stupar went on to claim the title.[5]

A year later, on February 12, 1940, Bobby Marshall Jr. won a Golden Gloves light heavyweight bout against George Wabashaw. It was a busy night, during which 3500 spectators watched 102 matches with the action lasting until after 1 a.m.[6] In the spring of that year, Bobby Marshall,

Bobby Jr. vs. George Wabashaw

Sr. couldn't stay away from athletics himself, and he played catcher for the Minnesota State Grain Commission team.[7]

November 6, 1940, was quite a night for Marshall's sons at the Eagles boxing show. An excited crowd of more than a thousand watched Billy defeat Jim Boyette in the 147-pound class, and Bobby, Jr. won a light heavyweight bout against Clyde "Red" Rasley.[8] This was an enormous achievement for Bobby Marshall Jr., considering that fifteen months earlier, he had fallen asleep at three a.m. while driving a car and hit a trolley pole at Fourth

Marshall with sons Bobby Jr. and Billy

Ave. South in Minneapolis. When admitted to the hospital his condition was listed as poor with a fractured jaw and a possible head injury.[9]

In early January, 1941 Bobby Jr. defeated Earl Doran at the Minneapolis Golden Gloves tournament held at the Minneapolis Ascension Club, and Billy defeated George Roman. Both Billy and Bobby Jr. advanced to the semifinals of the tournament.[10] A few days later, Billy and Bobby Jr. both won their divisions in the Minneapolis Golden Gloves tournament. Regarding his sons' victories, Bobby said, "I don't think I ever got as big a kick out of competing in football, baseball or hockey as I did out of seeing those two kids win the city titles. Billy fought like I hoped he would and I didn't worry about him. But Bobby had a tough night with Clyde Rasley. That was a close one but I was proud of the way he rallied."[11] (Bobby Marshall Jr. enlisted in the Army Air Corps in 1941, attending a training camp for African Americans in Illinois. The American armed services were still segregated and would remain so until President Harry Truman desegregated the military in 1948. After beating all the other boxers at the camp, including the boxing instructor, Marshall Jr. became the camp boxing instructor and then a lieutenant in the U.S. Army, receiving his commission from officer candidate school in Miami Beach in 1943.[12] This was quite a distinction for an African American in the 1940s.

Meanwhile, Billy Marshall entered the Golden Gloves Chicago Tournament of Champions along with 300 other boxers from 23 states. On February 24, 1942, at Chicago Stadium, he

Billy Marshall

knocked out Ralph Hill of Omaha, Nebraska, 52 seconds into the first round with a hard left hook to the stomach. George Barton of the *Minneapolis Morning Tribune* described it as "the hardest punch" Marshall had ever thrown."[13] The next night Billy lost to Bob Burns of Ft. Wayne, Indiana.[14]

On December 7, 1942, the United States entered World War II. Bobby Marshall sold war bonds to assist in the war effort.[15]

Billy Marshall wasn't able to join the armed forces due to sinus problems and asthma, but by 1944 he had fought 130 amateur fights in the welterweight division, winning 115. His sparring partner was Holman Williams—the same one that Joe Louis, who was then world heavyweight champion, used. It was Billy's goal to be a top-level athlete like his father.[16] Billy Marshall won his professional debut before 5,000 fans at Minneapolis Auditorium on February 1, 1944, defeating Ernie Peters by decision in six rounds with Louis acting as the referee.[17]

Bobby Marshall Jr. came back to Minneapolis to visit his

family on August 13, 1945, one day before V-J Day, the armistice with Japan that ended World War II. During his visit he said, "I'd like to make one more bid for the light heavyweight championship in the *Star-Journal* and *Tribune* Northwest Golden Glove tournament and then take a fling at professional boxing." At the time Marshall Jr. was serving as boxing instructor at the Tuskeegee, Alabama, army aircraft maintenance base. He weighed in at 180 pounds and felt he was in excellent condition to box.[18]

More than five thousand fans were on hand at the Minneapolis Auditorium on June 14, 1946, to see Billy Marshall, weighing in at 147 pounds, defeat Art Lambert in the first round of a six-round bout. Billy had returned home to Minneapolis from Detroit for the fight.[19] His father had seen what happened too often to boxers who ended up punch drunk and poor, and he took the opportunity to have a talk with his son. The gist of it was: "You're too smart for boxing." Billy took his father's advice and ended his boxing career in 1946.[20]

Donald Marshall, Bobby's other son, also boxed, winning a couple of fights as a bantamweight in 1946 while showing a "sturdy right and good boxing technique."[21] Donald had been in the U.S. Navy during World War II, serving as an Able Bodied Seaman, First Class.[22]

After World War II Bobby Marshall Jr. returned to Minneapolis and resumed his boxing career, entering the Northwest Minneapolis Golden Gloves tournament. On February 17, 1947 in his first Golden Gloves match at the Minneapolis Auditorium, before an overflow crowd of 10,112, he defeated Elias Wotzka of Brainerd. George A. Barton, writing for the *Minneapolis Tribune*, described Marshall Jr. in the fight with Wotzka as follows. "Marshall (was) boxing cleverly and punching sharply and viciously with both fists..." In the second match that evening Bobby Jr. defeated Bob Huttel of Duluth to win the Northwest Golden Gloves light heavyweight class.[23] It may seem strange to fight twice in the same night. According to Golden Gloves rules, fights last only three or four rounds.[24]

After winning the Minneapolis Golden Gloves tournament Marshall Jr. went off to compete in the Tournament of Champions in Chicago on February 25. This was a national Golden Gloves championship involving boxers from 37 cities and 29 states. A crowd of 11,500 fans at Chicago Stadium saw Bobby Jr. lose in a split decision to Richard Cunningham of Cleveland. The referee voted for Bobby but the judges saw it differently, making Cunningham the winner due to his aggressiveness.[25]

After the Tournament of Champions in Chicago, Bobby Jr. turned pro. On April 18 at the Minneapolis Auditorium before 8,540 fans he won a four-round light heavyweight decision over Dominic Berardo of Detroit.[26] And on October 17 at the Minneapolis Auditorium before a crowd of 3000, he scored a technical knockout victory over John Risko of Detroit. Bobby Jr. knocked down Risko three times and won by a technical knockout.[27] Just two weeks later on Halloween night, 4,121 fans saw Bobby Jr. fight in the heavyweight division at the Minneapolis Auditorium against Chief Don Eagle of Chicago. For Bobby Jr., who was ten pounds lighter than the Chief, it was a trick, not a treat. Bobby Jr. lost by a technical knockout and one wonders why Bobby Jr. went from light heavyweight to heavyweight class?[28] After the fight, Bobby Marshall Sr. said to Bobby Jr., "Son, you don't have the heart for boxing." Bobby Jr., like his brother Billy, listened to his father's advice and ended his boxing career in 1947.[29] Prior to his loss to Chief Don Eagle Bobby Jr. had won six straight pro fights, three by a knock-out.[30]

After a brief stint in the insurance business in Chicago, Bobby, Jr. returned to Minneapolis and went to work for Northwest Airlines doing repair work on delicate aeronautical instruments at Holman Field maintenance base.[31] But he later went back into the Army and became a career soldier. His nephew, Bill Marshall says, Bobby Jr. loved serving his country in the U.S. military.[32]

Marshall never coached his own sons in boxing because he felt parents would make poor coaches for their own children, being either too hard or too easy on them.[33]

Marshall celebrated his children's victories with them, but he wasn't afraid to tell them the hard truth when they needed to hear it.

15

Marshall's Later Years

What is the measure of a great athlete? His performance on the field? His longevity at the highest level of play? His example as a role model? His service to the community? The success of his children and grandchildren? His integrity?

On June 28, 1939, the *Minneapolis Star* reported that Bobby Marshall "was granted a divorce from Irene B. Marshall, 39, in District Judge Levi M. Hall's court. She had filed the original complaint but he [Marshall] filed a cross bill charging cruel and inhuman treatment and infidelity, and her complaint which included physical abuse was withdrawn. He was awarded custody of their four children."[1]

George A. Barton, a sportswriter for the *Minneapolis Morning Tribune*, interviewed Marshall for a column that appeared on February 27, 1942. Barton asked Marshall which sport was the roughest. Bobby replied, "HOCKEY…Boys knowing how to use their skates and sticks can give you a lot of abuse. And, do it so neatly officials miss much of it. Hockey takes more out of a player physically than any other sport. You're on the go every second—skating at top speed, twisting, turning, always with your eyes on the puck. Body-checks take a lot out of you when you are set for the shock, much less when you're not expecting it. You burn up far more energy in hockey than football and basketball as played nowadays. You can stall for a rest in football and you're not bumped around much in basketball because of the strict rules now in effect. No matter how much they change hockey rules, a stick, skate, or body-check hurts just as much."[2]

In 1942 the Pittsburg Pirates offered three Negro League players a tryout. Barton said in an article in the *Minneapolis Morning Tribune* of August 5, 1942, that an unnamed Minneapolis minister hoped these African Americans wouldn't play in Major League Baseball. The minister was quoted as saying, "Billy Williams and Bob Marshall played with white teams in the northwest. But I believe both will agree with me that THEY WOULD NOT HAVE ACCEPTED OFFERS FROM TEAMS IN ORGANIZED BASEBALL because they are too intelligent and have too much pride to court humiliation from white players in major and minor leagues."[3] A picture of Marshall accompanied the article, though Barton had never contacted Marshall about it. The Twin Cites African American newspaper, *The Spokesman*, responded, saying it was not okay that Marshall was not contacted before the article went to print. Marshall said nothing, letting *The Spokesman* speak for him.[4] Barton apologized to the *Spokesman*, but claimed he was stating the view of "prominent Negroes."[5] As he had done all his life, Marshall let his actions, not his words, speak for him. The Pirates cancelled the tryout, and it would be five more years before the first African American, Jackie Robinson, would play Major League Baseball.[6]

In an interview in the 1940s Bobby commented, "Pro ball a few years ago probably was more dangerous than football today, but players now have to be smarter and faster. In the old days it used to be power and plenty of it, but now it's power plus speed and deception. Forwards [forward passes], laterals and criss-crosses really open a game up."[7]

Bobby had strong opinions about baseball, too, stating that, "They say it's tough for the pitchers now. Sure it is, with the lively ball, but I often think they had it tougher in the old days. I liked that style of ball too, where you got the hit and run when it meant something and the stolen base. The sacrifice has sort of gone out, too."[8]

On Jan 28, 1947, Marshall attended an annual winter baseball event called the On to Nicollet party. The audience of 602 people, many local baseball players, listened as Waite Hoyt, a Yankee great, told humorous stories. Charles Johnson, sportswriter for the *Minneapolis Star*, described the event the next day: "Waite was at his best when he talked about Ruth. [On the same day Babe Ruth entered the hospital. He would be dead a year later.] Tops were his narration of how Babe greeted notables. He was telling of the time when Marshall Foch, hero of the First World War, visited Yankee Stadium. 'We Yankees all lined up in front of the Marshall's box to shake hands,' Hoyt explained. 'Ruth, of course, was the last. When he approached the famous officer, bedecked with ribbons, medals, Babe was at a loss for words. As he shook hands the big fellow blurted out, "They tell me you were in the war, general." That was the payoff and we all fairly howled.'"[9]

On May 5, 1947, 350 football fans packed the Calhoun Beach Club, across the street from Lake Calhoun in Minneapolis, to honor past University of Minnesota football greats, including Marshall.[10]

On December 30, 1949, *Minneapolis Star* sports reporter Dick Gordon did a story about whether college football players should be paid for playing. Gordon asked a number of former University of Minnesota football stars what they thought about this. Marshall said, "It is almost impossible to do all three things (football, studies, job) well. I think an athlete should get his room and board for nothing but I'm against actually paying college boys for playing."[11] In 2014 the National Labor Relations Board of the U.S. Government said it was okay for Northwestern University football players to organize a union to get paid to play.[12]

After thirty-nine years, Marshall retired from his position as state grain inspector in 1950. In his March 30 column on the sports page of the *Minneapolis Morning Tribune*, Dick Cullum had the following to say about Marshall. "The teams upon which Marshall played under Dr. H.L. Williams were among the first which must be credited with launching the Minnesota tradition in football…It may be said that Marshall was among the founders of what we have had ever since. So give him a hand. The way to do that is to be at the Dyckman [Hotel] at 6 P.M. Friday when he will be honored on the occasion of his retirement from the state grain weighing division. Bobby was a great one."[13] The testimonial dinner, which took place the next day, was sponsored by Marshall's union, the Minnesota Grain Weighers Association, and was attended by 600 people. Minnesota Governor Luther W. Youngdahl, Gophers football coach Bernie Bierman, and Bobby's teammate and best friend, Sig Harris all gave speeches that night to honor Marshall.[14] During his time at the podium Marshall recalled his grand slam home run in a championship baseball game against the Minneapolis Keystones. At the time Bobby was playing for the St. Paul Colored Gophers. "That was the hardest hit I ever got in my life. Boy, it went."[15] Hubert Humphrey, then the mayor of Minneapolis, didn't show up at the dinner. Bill Marshall, Bobby's grandson, remembered that there were some hurt feelings over that.[16] Then again, Humphrey was a Democrat and Bobby was a lifelong Republican. One man who went to Bobby's testimonial dinner was Nick Kahler. Nick knew a thing or two about ice hockey, and he said Bobby "was potentially a great hockey player…He had that same knack Ching Johnson used to have of looking so innocent and good natured while dishing out punishment that no one could suspect him of being a real trickster."[17]

Marshall, now retired, spent his time doing church activities, working with Minneapolis youth, and going to sporting events. He had a lifetime pass to Nicollet Park where the Minneapolis Millers played minor league baseball, and he also attended University of Minnesota athletic events regularly. Bobby also spoke to high school teams, the VFW, Boy Scouts, church groups, University of Minnesota events, anything to inspire young men to lead a better life.[18]

About a year after the death of her second husband, Irene left Great Falls, Montana, and came back to Minneapolis. Before long she and Bobby were living together again. I suspect that he felt that a prayer of his had been answered. According to Bobby's grandson Bill Marshall, Bobby and Irene lived in a common law relationship for a few years, but decided to get married again in 1952, when they went to Detroit to visit their daughter, Bette Session.[19] At the time of their second wedding, which took place in Detroit, Marshall was 72 years old. Back in Minneapolis once again, Irene participated in the Ladies Auxiliary of St. Peter's A.M.E. Church, where she and Bobby were members. Irene was also active in the local P.T.A. and the neighborhood community association.[20]

Bobby with Sig

Sig Harris and Bobby Marshall got together on Friday, November 7, 1952, for a meeting of the M Club, an organization of University of Minnesota athletic lettermen. The meeting was held at the Nicollet Hotel in the Gateway District of downtown Minneapolis. The purpose of the meeting was to honor Johnny McGovern, an All-American football player for Minnesota in 1909. More than five hundred M Club members attended, and the next day the *Minneapolis Star* ran a photo of Harris and Marshall standing together.[21] These two fellows had been friends for more than sixty years. Harris had been a vice-president of the M Club in 1936, and he'd also been a scout and assistant coach for Gopher football.[22] He even acted as head coach for one game when Doc Williams couldn't be there. The Gophers beat Indiana that day, 6-0, making Harris the only Minnesota head football coach who never lost a game.[23]

On Friday, October 23 and Saturday, October 24, 1953, a celebration was held in Minneapolis, for the fiftieth anniversary of the inception of the Little Brown Jug game between the University of Michigan and the University of Minnesota. On Saturday the two teams renewed their football rivalry. The temperature was in the 60s and the weather was sunny. Players from the 1903 Gophers team were honored, including Marshall, Sig Harris, Edward L. Rogers, Dr. M. Stranthern, M.W. Thorpe, Jim Kremel, O.N. Davies, and U.S. congressman from North Dakota, Usher L. Burdick. Michigan was previously undefeated that season and was a one touchdown favorite.[24] Perhaps, Marshall and his Gopher teammates inspired the current team because Minnesota won 22-0. After the game, Marshall said, "Those kids looked just like we did when Sig Harris was quarterbacking us and telling us to play ball. I was surprised but I haven't seen a Minnesota team play that fine a game in a long time." Sig Harris remarked, "Those kids really came through and I never saw anyone ever play better offensively and defensively than Paul Giel [of the 1953 Gopher football team]."[25]

A few years later *Minneapolis Star* sportswriter Dick Gordon interviewed Bobby regarding the prospects for the 1957 Gophers football team. In that same article Gordon writes, "Peerless Bobby (Marshall) was the first of his race to make a name for himself with the Gophers and one of the Negro pioneers in Big Ten football...Aided by Marshall's all-around play the Gophers won conference championships in 03 and 04. Now there is just a chance that they may end their 16-year title drought by exploiting a two ply Negro punch (Bob Blakely and Billy Martin) in the backfield."[26] Blakley and Martin did not become superstars, and the Gophers went 4-5.[27]

But a few years later, in 1961, Sandy Stephens, playing under Coach Murray Warmath at the University of Minnesota, became the first African American All-American quarterback at a major college. Stephens led the Gophers to a national championship and Big Ten championship in 1960, and to Rose Bowl appearances in 1961 and 1962. On New Year's Day 1962 Stephens led the Gophers to a 21-3 victory over UCLA in a game that remains

Sandy Stephens

the only Gophers victory in the Rose Bowl.[28] The Gophers actually finished second to Ohio State in the Big Ten that season, but the Ohio State Faculty Council voted 28-25 to deny the Buckeyes the opportunity to go to the Rose Bowl so the players could focus on their studies.[29]

Having an African American at quarterback seems commonplace today, but in the 1950s it was not. Stephens had received scholarship offers from more than fifty schools, but he enrolled in Minnesota because he knew that Minnesota had a more enlightened view of equal opportunity on the field than many other universities, and he felt he'd get the chance to play quarterback there.[30] The Sandy Stephens Endowed Scholarship was established in 2001, "…given each year to a deserving African-American student-athlete in the university's football program who has demonstrated leadership, courage and a commitment to civic and community responsibilities."[31] The Sandy Stephens Endowed Scholarship is still active. The recipient for 2019 was Tyler Nubin.[32]

If Bobby Marshall had not paved the way for African American athletes in University of Minnesota athletics by his example over 50 years, would things have been different? Would the culture of the University of Minnesota football program regarding people of color have been less favorable? Would Sandy Stephens have played at another college? Would Stephens have played quarterback in collegiate football at all? I think Bobby Marshall's example had something to do with Stephens' success with the Gophers.

16

The Last Days of a Hero

Including high school, college, and the pros, Marshall played in 315 football games, averaging nine games a year for 35 years.[1] Bill Hengen of the *Minneapolis Star* described him as "A tremendously conditioned athlete…"[2] In all his years of playing football he never sustained a major injury.[3]

Marshall continued to play baseball until he was 60, and softball until age 65. His advice about physical conditioning was simple: "Keep active. Never give up. Skate, play tennis, everything. Never let those muscles tighten up." In an interview with Joe Hendrickson on March 31, 1950 Bobby said, "They took me out of the Northwestern game once because of a bad shoulder. Otherwise, I played the full game all the time. In all my years I guess my injuries were only some twisted knees or ankles and some cracked fingers."[4]

Marshall's granddaughter Kathy Washington described him as "a gentle, quiet, private person, easy to get along with and fun loving. He enjoyed his grandchildren…A gentle giant you might say."[5] His son Donald stated, "Marshall probably resented the racial prejudice he encountered in the early 1900s. I think he never really voiced it. He was a very quiet guy."[6]

Quiet he may have been, and not a man to hold a grudge, but Marshall also had the courage to take a stand for what he thought was right. Bobby fought for the rights of farmers in the

Minnesota State Grain Commission. He had the tenacity to pursue and win the lawsuit to gain custody of his four children and often took a stand in defense of fair play on the field, as we've seen at various points in this narrative.

Marshall's grandson, Bill Marshall, spent a lot of time with Bobby as a young boy, and he describes Bobby as "confident, relaxed and comfortable in his own skin as he walked through his daily life…Bobby was always under control. I never saw him lose his temper."[7] He stressed that his grandfather was the type of guy who "put other people first, ferocious on the playing field, but kindly and soft-spoken everywhere else. But if you were not doing what you were supposed to, he had no problem setting you straight."[8]

His grandson noted that Marshall emphasized the importance of education. "He took the general attitude about race and racism that these were by and large ignorant people. His feeling was people would have to respect you if you were educated."[9]

Bill quoted his grandfather as saying "you have to look past racism, you can't let the past drag you down." He added that "Bobby didn't get mad at racists. He felt sorry for them." Bobby considered sports as "the great equalizer."[10]

Bill Marshall, in an interview on April 17, 2018, said the following about his grandfather. "Bobby Marshall was not into flaunting victory. He was not narcissistic because he believed when you won, the whole team won. The name of the jersey was not Marshall, it was Minneapolis Central. And that's the way he taught and his children, he made sure they understood that, too. He was a humble person, for being the person he was, he was a very humble man. And he never thought of himself as being better than others." Once, after one of Bobby Jr.'s boxing victories, Bobby scolded his son, telling him to never flaunt victory again. Bobby Jr. never did.[11]

Bill Marshall remembers that, "He [Bobby] was a serious person but yet had a humorous side that was facetious at times. He always tried to look to the high side of things in life and I cannot recall him ever raising his voice, using bad language, or in any way being anything other than a gentleman. Sometimes his wife Irene would get angry and Bobby would tell her to calm down. He took a lot of interest in his kids and grandchildren and by in large his neighborhood. He was well known in south Minneapolis and very respected in his community. He was a punctual type person and was demanding in that how people acted, dressed and their general outlook and would correct you when you used bad grammar, especially double negatives. He did not care for that at all. People would say, 'I ain't got any' instead of 'I don't have any.' I remember that from being a kid, being corrected numerous times on double negatives." Bill added, "Bobby felt children needed to be taught to listen so they could learn something.[12]

Bill Marshall

Bill said as a coach, "Bobby was sensitive to the needs of others; he had a great sense of humor; yet he was very demanding about doing things the right way, not fooling around. This made him an excellent coach."[13]

Bobby shaved every day, was a dapper dresser, and would stand when a woman entered the room. He had a deep faith in God and was active for 40 years at St. Peter AME Church in Minneapolis, where he was a deacon. He liked fire and brimstone in his religion, and thought the Presbyterian Church of grandson Bill was too lax. He went to church every Sunday and every Wednesday too, for prayer meetings. He insisted on standing for the National Anthem at public events and in front of the TV at his home on 3650 4th Ave. South in Minneapolis. He raised an American Flag each morning and took it down each night.[14]

Sig Harris, Bobby's lifelong friend, was an assistant coach and scout for the Gophers for many years. In a *Minneapolis Tribune* article on Sunday, September 12, 1937, Harris describes an incident between Marshall and Gophers head football coach, Dr. Henry Williams. In 1907 "Doc Williams engaged him (Bobby) as an assistant coach and scout. Bobby was assigned to scout Wisconsin that year while we went down to play at Chicago. Along about game time who should pop up on the bench down at Chicago but Bobby, who was supposed to be down in Madison."

"Bobby," shouted Doc, "'Why the blankety blank aren't you in Madison?'"

"'Doc,' said Bobby, grinning all over. "'It's this way. I missed the train.'"[15]

In a *Minneapolis Star* article from January 28, 1941, Bobby tells another story, this time about why he quit football. He said, "I started to look for my uniform and couldn't find it. Little Billy and Bobby would sneak away with a head-gear, a shoulder pad and a pair of shoes now and then, and when it came time to suit up I didn't have a complete outfit. So I decided to quit and let the kids play football."[16]

Bobby Marshall's house on 4th Avenue S.

Bill Marshall took me to see his grandfather's former home at 3650 4th Ave. South in Minneapolis, which is today a well-kept predominantly Hispanic neighborhood. Bill said the neighborhood looks much the same as it did in the 1950s. The old Central High School, then right down the street, was closed in 1982 and later torn down. Green Central Elementary now sits on the same site. Marshall bought the house on 4th Ave. South in the mid-1920s when the neighborhood was predominantly white.[17]

Bill told me that Bobby was an excellent money manager, investing wisely in property and in the stock market, while buying tools and other household goods second-hand to save money. Bill called Bobby "Pappy" and Irene "Nanna," and spent a great deal of time with them because he lived only two blocks away. Bobby and Irene loved to read, and they made good use of the public library just down the block. Bill would come over to the house after school and Bobby would ask him, "What did you learn in school today? Bobby would give Bill a nickel to get an ice cream cone from a nearby store.[18]

Nanna, a first-rate homemaker and very gracious person, would start cooking at 3 in the afternoon. At 6 p.m., on the dot, dinner would be served. Marshall was a stickler for punctuality, in the same way that he encouraged the proper use of language. The dinner would often consist of beef or pork procured from a nearby butcher shop accompanied by fresh vegetables from the garden in the back of the house. Bobby didn't trust supermarkets, preferring to patronize local family-owned businesses. After dinner Pappy and Nanna would step out to the front porch and socialize with their neighbors, the Millers and the Thompsons. They were very moderate drinkers, though Bobby liked a drink with three fingers worth of bourbon. Irene would occasionally smoke a cigarette but only on the porch since Bobby wouldn't allow it in the house. About a third of Pappy and Nanna's friends were Jewish, a third African American, and a third white Christians. Bobby always acknowledged both his Jewish and African American heritage. Pappy and Nanna had a black and white TV and Irene loved radio shows, but reading and socializing were much more important to them. Irene loved to play bridge with her daughter Bette as well as whist, hearts, and canasta. Two Siamese cats, Ming and Chan, roamed around the home.[19]

Marshall's granddaughter Kathy Washington came to live with Bobby and Irene when she was 12. Kathy describes both Bobby and Irene as strong-willed people, adding that Irene in particular had a great sense of humor. Bobby loved to play with

From left: Lesley Perkins (Kathy's daughter), Kathy Washington, Laurie Washington (Kathy's great granddaughter), and Taleah Blandon (Kathy's oldest daughter).

babies, saying, "Whop, whop," to them. When he said to Kathy, "Come inside now," he meant *right now*.[20]

Bobby's daughter, Bette Session, recalled times when Bobby had former teammates Sig Harris and Fred Chicken over for a visit. "They would sing old songs—not very well," and that Bobby "played plenty of poker with his buddies, too."[21] *Minneapolis Star* sports writer Joe Hendrickson wrote, "Bobby Sr. likes to talk about the old days. He likes to recall those twelve years he was a teammate of Sig Harris—four years each at Madison grade school, Central High, and Minnesota."[22] Bobby would take his grandson Bill to University of Minnesota football games in the mid 1950s. While sitting in the stands he would comment to nearby fans, "Sig Harris would never run a play like that." After the game he'd take Bill to the Gophers locker room to meet the players and coaches.[23]

Bobby's son Billy quit boxing on his father's advice, as mentioned earlier, and during the 1950s he became an excellent golfer, playing on the African American "Chitlin Tour." In the mid 1950s he won the Bronze Open, a tournament established locally in 1939 for African Americans at the Hiawatha Golf Course in Minneapolis. Billy owned and was landlord for a duplex and a triplex apartment in Minneapolis.[24]

On August 27, 1958, in Minneapolis, Marshall died of arteriosclerosis after a two week stay at St. Peter State Hospital in Nicollet County, Minnesota. He was 78.[25] St. Peter State Hospital was established as a hospital for the insane, and Bobby suffered from Alzheimer's disease that came on very quickly near the end of his life, around 1956 or 1957. Bobby's granddaughter Kathy says, "He was a little combative during that time but easy to get along with."[26] Forty years of punishing hits from football, baseball, or hockey probably contributed to his condition.[27] Bobby's wife Irene would go out to the garden in the back of the house to get the clothes off the clothes line and Bobby would lock the door.[28] Bobby would drive to a baseball game and take the bus home until Bobby's old friend Sig Harris or other financially well-off University of Minnesota friends of Bobby prevented this from continuing by renting limousines to take Bobby to and from ball games.[29] Near the end of his life Bobby began talking as if he were living in the 1920s.[30]

Bobby's son Billy had died a month earlier at the age of 35, collapsing at nearby Keller golf course.[31]

Bobby's funeral was held at Werness Brothers Mortuary and his interment was at Lakewood Cemetery in Minneapolis. He was the first African American to be buried there. Other family members are now buried nearby.[32]

Irene never remarried, but moved to Detroit in 1963 to be near her daughter, Bette. Healthy up to the end of her life, Irene

From left: Jeremy Marshall (son of Marcella Mallett), Marcella Mallett (former wife of grandson of Bobby Marshall), Lauren Marshall (daughter of Marcella Mallett), Joshua Marshall (son of Marcella Mallett), and Noah Marshall (son of Joshua Marshall).

died in 1986 at the age of 89. Her ashes were spread from an airplane over Great Falls, Montana, where she grew up.[33]

Although the details of Bobby Marshall's extraordinary career have faded and been forgotten by many, efforts have also been made to explore his legacy and preserve his memory by sports fans, historians, and family members. The former wife of one of Bobby's grandsons, Marcella Mallett, issued a proclamation at the Super Bowl held in Minneapolis in February, 2018, under-

Oliver Sims and his son

scoring Marshall's contribution to breaking down racial barriers in sports. Marcella says, "Bobby Marshall broke barriers to make opportunities possible for other African Americans. There has to be somebody who goes first."[34] Marshall's great grandson, Oliver Sims,

Shaun Hansen

has produced a video on Bobby's life, "Lost Legends The Magnificent Bobby Marshall." Oliver's grandfather was Bobby Marshall's son, Donald.[35]

One of Marshall's great grandsons, Shaun Hansen, was, like Bobby, a baseball player. Shaun pitched for Palm Beach, Florida Community College and for the Cub's summer league. Presently, Shaun is a general contractor, specializing in roofing. In 2020 he ran for the Minnesota State Senate as a Republican. Shaun says of his great grandfather, "Thinking of what Bobby Marshall achieved, has given me a great work ethic." [36]

In my mind's eye I picture Bobby Marshall as he was—standing straight and tall with great dignity and integrity, immaculately dressed in suit and tie, with a smile on his face.

Epilogue

Why isn't Bobby Marshall's name said in the same breath as Babe Ruth's, Tom Brady's, Michael Jordan's, Wayne Gretzky's, LeBron James's, or Jackie Robinson's? By the time of his death in 1958, Marshall's long list of athletic achievements had been forgotten by many, and none of the newspapers carried a lengthy obituary. But aficionados of local sports and the early years of the N.F.L. continued to champion his career, and in 1991 he was selected for the University of Minnesota M Club Hall of Fame alongside a stellar athlete from a more recent generation with an equally diverse career: Bronko Nagurski.[1] Nagurski earned All-American status on both sides of the line—as both fullback and defensive tackle. He went on to play for many years in the N.F.L., and also had a distinguished career as a professional wrestler.[2] Marshall played at a time when professional football and baseball were regionally based, while also holding down a steady job. Bobby's star doesn't shine quite so brightly. Yet Dr. Steven R. Hoffbeck, a history professor at Minnesota State University, Moorhead, says, "Had Marshall been white, he would have been remembered in the same terms as Nagurski."[3]

Jackie Robinson wore the number 42 on the back of his baseball uniform. That number is now retired and no one in Major League Baseball can now wear 42 on their back. When Bobby stepped on the playing field at Douglas Park in Rock Island, Illinois, in 1920, he, like Robinson, was breaking the color barrier. Shouldn't the N.F.L. honor his achievement in some way?

When Marshall broke the color line in the N.F.L. in 1920, it was a momentous, earth-shaking occasion. It is something I want to celebrate the same way I celebrate Jackie Robinson in M.L.B. in 1947, Earl Lloyd in the N.B.A. in 1950, and Willie O'Ree in the N.H.L. in 1958. Each of these men was the first to break the color line in his professional sport and that took courage. Marshall's great granddaughter, Loren Marshall commented, "I get ambition, knowing what Bobby did."[4]

Civil rights leader, family friend, and Minneapolis school board member W. Harry Davis said about Bobby, "He may have been quiet, but quite a few people patterned themselves after him, not only as an athlete but in his demeanor on the street and in church."[5]

At this distance, there is no way for us to ascertain how good Bobby Marshal *really* was. The comments of those who saw him play are impressive. Then again, such "back in my day" arguments are often inspired by nostalgia and tired assertions of "they don't make them like they used to." Yet it would be impossible to deny that Marshall impressed everyone who saw him play. This description of his play came from the *Minneapolis Journal* newspaper. "Those who watched him work will never forget the way in which he used to leave his feet and sail through the air as though gravity had never been invented. When he made one of his flights into the opposing team, the interference crumbled like a card house and usually the runner went down with the rest of them, but even if the runner escaped his grasp, the interference was shattered and Bobby skidded along on his chest with his heels still in the air as gracefully as an airplane coming to earth… He played with a rare combination of strength and craftiness, depending on leverage and experience to handle his opponents across the line."[6] Ossie Solem, University of Minnesota end and tackle and then football coach at Syracuse, Iowa, and Springfield College, has this to say about Bobby: "First of all, the greatest football player I ever saw, anywhere, was Bobby Marshall. Bobby could not only tackle a man with his arms but, if he missed could tackle him with his legs."[7]

There are a lot of "firsts" attached to Bobby Marshall; first African American in the N.F.L., among the first African Americans to be selected for the All Pro N.F.L. team (1920), first African American in the Big Ten on an All-American team (1905), first African American Big Ten coach (1907), probably the first African American pro ice hockey player, the first African American professional quarterback and head coach (12 years before the founding of the NFL), the first African American high school, college, and pro football coach in Minnesota, and the first African American to graduate from the University of Minnesota Law School.

Bobby was honored at the American Negro Exposition in Chicago in August of 1940 as one of the "greatest Negro athletes extant."[8] In 1949, sports writer Dick Cullum selected Bobby to the "All Time Gophers" football team. Sports writer Dick Gordon said Marshall "may well have been the best end in Gopher history."[9] On October 30, 1971, during halftime at the University of Minnesota Ohio State football game, Bobby was inducted into the National Football Foundation Hall of Fame for Pioneer College Players.[10] Bobby's wife Irene, daughter Bette, and sons Donald and Bobby Jr. attended the ceremony with Donald accepting the award.[11] On October 24, 1999 he was placed as an end on the "Gophers: All Time Eleven" football team by sports writer Patrick Reusse of the *Minneapolis Star Tribune*.[12] Jay Weiner of the *Minneapolis Star Tribune* placed Bobby as number 51 on the "Millennium Top 100 Sports Figures" on December 25, 1999.[13]

Dick Cullum, *Minneapolis Tribune* sports writer, summed up Bobby's career as follows. "Marshall was a fast and rangy end, and famed for the trickery which drew opponents into traps. He made a study of the business of playing end, and at the end of his career, could have been the man who wrote the book. He continued to play independent and professional football for years after leaving college and was still one of the most respected ends in the game when close to his 50th birthday."[14]

Walter Robb, a teammate from Central High School, said that Bobby was "really (like) one of my older brothers." Bobby's high school and college teammate, Sig Harris, considered Bobby "a true friend." James S. Griffin, Deputy Police Chief of St. Paul, considered Marshall to be "the outstanding man of the Minneapolis African American community." Harry Davis considered Marshall to be the "image, the mentor, and the star" of the same community. Sportswriter Bill Hengen said that Marshall was "a great man because he spent so much of his time sharing his knowledge with younger people." Coaching young people in football and boxing at the Phyliss Wheatley House in Minneapolis, working in Golden Gloves boxing, and acting as an official for youth football were some of Marshall's efforts in the 1930s.[15]

On October 5, 2018 Bill Marshall and I visited Bobby Marshall's grave. An appropriate inscription on Bobby Marshall's tombstone would be the following quote from *The Appeal*, "… he carried with him an unconquerable love of athletics…"[16] That love sustained him and contributed to his many achievements.

The next day Bill and I attended a football game in Minneapolis between the University of Iowa and the University of Minnesota. Even though it was early October, it was a cold and overcast day, typical for Minnesota, and sad to say, the Gophers lost 48-31. With thousands of fans at TFC Bank Stadium cheering on the home team, Bill recalled how much Bobby loved playing for the Gophers—more than he ever loved playing professional sports.[17]

This is probably the greatest lesson we can learn from his life-his ability to live with dignity and not resort to hate and violence when faced with exactly that. The washboard he wore around his abdomen to protect against injury while playing football is something I often think about. Bobby said the modern passing game had "brought the need for extra armour."[18] For me that washboard is a metaphor for living in a sometimes mean world, maintaining dignity and not resorting to hate.

Sports writer Ed Shave said Marshall, "made a very definite lasting contribution to athletics for the entire nation." Historian, Steven R. Hoffbeck, wrote Bobby "…developed a hard exterior to

The author and Bill Marshall at a Gophers football game, 2018

protect himself from hostile stares, gestures, and words at various times in his life, but underneath it all was the fine-grained wood of the gentleman, father, and sportsman who became an institution in Minnesota's African American community."[19] Bobby had an indomitable spirit.

Bobby Marshall, throughout his life, loved watching Minneapolis Millers baseball games at Nicollet Park. That park was torn down in 1955 and a plaque commemorating the old location of the park was erected in 1983.[20] Dick Cullum, in his sports column for the *Minneapolis Morning Tribune* went into detail on Bobby's love for the Millers. Cullum wrote, "No one in the park today (April 28, 1954) will have seen more games, opening games and otherwise, than Bobby Marshall, one of the all-time great ends of Minnesota football. He saw his first opener in 1902 which was the first day of play in the history of the American Association. He had been one of the most regular attendants throughout the season ever since. He had some seasons when he did not miss a game. He's never had a season when he missed very many. The count runs into thousands of games."[21] I picture Bobby sitting in the stands, watching a Millers game, as a young man and as a much older man, watching a team he would have been a superstar on, if African Americans were then allowed to play for teams connected to Major League Baseball. He was denied that opportunity and yet he was a fan of the team. I don't think there was any bitterness at all in the heart of Bobby Marshall. He seemed to have the patience to let America catch up to the love and understanding already present in his soul.

Bill Marshall tells what it was like to grow up around Bobby: "We were raised to be Americans…God first, family second, America third…Bobby saw a better time coming for everyone. To him, education was the answer to minority problems. He thought America was a place that was evolving to something better. He believed America was ordained by God."[22]

Bobby's greatest contribution may not have been on the field of play. As I researched this book I was amazed by how many times I discovered news articles regarding Marshall's presence at University of Minnesota alumni gatherings and other sports related social events. Bobby Marshall stood as a reminder to all Minnesotans that African Americans had integrity and ability on and off the playing field during decades when African Americans were banned from professional sports and many other opportunities.

Much has been said here about the racism in Minnesota during the first half of the 20th Century. Historian Peter Gorton acknowledges that racism in Minnesota but points out that, "There was a place where an African American could play baseball, football, and ice hockey on white teams in the first half of the 20th Century and that place was Minnesota."[23] Bobby's achievement would have been impossible in some other regions of the United States.

Learning about Bobby Marshall's life has been an inspiration for me. I hope it has been an inspiration for you.

Notes

Chapter 1

1. "Milwaukee, Wisconsin, 1880s," Google Images, last modified February 25, 2018. https://images.google.com/.
2. "If Bobby Marshall Took a Notion to Be King," *Mpls Journal*,13 January 1924. Magazine Section; Paul Haubrich, "Class of 1846: Ezekiel Gillespie," *Milwaukee Independent*, last modified March 27, 2016, http://www.milwaukeeindependent.com/articles/class-of-1846-ezekiel-gillespie/.
3. S. Hoffbeck (ed), *Swinging for the Fences*, 58, 59.
4. "Bobby Marshall," Datab.us, last modified February 25, 2018. http://datab.us/i/Bobby%20Marshall; S. Hoffbeck, "Bobby Marshall: Pioneering African American Athlete," 159.
5. Bill Marshall interview, April 17, 2018.
6. David Vassar Taylor, *African Americans in Minnesota*, 17.
7. S. Hoffbeck (ed), *Swinging for the Fences*
8. Bill Marshall interview, April 17 and October 5, 2018.
9. S. Hoffbeck (ed), *Swinging for the Fences*.
10. Bill Marshall interview, February 1, 2019.
11. David V. Taylor, *African Americans in Minnesota*, 15-17.
12. Bill Marshall interview, April 17, 2018.
13. S. Hoffbeck, "Bobby Marshall: Pioneering African American Athlete," 160
14. Ibid.
15. John Carroll, *Fritz Pollard: Pioneer in Racial Advancement*, 24.
16. Neal Rozendaal, *Duke Slater: Pioneering Black NFL Player and Judge*,22.
17. S. Hoffbeck (ed), *Swinging for the Fences*, 69.
18. Randy York, "The Legends of George Flippin + Four More."
19. Chuck Fouts, "Chicago baseball legend Cap Anson should not be in the Hall of Fame."
20. S. Hoffbeck (ed), *Swinging for the Fences*, 48-49.
21. Bill Marshall interview, April 15, 2018.
22. Ibid.
23. S. Hoffbeck, "Bobby Marshall: Pioneering African American Athlete,"
24. Ibid.

25. Bill Marshall interview October 5, 2018.

26. S. Hoffbeck (ed), *Swinging for the Fences*, 59.

27. Bill Marshall interview, April 15, 2018.

28. Abe Altrowitz, "Abe's Pierless Bridge Idea for Calhoun Seems Doomed," *Mpls Star*, (6 August 1967): 2, https://www.newspapers.com/image/188427374/?ter ms=%22Bobby%2BMarshall%22.

29. "No Scores," *Mpls Tribune*, 16 September 1900, 8.

30. "Football at Minnesota The Story of Thirty Years' Contests on the Gridiron," *The Minnesota Alumni Weekly*,11-9-1914, 18.

31. "Central Wins," *Mpls Star Tribune*, 25 November, 1900.

32. S. Hoffbeck (ed), *Swinging for the Fences*, 59.

33. S. Hoffbeck, "Bobby Marshall: Pioneering African American Athlete," 161.

34. Bill Marshall interview, October 5, 2018.

Chapter 2

1. "Defeated the H.S. Team," Mpls Journal, 22 February 1902, 4.

2. Todd Peterson, *Early Black Baseball in Minnesota,*, 216-217.

3. Bill Marshall interview, April 17, 2018.

4. "Sports Scholarships: A Look Back at History," *Sportscholarship.com*, last modified 2016, http://sportsscholarship.com/about/history-of-sports-scholarships/.

5. Dick Gordon, "Gopher Grid Greats Oppose Paying College Football Players," *Mpls Star*, (30 December 1949): 13.

6. Bill Marshall, interviewed April 17, 2018.

7. Neal Rozendaal, *Duke Slater: Pioneering Black NFL Player and Judge*, 182.

8. John Carroll, *Fritz Pollard: Pioneer in Racial Advancement* 60.

9. S. Hoffbeck, "Bobby Marshall: Pioneering African American Athlete," 161.

10. Neal Rozendaal, "African Americans in Big Ten Football, 1890-1963," last modified February 16, 2013, http://nealrozendaal.com/2013/02/26/african-americans-in-big-ten-football-1890-1963/. "Race and Football in America, The Life and Legacy of George Taliaferro," IU Gameday Central, 4 May 2020, https://iuhoosiers.com/news/2020/5/14/race-and-football-in-america-the-life-and-legacy-of-george-taliaferro-part-1.aspx; Rachel Reed and Grefg Kinney, "Celebrating George Jewett," Bentley Historical Library, 2021,https://bentley.umich.edu/features/celebrating-george-jewett/; Robert Tate, "C.R. Patterson & son Fred, 1st African American car makers," motorcities, 7 November 2018, https://www.motorcities.org/story-of-the-week/2018/c-r-patterson-son-fred-1st-african-american-carmakers.

11. Bill Littlefield, "First Black All-american college Football Player Honored, Belatedly," WBUR News, 19 December 2009, https://www.wbur.org/news/2009/12/19/football-fame-lewis

12. Bill Marshall, interviewed April 17, 2018.

13. S. Hoffbeck (ed), *Swinging for the Fences*, 60.

14. Beating Chicago By '06 Field Goal is Marshall's Fondest Grid Memory," *Mpls Star-Tribune*, (4 October, 1939): 20.

15. "Minnesota Golden Gophers School History," Sports Reference, 2020; "1905 Football Schedule," University of Minnesota Athletics," 2020.

16. "African-Americans in Big Ten Football- Minnesota," *Ohio State Black Alumni Society*.

19. John Kryk, "Why American Football Added a 4th Down," *Toronto Sun*, (2 February 2012): http://torontosun.com/2012/02/02/college-football-a-different-game-century-ago/wcm/60a38e5f-5e6b-45bb-bcf2-43e02c481bca. *The Minnesota Alumni Weekly*, 11-9-14, Vol. XIV, No. 9: 57.

20. Al Pappas Jr, *Gophers illustrated:* 15.

21. S. Hoffbeck, "Bobby Marshall: Pioneering African American Athlete," 161.

22. "Michigan Minnesota The Little Brown Jug Series," *Board of Regents of the University of Michigan*, last modified June 17, 2009, http://www.mgoblue.com/sports/m-footbl/spec-rel/061709aaa.html.

23. Dick Rainbolt, "Gophers' History Dr. Williams, The great innovator," *Mpls Star*, (22 September 1972): 33, https://www.newspapers.com/image/190554421/?terms=%22Bobby%2BMarshall%22%2Bfootball%2BMinnesota.

24. Robert W. "Bobby" Marshall, "My Greatest Thrill in Football," *Mpls Star Tribune*, 1 November 1932, 17.

25. "Football at Minnesota The Story of Thirty Years' Contests on the Gridiron," *The Minnesota Alumni Weekly* 11-9-14 vol. XIV No. 9, (9 November 1914): 17.

26. Robert W. "Bobby" Marshall, "My Greatest Thrill in Football," *Mpls Star Tribune*, 1 November 1932, 17.

27. William J. McNally, "Personal," *Mpls Star Tribune*. (23 October 1943): 4, https://www.newspapers.com/image/182241072/?terms=William%2BJ.%2BMcNally%2B%22Little%2BBrown%2BJug%22.

28. "No Doubt of Rough Usage: More Stories of Minnesota's Fighting Tactics; Gopher Players Instructed to 'Kill Off' Heston," *Detroit Free Press, 3 November 1903, 3, https://www.newspapers.com/image/118575590;* Bill Dow, "Willie Who? Willie Heston, U. of M.'s First Football Star," last modified September 25, 2010. https://www.detroitathletic.com/blog/2010/09/25/willie-who-willie-heston-u-of-m%E2%80%99s-first-football-star/.

29. S. Hoffbeck, "Bobby Marshall: Pioneering African American Athlete," 161.

30. Dick Rainbolt, "Gophers' History Dr. Williams, The great innovator," *Mpls Star*, (22 September 1972): 8.

31. Charles Johnson, ed.,"People's Column," *Mpls Star*, (24 October 1953): 13.

32. S. Hoffbeck, "Bobby Marshall: Pioneering African American Athlete," 161.

33. Dick Rainbolt, "Gophers' History Dr. Williams, The great innovator," *Mpls Star* (22 September 1972): 8.

34. S. Hoffbeck, "Bobby Marshall: Pioneering African American Athlete," 161.

35. Dick Gordon, "03 Star Recalls Tying Kick," *Mpls Star Tribune*, (4 June 1953).

36. Charles Johnson, ed., "People's Column," *Mpls Star*, (24 October 1953): 13.

37. Marvin Quinn, "35 Years of Football Not Enough, Marshall Thinks of Comeback," *Mpls Star Tribune*, (14 June 1936): 20.

38. "Michigan Minnesota The Little Brown Jug Series," *M Go Blue*, last modified June 17, 2009, https://mgoblue.com/news/2009/6/17/michigan_minnesota_ the_little_brown_jug_series.aspx.

39. "1903 World Series Game 1 Pirates at Americans," Baseball Reference, https:// www.baseball-reference.com/boxes/BOS/BOS190310010.shtml.

Chapter 3

1. O'Loughlin, "Carleton's Game Fight Did Not Check Gophers," *Mpls Journal*, (03 Oct. 1904): 45.

2. "Mpls," *The Appeal*, (Saint Paul, MN), 8 October 1904, 3.

3. "Marshall's Plight," *Mpls Journal*, 12 October 1904, 18.

4. "Gophers Play a Strong Defense," *Mpls Star Tribune*, (16 October 1904): 33.

5. Dr. L.J. Cooke, "Doc Cooke's Days at Minnesota," *Mpls Star Tribune*, (26 February 1936): 17.

6. Chandler Forman, "Northwestern a Push Over---But That Was Back in Days of the V-Rush," *Mpls Star Tribune*, (29 October 1932): 23.

7. Joe Cutting, "My Greatest Thrill in Football ...," *Mpls Star Tribune*, (1 December 1932): 18.

8. "Mpls," *The Appeal*, (Saint Paul, MN), 3 December 1904, 3.

9. Christopher R. Reed, "A century of civics and politics: the Afro Americans of Chicago," last modified July 1987. http://www.lib.niu.edu/1987/ii870732. html.

10. "Year By Year Records, 1904," *M Football*, last modified 2018, https:// gophersports.com/schedule.aspx?path=football.

11. S. Hoffbeck, "Bobby Marshall: Pioneering African American Athlete," 162.

12. "Harris, Sig," *Jews in Sports*, http://www.jewsinsports.org/profile. asp?sport=football&ID=9.

13. Frank E. Force, "Gophers Getting Ready for Football Practice," *Mpls Star Tribune*, (23 July 1905): 35.

14. Frank E. Force, "Gophers Training to Defeat Iowa," *Mpls Star Tribune*, 15 October 1905, 43.

15. Frank E. Force, "Lawrence," *Mpls Star Tribune*, (29 October 1905): 37.

16. "1905 Golden Gophers Schedule and Results," *Sports Reference LLC*, last modified 2018, https://www.sports-reference.com/cfb/schools/ minnesota/1905-schedule.html.

17. "The Men Who Wear the 'M,'" *Minnesota Daily*, 20 December 1905, 2.

18. "Central Vets Win Out," *Mpls Journal*, 28 Dec. 1905, 9.

19. Earl Current, "8 Points But No TD," *Mpls Star Tribune*, (30 September 1959): 67.

20. Halsey Hall, "Marshall Boots Victory," *Mpls Star Tribune*, (15 November 1939): 22.

21. *Mpls Journal*, 19 December 1920; O' Loughlin, "How the Minnesotan 'Showed Chicago,'" *Mpls Journal*, (11 November 1906): http://chroniclingamerica.loc. gov/lccn/sn83045366/1906-11-11/ed-1/seq-30/.

22. John R. Schuknecht, "My Greatest Thrill in Football...," *Mpls Star Tribune*, (2 December 1932): 18.

23. S. Hoffbeck, "Bobby Marshall: Pioneering African American Athlete," 162.

24. Charles Johnson, "People's Column," *Mpls Star Tribune*, (16 November 1963): 13.

25. S. Hoffbeck, "Bobby Marshall: Pioneering African American Athlete," 162.

26. Ibid; Charles Hallman, "Early Black Gopher earned place of honor," *Mpls Spokesman*, August 28, 2014, 10.

27. S. Hoffbeck, "Bobby Marshall: Pioneering African American Athlete," 162.

28. "Mpls," *The Appeal*, (St. Paul, MN), 17 November 1906, 3.

29. S. Hoffbeck, "Bobby Marshall: Pioneering African American Athlete," 162.

30. *University of Chicago Department of Athletics and Recreation*, 2019, https:// athletics.uchicago.edu/about/history/amos-alonzo-stagg.

31. Todd Peterson, *Early Black Baseball in Minnesota* , 216.

32. "Bobby Marshall, Whose Kick Won the Game for the Gophers," *Mpls Star Tribune*, 11 November 1906, 12. "Minnesota Defeats Chicago 4-2; Regains Championship of the West," *Mpls Star Tribune*, 11 November 1906, 1,

33. Halsey Hall, "Marshall Boots Victory," *Mpls Star Journal*, 15 November 1939, 22.

34. Chandler Forman, "Earl Current, Gopher Back 25 Years Ago, Recalls 4 to 2 Victory Over Chicago in 1906," *Mpls Star Tribune*, (20 October 1928): 30.

35. John Kryk, "Why American Football Added a 4th Down," *Toronto Sun*, (2 February 2012).

36. Bill Marshall, interviewed April 17, 2018.

37. "Great Ovation for Gopher Champions," *Mpls Star Tribune*, 13 November 1906, 3

38. Bette Sessions, "Fan's Corner," *Mpls Star Tribune*, (13 April 1971): 2e.

39. S. Hoffbeck, "Bobby Marshall: Pioneering African American Athlete," 163.

40. Ibid., 163-164; Murray T. Davenport, "Minnesota Fails to Score Against Carlisle Indians," *Mpls Star Tribune*, 18 November 1906, 37; Gordon Hanson, "Pierre Resident Recalls Playing Days with Carlisle's Jim Thorpe," *Argus-Leader* (Sioux Falls, South Dakota), 16 May 1965, 41.

41. "Football Year's Death Harvest," *Chicago Tribune*, (26 November 1905): 1.

42. "History of the Forward Pass," *The Biletnikoff Award*.

43. "The One and Only Bobby Marshall Enters Football's Hall of Fame," *Mpls Spokesman*, 28 October 1971.

44. S. Hoffbeck, "Bobby Marshall: Pioneering African American Athlete," 163

45. "Robert W. Marshall Athlete, Mpls," *The Appeal*, 25 October 1913, 10.

46. "The One and Only Bobby Marshall Enters Football's Hall of Fame," *Mpls Spokesman*, 28 October 1971.

47. Ibid.

48. S. Hoffbeck, "Bobby Marshall: Pioneering African American Athlete," 163.

49. Bill Marshall, interviewed April 17, 2018.

50. Peter Gorton, "Bobby Marshall Information For Terry McConnell," November 2019.

51. "St. Paul Team Wins," *Mpls Star Tribune*, (7 January 1907): 3 .

52. Oliver "Cougar" Sims, Lost Legends The Magnificent Bobby Marshall, 2019, courgarsims.com.

53. *Mpls Journal*, 23 January 1907, 10.

54. "University News," *Mpls Star Tribune*, 20 January 1907, 6,

55. Bill Marshall, interviewed April 17, 2018; S. Hoffbeck (ed), *Swinging for the Fences* 60.

56. Bill Marshall, interviewed October 6, 2018

57. S. Hoffbeck, "Bobby Marshall: Pioneering African American Athlete," 164.

Chapter 4

1. S. Hoffbeck, "Bobby Marshall: Pioneering African American Athlete," 164.

2. "Mpls," *The Appeal*, (St. Paul, MN), 17 August 1907, 3.

3. S. Hoffbeck (ed), *Swinging for the Fences*, 73; Terry Bohn, "From the Buffalo Soldiers to Satchel: Early Black Baseball in Minnesota," *North Dakota Baseball History*, https://ndbaseball.weebly.com/uploads/2/1/1/9/21192418/black_baseball_in_nd.pdf

4. S. Hoffbeck (ed), *Swinging for the Fences*, 61.

5. Todd Peterson, *Early Black Baseball in Minnesota*, 37-38.

6. S. Hoffbeck, "Bobby Marshall: Pioneering African American Athlete," 164

7. Ibid.

8. S. Hoffbeck, "Bobby Marshall: Pioneering African American Athlete," 168.

9. Robert W. Peterson, *Pigskin The Early Years of Pro Football*, 173.

10. Chris Lamb, "Catcher's Tears Were a Likely Inspiration for Rickey," *New York Times*, (14 April 2012): https://www.nytimes.com/2012/04/15/sports/baseball/branch-rickey-found-inspiration-in-catchers-tears.html.

11. S. Hoffbeck, "Bobby Marshall: Pioneering African American Athlete," 167.

12. "League Football," *Mpls Star Tribune*, (4 November 1907): 3; "Our Seals Defeated By the Deans," *New Prague Times*, 7 November 1907, 1, 4.

13. "Marshall's Team Fast," *Mpls Star Tribune*, (18 November 1907): 3, https://www.newspapers.com/image/179050365.

14. "Mpls," *The Appeal*, (St. Paul, Minn.), 23 November 1907, 3.

15. "North and Central Meet in Final Contest Next Friday," *Mpls Star Tribune*, (10 November 1907): 34;"North High Wins City Championship," *Mpls Star Tribune*, (16 November 1907): 18.

16. "Freshman and Sophomores Will Meet on the Gridiron," *Mpls Star Tribune*, (26 October 1907): 14.

17. "Mpls," *The Appeal*, (St. Paul, Minn.), 18 May 1907, 3.

18. Dylan Matthews, "Woodrow Wilson was extremely racist—even by the standards of his time," *Vox*, last modified November 20, 2015, https://www.vox.com/policy-and-politics/2015/11/20/9766896/woodrow-wilson-racist.

19. Bill Marshall interview, April 17, 2018.

20. "Lake Shores Beat St. Paul Boat Club," *Mpls Star Tribune*, 5 January 1908;

21. *Mpls Journal*, 7 January 1908, 10.

22. "Wanderers Defeat Lake Shore Team," *Mpls Star Tribune*, 2 February 1908, 30.

23. S. Hoffbeck, "Bobby Marshall: Pioneering African American Athlete," 168.

24. *Mpls Journal*, 26 December 1908, 3.

25. S. Hoffbeck, "Bobby Marshall: Pioneering African American Athlete," 168.

26. Bill Hengen, "Marshall Now Grid Immortal," *Mpls Star*, 22 March 1971, 24.

27. S. Hoffbeck, "Bobby Marshall: Pioneering African American Athlete," 165.

28. Ibid.

29. Ibid.

30. "Keystones Blank Coughlin's Men," *Mpls Star Tribune*, (27 April 1908): 5.

31. Todd Peterson, *Early Black Baseball in Minnesota*, 80.

32. Ibid. 90.

33. Ibid.

34. Ibid. 91.

35. S. Hoffbeck, "Bobby Marshall: Pioneering African American Athlete," 165.

36. Ibid.

37. Todd Peterson, *Early Black Baseball in Minnesota*, 100.

38. W.F. Allen, "Hard Scrimmage Is Lot of Gophers," *Mpls Star Tribune*, 8 October 1908, 12.

39. "Dean Team Defeats Ascensions 16-0," *Mpls Star Tribune*, (19 October 1908): 3.

40. "Deans and Adams Line Up at Minnehaha Park Today," *Mpls Star Tribune*, 25 October 1908, p. 43.

41. "Deans-Adams Game on for Next Week," *Mpls Star Tribune*, (26 October 1908): 5.

42. "Heston May Play Against Dean Team," *Mpls Star Tribune*, (30 October 1908): 10.

43. S. Hoffbeck, "Bobby Marshall: Pioneering African American Athlete," 167-168.

44. "Deans Again Rout St. Paul Quicksteps," *Mpls Star Tribune*, (16 November 1908): 3.

45. "Deans Too Speedy for Husky Adams," *Mpls Star Tribune*, (2 November 1908): 5.

46. "Deans and Adams Play at 'Haha Today," *Mpls Star Tribune*, (1 November 1908); 55.

47. W.F. Allen, "New Prague Plays the Deans at Minnehaha Eckersall Opposes

Capron on Thursday Football," *Mpls Star Tribune*, (22 November 1908): 50.

48. Frank E. Force, "Sporting Gossip of the Day," *Mpls Star Tribune*, (26 November 1908): 5.

49. Ibid.

50. W.F. Allen, "Eckersall Stars Arrive to Battle With Deans Today," *Mpls Star Tribune*, (26 November 1908): 5.

51. "Thanksgiving Day Celebrated Joyously in Mpls," *Mpls Star Tribune*, (27 November 1908): 2.

52 W.F. Allen, "Tie-Score in Dean and Eckersall Game," *Mpls Star Tribune*, (27 November 1908): 6, https://www.newspapers.com/image/180344388.

53. "Football Special Teams: Field Goals and PATs," dummies, https://www.dummies.com/sports/football/special-teams/football-special-teams-field-goals-and-pats/.

54. "Drop It Like Its Hot," *Pro Football Hall of Fame*, last modified December 6, 2015, https://www.profootballhof.com/the-last-dropkick/.

55. "Flutie converts first drop kick since 1941 championship," *ESPN.com news services*, last modified January 2, 2006, http://www.espn.com/nfl/news/story?id=2277308.

56. S. Hoffbeck, "Bobby Marshall: Pioneering African American Athlete," 164.

57. Bill Marshall, interviewed April 17, 2018.

58. Greg Leedham, "Jack Johnson: 100 years on... the story of the race-hate fight that split America," *Daily Mail*, (2 April 2015).

58. "Roller Skating Rink," *The Appeal*, (St. Paul Minn.), 10 October 1908, 3.

Chapter 5

1. Todd Peterson, *Early Black Baseball in Minnesota,* 100.

2. "Red Wings Booked to Play at Rochester Today Semi-Pro Teams Fighting It Out for Championship Baseball," *Mpls Star Tribune*, 18 July 1909, p.41.

3. Todd Peterson, *Early Black Baseball in Minnesota:* , 109.

4. Ibid. 110.

5. "Saint Paul Colored Gophers vs. Leland's Chicago Giants At Lexington Park July 24, 25, 26, 27, 28," *The Appeal*, (St. Paul Men.), 23 July 1910, 3.

6. "Red Wings Booked to Play at Rochester Today Semi-Pro Teams Fighting It Out for Championship Baseball, *Mpls Star Tribune*, 18 July 1909, p.41.

7. S. Hoffbeck, "Bobby Marshall: Pioneering African American Athlete," 166.

8. Todd Peterson, *Early Black Baseball in Minnesota:* 111, 133.

9. Ibid. 114; S. Hoffbeck, "Bobby Marshall: Pioneering African American Athlete," 166.

10. Ryan Whirty, "For one shining season in 1909, the eyes of baseball were on St. Paul's black baseball team," *Citypages*, 1 April 2015, http://www.citypages.com/news/for-one-shining- season-in-1909-the-eyes-of-baseball-were-on-st-pauls-black-baseball-team-6536145.

11. Todd Peterson, *Early Black Baseball in Minnesota*, 240.
12. Ibid. 100.
13. S. Hoffbeck, "Bobby Marshall: Pioneering African American Athlete," 165.
14. S. Hoffbeck (ed), *Swinging for the Fences* (St. Paul: Minnesota Historical Society Press, 2018), 69.
15. S. Hoffbeck, "Bobby Marshall: Pioneering African American Athlete," 165.
16. Ibid.
17. S. Hoffbeck (ed), *Swinging for the Fences*, 69, 70.
18. Bryon Bennett, "Chicago's West Side Grounds- Where the Cubs Last Won the World Series," *deadballbaseball.com*, last modified 2016. http://deadballbaseball.com/?p=2358.
19. Todd Peterson, *Early Black Baseball in Minnesota*, 119.
20. S. Hoffbeck, "Bobby Marshall: Pioneering African American Athlete," 166, 167.
21. "Black Sporting Experience at Dartmouth," last modified January 22, 2013, http://sites.dartmouth.edu/blacksportingexperience/matthew-bullock-04/.
22. *Winnebago City Press-News*, 25 September 1909, 1.
23. *Winnebago City Press-News*, 13 November 1909.
24. S. Hoffbeck, "Bobby Marshall: Pioneering African American Athlete," 164.
25. Ibid. 158.
26. "Jack Johnson's Brother a Distinguished Gen'man," *Mpls Star Tribune*, (24 November 1909): 10.
27. "Deans Easily Defeat New Prague's Eleven," *Mpls Star Tribune*, (29 November 1909):12.
28. S. Hoffbeck, "Bobby Marshall: Pioneering African American Athlete," 167.
29. Todd Peterson, *Early Black Baseball in Minnesota*, 120.
30. "Unforgivable Blackness" a film directed by Ken Burns, *WETA*, last modified January 11, 2005, https://www.pbs.org/unforgivableblackness/knockout/women.html.
31. S. Hoffbeck (ed), *Swinging for the Fences*, 71.
32. "Flag Day at Auburn Park," *Chicago Broad Ax*, (14 May 1910): 2, https://drive.google.com/file/d/0B1Wcncq5-bHdcnh1dUwxelpMUUE/view?pli=1.
33. S. Hoffbeck, "Bobby Marshall: Pioneering African American Athlete," 167.
34. Bill Marshall, interviewed April 17, 2018.
35. Todd Peterson, *Early Black Baseball in Minnesota*, 126.
36. Bill Marshall, interviewed April 17, 2018.
37. Todd Peterson, *Early Black Baseball in Minnesota*, 126.
38. Greg Leedham, "Jack Johnson: 100 years on…the story of the race-hate fight that split America," Daily Mail, (3 April 2015): http://www.dailymail.co.uk / sport/boxing/article-3023768/Jack-Johnson-100-years-story-race-hate-fight-split-America.html.
39. Todd Peterson, *Early Black Baseball in Minnesota:* , 126, 127, 130, 131.
40. Ibid. 132 -135.

Chapter 6

1. Todd Peterson, *Early Black Baseball in Minnesota,* 139, 143, 144.

2. S. Hoffbeck, "Bobby Marshall: Pioneering African American Athlete," 168; Todd Peterson, *Early Black Baseball in Minnesota,* 139.

3. S. Hoffbeck, "Bobby Marshall: Pioneering African American Athlete," 168.

4. Bill Marshall, interviewed April 17, 2018.

5. "Gopher Coach Tells Team About Things as They Really Should Be," *Mpls Star Tribune,* 11 October 1910, 10.

6. Todd Peterson, *Early Black Baseball in Minnesota,* 145.

7. *The Appeal,* (St. Paul, Minn.), 15 April 1911, 3.

8. *Evening Times,* (Grand Forks, ND) (11 April 1911): 1.

9. Todd Peterson, *Early Black Baseball in Minnesota:* , 31, 32, 131, 144; Frank M. White, *They Played for the Love of the Game.*

10. Todd Peterson, *Early Black Baseball in Minnesota,* 146.

11. Ibid. 147.

12. Ibid. 149.

13. Ibid. 149, 150.

14. Ibid. 153.

15. Ibid. 155.

16. Ibid. 160, 161.

17. Ibid. 161.

18. Ibid. 162-164.

19. Ibid. 170.

20. S. Hoffbeck, "Bobby Marshall: Pioneering African American Athlete," 168.

21. Todd Peterson, *Early Black Baseball in Minnesota:* 171,173.

22. S. Hoffbeck, "Bobby Marshall: Pioneering African American Athlete," 168.

23. Kathy Washington, interviewed, May 30, 2018; Bill Marshall interview April 17, 2018.

24. S. Hoffbeck, "Bobby Marshall: Pioneering African American Athlete," 168.

25. Ibid. 168, 169.

26. Bill Marshall, interviewed April 17, 2018.

Chapter 7

1. Todd Peterson, *Early Black Baseball in Minnesota:* , 171.

2. Bill Marshall, interviewed April 17, 2018.

3. "Robert W. Marshall Athlete, Mpls," *The Appeal,* 25 October 1913, 10.

4. Dr. Jerry Bergman, "A Brief History of the Eugenics Movement," last modified May 2000, http://users.adam.com.au/bstett/BEugenics72Bergman73Potter77.htm; "Introduction to Genetics," *Genetics Generation,* last modified 2015, http://knowgenetics.org/history-of-eugenicsinois&date2=1922&proxtext=%22Bobby+Marshall%22& y=14&x=8&dateFilterType=yearRange&page=1.

5. Ben Westhoff, "Eugenics & Me: How a Hitler fan paid my mother's college tuition and sent me down a rabbit hole," CITYPAGES, last modified May 10, 2017, http://www.citypages.com/news/eugenics-me-how-a-hitler-fan-paid-my-mothers-college-tuition-and-sent-me-down-a-rabbit-hole/421797153.

6. Todd Peterson, *Early Black Baseball in Minnesota*, 177-179.

7. "Athletics Down St. Joes in Heavy Hitting Game," *Mpls Star Tribune*, 29 July 1912, p. 9.

8. "Werden's and St. Joes Battle at the Nicollet Pasture Today," *Mpls Star Tribune*, 4 August 1912, p. 43.

9. "St. Joes Easy for Werdens," *Mpls Star Tribune*, 5 August 1912, p. 8.

10. "Knockout," *PBS.org*, last modified January 2005, http://www.pbs.org/unforgivableblackness/knockout/.

11. "Beavers Triumph Over Marines, 7-3," *Mpls Star Tribune*, 18 November 1912, 9. Stars Squelch Beavers in Wonderful Game," *Mpls Star Tribune*, 29 November 1912, 10.

12. Todd Peterson, *Early Black Baseball in Minnesota*, 178.

13. "Camerons Down West Siders," *Mpls Star Tribune*, 30 June 1913, 10.

14. Todd Peterson, *Early Black Baseball in Minnesota*, 178-179.

15. S. Hoffbeck (ed), *Swinging for the Fences*, 73.

16. S. Hoffbeck, "Bobby Marshall: Pioneering African American Athlete," 170.

17. Jim Quirk, "The Mpls Marines: Minnesota's Forgotten NFL Team," *The Coffin Corner*. Vol. 20, No. 1 (1998), last modified 1998, www.profootball/researchers.org/archives/.

18. "Bobby Marshall," *Mpls Star Tribune*, (22 November 1913), 24.

19. "Marines Win at Duluth," *Mpls Star Tribune*, 27 October 1913, p. 8.

20. "Mpls," *The Appeal*, (St. Paul, Minn.), 1 November 1913, 3.

21. Todd Peterson, *Early Black Baseball in Minnesota*, 214.

22. "All Stars Possess Too Much Class for Marines," *Mpls Star Tribune*, 28 November 1913, 14.

23. Todd Peterson, *Early Black Baseball in Minnesota*, 179, 181.

24. "Bob Marshall To Ride Cycle," *Virginia Enterprise*, (St. Louis County, Minn.) (1 July 1914): http://chroniclingamerica.loc.gov/lccn/sn90059180/1914- 07-03/ed-1/seq-3/.

25. Todd Peterson, *Early Black Baseball in Minnesota*, 179, 180.

26. "Indians Defeat All-Stars," *Mpls Star Tribune*, (5 October 5 1914): 12,

27. "Marines Play Horse with Laurels, 43-0," *Mpls Star Tribune*, 2 November 1914, 8.

28. "Marines Play Horse with Laurels, 43-0," *Mpls Star Tribune*, 2 November 1914, 8.

29. "Just a Missed Goal Try Gives All-Stars Victory," *Mpls Star Tribune*, 27 November, 1914, 13.

30. Bill Marshall, interviewed April 17, 2018.

31. Ben Welter, "Oct. 14, 1914 Dight Ave.'s Hitler Connection," *Mpls Star Tribune*,

(22 June 2015).

32. "Thomas Dixon Jr., segregationist and author," *African American Registry*, last modified 2018, https://aaregistry.org/story/thomas-dixon-jr-segregationist-and-author/.

33. Malcolm Gay, "A century ago, protests sparked a movement," *Boston Globe*, (30 January 2017): B1, B8.

34. DeNeen L. Brown, "The preacher who used Christianity to revive the Ku Klux Klan," *Washington Post*, 10 April 2018.

35. S. Hoffbeck (ed), *Swinging for the Fences*, 74.

36. Jim Quick, "The Mpls Marines: Minnesota's Forgotten NFL Team," *The Coffin Corner*. Vol. 20, No. 1, last modified 1998, www.profootball/researchers. org/archives/.

37. Todd Peterson, *Early Black Baseball in Minnesota*, 214, 215; "Marines Barely Win From Laurels, 3 To 0," *Mpls Star Tribune*, 1 November 1915, 10.

38. "All-Stars and Marines Confident of Winning," *Mpls Star Tribune*, 25 November 1915, 12.

39. Fred R. Coburn, "All Stars Defeat Marines by Lone Touchdown," *Mpls Star Tribune*, 26 November 1915.

40. "Last Football Contest at Grand Tonight," *Bemidji Daily Pioneer*, 13 December 1915.

41. Hennepin County, Minnesota, Minnesota Official Marriage System (MOMS), Hennepin County Vital Records, Hennepin County, MN, v. 197:290, marriage of Robert W. Marshall and Irene B. Knott, 1916; SAM microfilm 447 microfilm reel 50, MN Historical Society Hubbs Microfilm Room, St. Paul.

42. Kathy Washington, interviewed, May 30, 2018.

43. "Mpls," *The Appeal*, (St. Paul, Minn.), 11 November 1916, 4.

44. Kathy Washington, interviewed, May 30, 2018.

45. "Mpls," *The Appeal*, (St. Paul, Minn.), 4 November 1916, 4.

46. "Marines Are Given Battle by East Ends," *Mpls Star Tribune*, 30 October 1916, 8.

47. "Marines Defeat Laurels Despite Salon's Playing," *Mpls Star-Tribune*, 13 November 1916, 10.

48. "Paid Attendance at Final Contest of Season 3,000," *Quad-City Times*, 4 December 1916, 8; Jerry Mack, "Marine Machine Play Crushes D.A.C. Defense, At Start to Win, 19 to 7," *Quad-City Times*, 4 December 1916, 8.

49. Todd Peterson, *Early Black Baseball in Minnesota*, 215.

50. "McGovern Switches Lineup for Game with Marines on Thanksgiving Day," *Mpls Star Tribune*, 29 November 1916, 16; Fred R. Coburn, "Marines Enter List of Football Dope Upsetters By Holding All-Stars to Scoreless Tie," *Mpls Star Tribune*, 1 December 1916, 11.

51. "Marines Win from Davenport Eleven," *Mpls Star Tribune*, 4 December 1916, 11.

52. "Paid Attendance at Final Contest of Season 3,000," *The Daily Times*, Davenport, Iowa; 4 December 1916, 8.

Chapter 8

1. Chad Williams, "African Americans and World War I," *Hamilton College Shomberg Center for Research in Black Culture*, last modified 2011, http://exhibitions.nypl.org/africanaage/essay-world-war-i.html.
2. "The Great Migration," History A&E Networks, 2020, https://www.history.com/topics/black-history/great-migration.
3. David Vassar Taylor, *African Americans in Minnesota* (St. Paul, MN: Minnesota Historical Society Press, 2002), 30, 32.
4. Leslie V. Tischauser, *Landmarks of the American Mosaic Jim Crow Laws* (Santa Barbara CA: Greenwood, an imprint of ABC Clio LLC, 2012), xi, 1,2.
5. John M. Carroll, *Fritz Pollard Pioneer in Racial Advancement* (Urbana and Chicago: University of Illinois Press, 1992), 119.
6. Ibid.
7. Elizabeth Dorsey Hatle, *The Ku Klux Klan in Minnesota* (Charleston S.C.: The History Press 2013), 15.
8. S. Hoffbeck (ed), *Swinging for the Fences* 74.
9. Bill Marshall, interviewed April 17, 2018.
10. Ibid.
11. Todd Peterson, *Early Black Baseball in Minnesota*, 215.
12. S. Hoffbeck, "Bobby Marshall: Pioneering African American Athlete," 169,
13. Johnny Walker, "Athletics and Independents Meet in Final Game of Season Sunday For Tri-City Pro Championship," *The Daily Times* (Davenport Iowa) 1 December 1917, 12.
14. Johnny Walker, "Gambling Seems to Have Superceded Sport in Tri-City Football," *The Daily Times* (Davenport Iowa) (3 December 1917) 9.
15. Neal Rozendaal, *Duke Slater: Pioneering Black NFL Player and Judge* (Jefferson NC: McFarland, 2012), 35.
16. Jim Quick, "The Mpls Marines: Minnesota's Forgotten NFL Team," *The Cofffin Corner*. Vol. 20, No. 1, last modified 1998, www.profootball/researchers. org/ archives/.
17. Neal Rozendaal, *Duke Slater: Pioneering Black NFL Player and Judge* (Jefferson NC: McFarland, 2012), 36.
18. "All Public Gathering Places Close At 6 Tonight By Order of Local and State Officers," *Rock Island Argus*, 16 October 1918, 2; "Final Rulings of Quarantine Removed Today," *Rock Island Argus*, 13 November 1918, 7.

Chapter 9

1. S. Hoffbeck (ed), *Swinging for the Fences*, 74.
2. Elizabeth Dorsey Hatle, *The Ku Klux Klan in Minnesota* (Charleston S.C.: The History Press 2013), 31.

3. S. Hoffbeck, "Bobby Marshall: Pioneering African American Athlete," 169.

4. Neal Rozendaal, *Duke Slater: Pioneering Black NFL Player and Judge* (Jefferson NC: McFarland, 2012), 160.

5. "Airmen Bested By Locals 6-0 In Bitter Game," *Rock Island Argus*, 18 November 1918, 5.

6. S. Hoffbeck, "Bobby Marshall: Pioneering African American Athlete," 169.

7. "Gangs of Workmen Are Engaged at Douglas Park in Preparing Field for Hard Fall Campaign," *Rock Island Argus*, 6 September 1919, 12.

8. Ibid.

9. "Ursella, Ex-Marine Star, to Coach Independents," *Rock Island Argus*, 8 September 1919, 10; "Coach Ursella Will Size Up Candidates Tonight," *Rock Island Argus*, 9 September 1919, 12; "Crowd of 500 Grid Fans Look Independents Over in Initial Rehearsal Staged Last Night," *Rock Island Argus*, 10 September 1919, 12.

10. "Flanagan Makes Proposition to Play Inter-City Contests on Basis of Winner Take All," *Rock Island Argus*, 12 September 1919, 18.

11. "Rock Island Ready for Coming of Billy Sunday," *Rock Island Argus*, 13 September 1919, 5; Malcolm H. Eddy, "Sunday Opens Fire on Devil in Tri-Cities," *Rock Island Argus*, 15 September 1919, 1.

12. "To Scrimmage Independents Thursday Eve," *Rock Island Argus*, 15 September 1919, 12.

13. "Secret Practice Is Ordered for Independents," *Rock Island Argus*, 16 September 1919, 10.

14. "Bashaw, Star Lineman, and Mansfield Report," *Rock Island Argus*, 17 September 1919, 18.

15. "Bueland, Giant Tackle, Is Latest to Join Team," *Rock Island Argus*, 23 September 1919, 14.

16. "Great Halfback Coming," *Rock Island Argus*, 24 September 1919, 14.

17. "Chicken Arrives Tomorrow with Giant Guard," *Rock Island Argus*, 26 September 1919, 22.

18. "Green Jerseys Open Tomorrow with Boom," *Rock Island Argus*, 27 September 1919, 12.

19. "Independents Win Opening Game by Score 20-0," *Rock Island Argus*, 29 September 1919, 12.

20. "Frank Olson Some Punter Say Hamburgs," *Rock Island Argus*, 1 October 1919, 15.

21. "Independents Tear Up Hamburgs for 21-0 Count," *Rock Island Argus*, 6 October 1919, 14.

22. "Marines Open Season with 36-0 Victory," *Mpls Star Tribune*, 6 October 1919, 15. "Independents Tear Up Hamburgs for 21-0 Count," *Rock Island Argus*, 6 October 1919, 14.

23. "Hammond Is Booked to Play Here Next Sunday," *Rock Island Argus*, 7 October 1919, 12; "Hammond Supporters Will Back Team Heavily," *Rock Island Argus*, 8 October 1919, 12; "Hammond Will Bring 23 Players to This City," *Rock*

Island Argus, 9 October 1919, 14;

24. "Thousand to Head for Douglas Park Tomorrow," *Rock Island Argus*, 11 October 1919, 14.

25. "Independents Fall Before Hammonds, 12-7," *Rock Island Argus*, 13 October 1919, 14.

26. "Tom Henry of Louisiana U Joins Independents," *Rock Island Argus*, 18 September 1919, 12.

27. Bill Marshall, , interviewed , April 17, 2018.

28. "Squirrel Food," *Rock Island Argus*, 18 October 1919, 14.

29. J.L. Hughes, "Team Ready on Eve of Big Inter-City Contest," *Rock Island Argus*, 19 October 1919, 14.

30. "Independents Batter Davenport to Tune of 33-0," *Rock Island Argus*, 20 October 1919, 12.

31. "High to Meet Moline- Cincy Celts on Sunday," *Rock Island Argus*, 21 October 1919, 12.

32. "Hard Battle Is Predicted- Celts Have 18 Players," *Rock Island Argus*, 22 October 1919, 12; "Celts Come as Second Big Grid Attraction," *Rock Island Argus*, 25 October 1919, 14; "Independents Smother Celts by Score 33 to 0," *Rock Island Argus*, 27 October 1919, 14.

33. "Unlimited Fund Behind Pine Village Gridders," *Rock Island Argus*, 28 October 1919, 15; "Pine Village Is Daffy About Football Team," *Rock Island Argus*, 29 October 1919, 14; Hege Clark, "Tells Why Pine Village Can Boast About Team," *Rock Island Argus*, 30 October 1919, 18; "Pine Village Holds Islanders to Scoreless Tie," *Rock Island Argus*, 3 November 1919, 15.

34. "Islanders Wallow in Mud to Crush Moline 57-0," *Rock Island Argus*, 10 November 1919, 12.

35. "Islanders in Easy Contest With Hammond," *Rock Island Argus*, 17 November, 1919, 12.

36. "Independents to Meet Columbus Panhandles," *Rock Island Argus*, 17 November, 1919, 12; "Victory Sunday Brings 'Em All to Rock Island," *Rock Island Argus*, 19 November 1919, 18; "Cleveland Writer Terms Then 'Manhandlers,'" *Rock Island Argus*, 21 November 1919, 28; "All Set for… (the rest of the title unavailable,)" *Rock Island Argus*, 22 November 1919, 13; "Panhandles Are Very Much Manhandled, 40-0," *Rock Island Argus*, 24 November 1919, 12.

37. "Independents Beat Davenport by 26 to 0 Score," *Rock Island Argus*, 28 November 1919, 26.

38. "Akron confident of Copping from Independents," *Rock Island Argus*, 29 November 1919, 13; "Canton Bulldogs Coming to Play Rock Island," *Rock Island Argus*, 1 December 1919, 12.

39. *Rock Island Argus*, 1 December 1919, 12; "First Day of Drive Nets $5,000 for Game," *Rock Island Argus*, 2 December 1919, 12; "This Is Thorpe," *Rock Island Argus*, 2 December 1919, 12; "Will Thorpe Give Up Title Without Struggle?," *Rock Island Argus*, 3 December 1919, 16; "Canton Develops Cold Feet; No

Chance for Game," *Rock Island Argus*, 5 December 1919, 24.

40. Todd Peterson, *Early Black Baseball in Minnesota:* , 215.

41. Simon Herrera, "Rock Islands Independents," last updated December 5, 2016, http://www.rockislandindependents.com.

42. "Great Football Next Year: Augie Secures Tourney," *Rock Island Argus*, 13 December 1919, 12.

Chapter 10

1. "Football Admission to be $1.65; Ursella Here," *Rock Island Argus*, 14 Sept 1920, 15.

2. Christopher Klein, "The Birth of the National Football League," A&E Television Networks, last modified September 4, 2017, https://www.history.com/news/the-birth-of-the-national-football-league.

3. Bruce Copeland, "Pro Grid Board Formed; Flanigan Gets Office," *Rock Island Argus*, 18 September 1920, 10.

4. John M. Carroll, *Fritz Pollard Pioneer in Racial Advancement* (Urbana and Chicago: University of Illinois Press, 1992), 137.

5. "1920 Akron Pros Schedule and Game Results," *Pro Football Reference*, last modified 2017, http://www.pro-footballreference.com/teams/akr/1920 _games. htm; "1920 Rock Island Independents Schedule and Game Results," *Pro Football Reference*, last modified 2017, http://www.pro-football-reference.com/ teams/rii/1920_games.htm.

6. John M. Carroll, *Fritz Pollard Pioneer in Racial Advancement* (Urbana and Chicago: University of Illinois Press, 1992), 147, 178, 179.

7. Christopher Klein, "The Birth of the National Football League," *A&E Television Networks*, last modified September 4, 2017, https://www.history.com/news/the-birth-of-the-national-football-league.

8. "1920 Rock Island Independents Starters, Roster & Players," *Pro Football Reference*, last modified 2018, https://www.pro-football-reference.com /teams/ rii/1920_roster.htm.

9. Robert W. Peterson, *Pigskin The Early Years of Pro Football*, (New York and Oxford: Oxford University Press, 1997, 74.

10. Bruce Copeland, "Speed and Brawn Win for Islanders; score, 48-0," *Rock Island Argus*, 27 September 1920, 12.

11. Bruce Copeland, "Championship Punch Crushes Muncie Flyers, 45-0" *Rock Island Argus*, 4 October 1920, 11.

12. "1920 Muncie Flyers Statistics and Players," Pro Football Reference, https://www.pro-football-reference.com/teams/mun/1920.htm.

13. Bruce Copeland, "Independents Hold Secret Sessions," *Rock Island Argus*, 15 October 1920, 26.

14. "Hopes of Independents At Stake," *Rock Island Argus*, 16 October 1920, 11.

15. Bruce Copeland, "The Sportscope," *Rock Island Argus*, 14 October 1920, 15.

16. Robert W. Peterson, *Pigskin The Early Years of Pro Football* (New York: Oxford

University Press, 1997), 53.

17. *Football at Minnesota*, (Mpls: General Alumni Association of the University of Minnesota, 1914), 21.

18. Bruce Copeland, "Staleys Tame Independents Punch," *Rock Island Argus*, 18 October 1920, 12.

19. Bruce Copeland, "The Sportscope," *Rock Island Argus*, 19 October 1920, 20.

20. Bruce Copeland, "Racine Cards Next Foes at Douglas Park," *Rock Island Argus*, 19 October 1920, 20.

21. Bruce Copeland, "Independents Scored for Lax Play," *Rock Island Argus*, 20 October 1920, 15.

22. Bruce Copeland "Independents Regain Lost Punch," *Rock Island Argus*, 25 October 1920, 14.

23. Bruce Copeland, "The Sportscope," Rock Island Argus, 26 October 1920, 15.

24. Oliver "Cougar" Sims, Lost Legends The Magnificent Bobby Marshall, interview with Kwame McDonald, 2019, courgarsims.com.

25. Bruce Copeland, "Super-Independents Crush Tigers," *Rock Island Argus*, 1 November 1920, 12.

26. Bruce Copeland, "Big Grid Game Bestirs Tri-Cities," *Rock Island Argus*, 6 November 1920, 13; Bruce Copeland, "Staleys Accept Rock Island's Bid," *Rock Island Argus,* 2 November 1920, 11.

27. Bruce Copeland, "Cripples Hold Staley to 0-0 Tie," *Rock Island Argus,* 8 November 1920, 12, 14; Bruce Copeland, "Five or Six Independents Not Likely to Play Chicagoans At Monmouth on Armistice Day," *Rock Island Argus,* 9 November 1920, 13.

28. S. Hoffbeck, "Bobby Marshall: Pioneering African American Athlete," 169.

29. Bruce Copeland, "Ursella Breaks Islanders' Jinx," *Rock Island Argus,* 12 November 1920, 25; Bruce Copeland, "How the Independents Were Almost Defeated by Plucky Thorn Team," *Rock Island Argus*, 12 November 1920, 25.

30. Bruce Copeland, "Flashy Passes Baffle Islanders," *Rock Island Argus,* 15 November 1920, 13.

31. Bruce Copeland, "Independents Crush 'Collegians,'" *Rock Island Argus,* 29 November 1920, 11; Simon Herrera, Independents Use All Star Team to Get Back on Track," last modified December 5, 2016, http://www. rockislandindependents.com.

32. "1920 Rock Island Independents Game Log," *Pro Football Reference*, last modified 2018, https://www.pro-football-reference.com/teams/rii/1920/gamelog/.

33. John M. Carroll, *Fritz Pollard Pioneer in Racial Advancement* (Urbana and Chicago: University of Illinois Press, 1992), 143.

34. Bruce Copeland, "All Star Professional Team," *Rock Island Argus,* 2 December 1920, 17.

35. Rossi Anastopoulo, "Meet Fritz Pollard," last modified November 25, 2012, http://www.sportsinblackandwhite.com/2012/11/25/meet-fritz-pollard/.

36. John M. Carroll, *Fritz Pollard Pioneer in Racial Advancement* (Urbana and

Chicago: University of Illinois Press, 1992), 137, 138, 159.

36. Peter Gorton, historian, interviewed November 20, 2019.

Chapter 11

1. Charles Johnson, "Stars' Great Defense Holds Marines Even," *Mpls Star*, 26 November 1920, 10; "All- Stars May Play Turkey Day Game at Hippodrome," *Mpls Star*, 22 November 1920, 10.

2. Charles Johnson, "Stars' Great Defense Holds Marines Even," *Mpls Star*, 26 November 1920, 10.

3. "Bob Marshall Is Perennial Star of The Gridiron; Plays at Age of 42," *Mpls Journal*, 19 December 1920, 3 Sport Section.

4. S. Hoffbeck, "Bobby Marshall: Pioneering African American Athlete," 170.

5. "Segregated Student Housing and the Activists Who Defeated It," *A Campus Divided Essays*, *University of Minnesota*, last modified 2017, http:// acampusdivided.umn.edu/index.php/essay/segregated-student-housing/.

6. Bill Marshall, interviewed August 2, 2018.

7. Elizabeth Dorsey Hatle, *The Ku Klux Klan in Minnesota* (Charleston S.C.: The History Press 2013), 31-33.

8. John M. Carroll, *Fritz Pollard Pioneer in Racial Advancement* (Urbana and Chicago: University of Illinois Press, 1992), 30.

9. "Tulsa Race Massacre," A&E Televison Networks, LLC, 2019, https://www. history.com/topics/roaring-twenties/tulsa-race-massacre.

10.. Charles Johnson, "'Big Ten' Will Decide Fate of Festus Tierney," *Mpls Star*, 27 September 1921, 8; "At Football Camps," *Chicago Tribune*, 27 September 1921, 14.

11. S. Hoffbeck, "Bobby Marshall: Pioneering African American Athlete," 169.

12. Todd Peterson, *Early Black Baseball in Minnesota*, 100.

13. "Liberties Trounced by Duluthians, 35-0," *Mpls Star Tribune*, 17 October 1921, 10.

14. "Kaysee Team Downs Liberties 7-6; Plays Duluth Next Sunday," *Mpls Star Tribune*, 24 October 1921, 6.

15. Stew Thornley, "Nicollet Park," last modified 2017, http://stewthornley.net/ nicollet_park.html.

16. "St. Louis Park Team Bows to Liberty Punch," *Mpls Star Tribune*, 31 October 1921, 7.

17. "Two All-American Players Sign for All-Star Game," *Mpls Star*, 31 October 1921, 8.

18. "Ironwood Squad Drills Hard This Week to Prepare for Hibbing Squad," *Ironwood Daily Globe*, 2 October 1923, 8.

19. "20 Years Ago Nov. 12, 1921," *Ironwood Times*, 12 November 1941, 6.

20. George A. Rhame, "Squad of 70 Works at Northrup Field," *Mpls Star Tribune*, 7 November 1921, 12.

21. "Marines Bump Old Rivals, 7-0, in Hard Game at Nicollet Park," *Mpls Star Tribune*, 25 November 1921, 15.

22. S. Hoffbeck (ed), *Swinging for the Fences*, 76; S. Hoffbeck, "Bobby Marshall: Pioneering African American Athlete," 170.

23. Todd Peterson, *Early Black Baseball in Minnesota*, 186.

24. S. Hoffbeck (ed), *Swinging for the Fences*, 74, 75.

25. "Former Aggie Star with Escanaba Grid," *Ironwood Daily Globe*, 9 November 1922, 6.

26. "20 Years Ago," *Ironwood Daily Globe*," 25 September 1942, 4.

27. S. Hoffbeck, "Bobby Marshall: Pioneering African American Athlete," 170.

28. Todd Peterson, *Early Black Baseball in Minnesota*, 185.

29. Charles Johnson, "Marines To Go Through With All-Star Game," *Mpls Star Tribune*, 28 November 1922, 10.

30. "Packers Win Opening Game From Hibbing," *Green Bay Press Gazette*, 24 September 1923.

31. "Blocked Punt, Lucky Catch and Breaks of Game Spell Defeat for Hibbing Eleven," *Hibbing Daily News*, 25 September 1923, 4.

32. "Shifts in All-Stars Lineup Are Announced- Buland To Remain Out of Early Game," *Hibbing Daily News*, 30 September 1923, 4.

33. "All-Stars Will Have Whole Team Together Tomorrow for Last Time Before Sunday," *Hibbing Daily News*, 14 September 1923, 4.

34. "Curly Lambeau Athlete, Coach, Football Player (1898-1965,)" *Biography*, last modified 2018, https://www.biography.com/people/curly-lambeau-21224337.

35. "Top 10 Oldest NFL Stadiums Still in Use," *TheRichest*, last modified 2018, https://www.therichest.com/sports/football-sports/top-10-oldest-nfl-stadiums-still-in-use/.

Chapter 12

1. "Charles Fremont Dight: An Inventory of His Papers at the Minnesota Historical Society," *Minnesota Historical Society*, Manuscripts Collection, last modified 2015, http://www2.mnhs.org/library/findaids/P1628.xml.

2. Gary Phelps, "The Eugenics Crusade of Charles Fremont Dight," *Minnesota History* (Fall 1984): 99-108, http://collections.mnhs.org/MNHistoryMagazine/articles/49/v49i03p099-108.pdf.

3. Ben Westhoff, "Eugenics & Me: How a Hitler fan paid my mother's college tuition and sent me down a rabbit hole," *City pages*, last modified May 10, 2017.

4. John Rosengren, "A Football Martyr," *SB Nation*, last modified Nov 25, 2014; Kay Johnson, "When the Klan Came to Minnesota," *Hutchinson Leader*, 24 October 2013, 1.

5. Elizabeth Dorsey Hale, *The Ku Klux Klan in Minnesota*, 83-86.

6. John Rosengren, "A Football Martyr," *SB Nation*, last modified Nov 25, 2014.

7. Elizabeth Dorsey Hale, *The Ku Klux Klan in Minnesota*, 54, 57.
8. John Rosengren, "A Football Martyr," *SB Nation*, last modified Nov 25, 2014.
9. Dick Gordon, "Gophers to "help" name stadium?" *Mpls Star*, 31 May 1974, 28.
10. John Rosengarten, "A Football Martyr," *SB Nation*, last modified Nov 25, 2014.
11. "Hibbing Outplays Gogebic Rangers and Win Game By 10 To 0 Count-'Tough' Gang," *Hibbing Daily News*, 9 October 1923, 4.
12. Neal Rozendaal, *Duke Slater: Pioneering Black NFL Player and Judge* (Jefferson NC: McFarland, 2012), 85.
13. Art Williams, "Ariel Route Wins For Independents, 27-7," *Rock Island Argus*, 22 October 1923, 16; Art Williams, "A Line on Sports," *Rock Island Argus*, 22 October 1923, 16; "The Game, Play By Play," *Rock Island Argus*, 22 October 1923, 16; https://www.newspapers.com/image/482135594/.
14. "Junior All-Stars Play Iveys on Nicollet Bill," *Mpls Star Tribune*, 28 Nov. 1923, 19.
15. "Marines-All Stars Meet in Annual Battle Tomorrow," *Mpls Star Tribune*, 28 November 1923, 8.
16. "Marines Victorious Over All-Stars, 7-0," *Mpls Star Tribune*, 30 Nov. 1923.
17. "If Bobby Marshall Took a Notion to Be King," *Mpls Journal*, 13 January 1924, magazine section.
18. Todd Peterson, *Early Black Baseball in Minnesota*, 187.
19. "Ironwood to Play at Duluth Today," *Mpls Star Tribune*, 21 September 1924, 7.
20. "Old Grads Swarm in for Football Classic, University Homecoming," *Mpls Star*, 31 October1924, 1.
21. "'Bobby' Marshall Sued for Divorce," *Mpls Star*, 5 August 1924, 9.
22. Bill Marshall, interviewed April 20, 2018.
23. Todd Peterson, *Early Black Baseball in Minnesota*, 188.
24. Peter Gorton and Sam Sinke, "John Wesley Donaldson," Last Modified 14 January 2020, http://johndonaldson.bravehost.com/eh.html.
25. Chuck Frederick, "Duluth Eskimos To Washington Redskins," *Duluth News Tribune*, 2 December 2006.
26. S. Hoffbeck, "Bobby Marshall: Pioneering African American Athlete," 169.
27. Cubby Campbell, "Rock Island Trounces Duluth With Brilliant Air Attack," *Duluth News Tribune*, 12 October 1925, 8; Neal Rozendaal, *Duke Slater: Pioneering Black NFL Player and Judge*, 96.
28. S. Hoffbeck, "Bobby Marshall: Pioneering African American Athlete," 169.
29. "Liberties and All Stars Play to 6-6 Tie," *Mpls Star Tribune*, 30 November 1925, 9; "Liberties and All Stars Play at Nicollet Sunday," *Mpls Star*, 28 November 1925, 14.
30. Ben Westhoff, "Eugenics & Me: How a Hitler fan paid my mother's college tuition and sent me down a rabbit hole," *City pages*, last modified May 10, 2017; Gary Phelps, "The Eugenics Crusade of Charles Fremont Dight," *Minnesota History* (Fall 1984): 99-108.
31. George A. Barton, "Watching the Sports Show Through the Referee's Eyes," *Mpls Star Tribune*, 13 December 1925, 30.

32. Todd Peterson, *Early Black Baseball in Minnesota:* (Jefferson NC: McFarland, 2010, 190.

33. "Former Liberty Grid Team Practices Tonight," *Mpls Star*, (2 September 1926): 11, https://www.newspapers.com/image/186805225/?terms=%22Bobby%2B Marshall%22.

34. "Bob Marshall to Play with All Star Team," *Mpls Star Tribune*, (25 September 1926): 27, https://www.newspapers.com/image/182059205/?terms=%22Bobb y%2BMarshall%22.

35. "Pro Gridders Will Clash at Lexington Park," *Mpls Star*, (25 September 1926): 16, https://www.newspapers.com/image/186806659/?terms=Olsen%2B%22B obby%2BMarshall%22.

36. Frank E. Murray, "Nevers and Eskimos Defeat Twin Cities All Stars, 7-0," *Mpls Star Tribune*, 27 September 1926, 10.

37. John Woods, "Hard-Working Nevers Did It All in One Day in 1929," *New York Times Blog*, last modified November 28, 2010; Chuck Frederick, "Duluth Eskimos To Washington Redskins," *Duluth News Tribune*, 2 December 2006.

38. "All Stars Down Eau Claire, 7-0," *Mpls Star Tribune*," 25 October 1926, 9.

39. "History," *Phyllis Wheatley Community Center*, last modified 2016; S. Hoffbeck, "Bobby Marshall: Pioneering African American Athlete," 171.

40. "All Stars to Meet Duluth Team Sunday," *Mpls Star Tribune*, 26 October 1926.

41. "Red Grange's Yankees Defeat Marines, 7-0," *Mpls Star Tribune*, 26 September 1927, 7.

42. S. Hoffbeck, "Bobby Marshall: Pioneering African American Athlete," 169.

43. John M. Carroll, *Fritz Pollard Pioneer in Racial Advancement*, 178, 179.

44. Neal Rozendaal, *Duke Slater: Pioneering Black NFL Player and Judge*, 110.

45. Frank Murray, "Grid Scouts Worry as Supposedly Weak Gophers Humble Team of Famous Stars," *Mpls Star Tribune*, 6 May 1928, 1.

46. "Score Upset in Park Grid Play," *Mpls Star*, 22 October 1929, 14.

47. "Segregated Student Housing and the Activists Who Defeated It," *A Campus Divided Essays, University of Minnesota*, last modified 2017, http://acampusdivided.umn.edu/index.php/essay/segregated-student-housing/.

48. David Vassar Taylor, *African Americans in Minnesota*, 34, 35; "History," *Phyllis Wheatley Community Center*, last modified 2016, http://phylliswheatley.org/history/.

Chapter 13

1. Bill Hengen, "Marshall Now Grid Immortal," *Mpls Star*, 22 March 22 1971, 24.

2. Charles Johnson, "The Lowdown on Sports," *Mpls Star*, 3 June 1931, 15.

3. "Fritz Crisler," *Sports Reference*, last modified 2018, https://www.sports-reference.com/cfb/coaches/fritz-crisler-1.html.

4. "Minnehahas Seek To Stop Phantoms," *Mpls Star Tribune*, 11 October 1931, 24.

5. "Bobby Marshall Will Play in Alumni Grid Tilt," *Mpls Star*, 5 Nov 1931, 18.

6. Irvin Rudick, "South, Central Grads Tie, 7-7," *Mpls Star Tribune*, 12 November

1931, 21.

7. Todd Peterson, *Early Black Baseball in Minnesota*, 194; S. Hoffbeck, "Bobby Marshall: Pioneering African American Athlete," 170.

8. Fred Hutchinson, "St. Paul Boys O.K.'d; Irish Are Favorites," *Mpls Star*, 3 September 1932, 8; "Scotch Ten Noses Out Slavs, 2-1, in Feature All-Nations Opener," *Mpls Tribune*, 7 September 1932, 14; "Irish Beat Scotch for Nations Title," *Mpls Tribune*, 14 September 1932, 16.

9. "Jack Manders Leads All Stars to 12-6 Win," *Mpls Star Tribune*, 5 December 1932, 12.

10. "Alumni Battle Valiantly, But Lose To Gophers," *Mpls Star Tribune*, 1 June 1933, 18.

11. "Minnesota All-Stars Smother Giants, 38-0," *Mpls Star Tribune*, 6 October 1933, 28.

12. "All-Stars Romp Over Eveleth-Virginia, 40-0," *Mpls Star Tribune*, 13 October 1933, 25.

13. "Football Greats Show Stuff in All-Star Game," *Mpls Star Tribune*, 12 November 1933, 3; "Gopher All Stars Beat Tommies, 6-0," *Mpls Star Tribune*, 12 November 1933, 13; "Hovde Joins All-Stars for Tommie Tilt," *Mpls Star Tribune*, 5 November 1933, 23.

14. "Biggie Munn, *Sports Reference*, last modified 2018, https://www.sports-reference.com/cfb/coaches/biggie-munn-1.html.

15. "Who Was 'Pudge?,'" *Pro Football Hall of Fame*, last modified November 12, 2012, https://www.profootballhof.com/news/who-was-pudge/.

16. Robert W. Peterson, *Pigskin The Early Years of Pro Football*, 171, 172.

17. Greg Howard, "A Ban on Black Players Cost the NFL Its Most Exciting Quarterback," *Deadspin*, last modified February 19, 2014.

18. Frank Foster, *Breaking the Color Barrier The Story of the First African-American NFL Head Coach, Frederick "Fritz" Pollard* (BookCaps Study Guides, 2014), 64, 65.

19. Todd Peterson, *Early Black Baseball in Minnesota: The St. Paul Gophers, Mpls Keystones and other Barnstorming Teams of the Deadball Era*, 214.

20. "Jimmy Page Gets Blanket for Services," *Mpls Star*, 6 June 1934, 17.

21. Charles Johnson, "The Lowdown on Sports, *Mpls Star*, 9 June 1934, 2.

22. Sonny, "Gogebic Panthers Tamed by Minnesota All Stars," *Ironwood Daily Globe*, 29 October 1934, 8,9; Sonny, "College Stars Coming Sunday," *Ironwood Daily Globe*, 23 October 1934, 7; Sonny, "Its – All – In – The - Slant," *Ironwood Daily Globe*, 27 October 1934, 5.

23. "Old Guards of Diamond..," *Mpls Star Tribune*, 24 January 1935, 13; Charles Johnson, "The Lowdown on Sports," *Mpls Star*, 26 January 1935, 17; "Past Lives Again as Old Guards of Diamond Meet," *Mpls Star Tribune*, 24 January 1935, 13.

24. Martin Quinn, "35 Football Years Not Enough, Marshall Thinks of Comeback," *Mpls Tribune*, 14 June 1936, 20.

25. S. Hoffbeck, "Bobby Marshall: Pioneering African American Athlete," 170.

26. Ibid. 171.

27. Bill Marshall, interviewed April 17, 2018.

28. Bob Beebe, "Morning, Sir," *Mpls Star Tribune*, 5 June 1936, 23.

29. David Vassar Taylor, *African Americans in Minnesota*, 32, 39, 40, 45, 46.

Chapter 14

1. "Legion Post Honors Prep Captains," *Mpls Star Tribune*, 5 October 1937, 15.

2. Bob Beebe, "'Morning, Sir," *Mpls Star Tribune*, 8 October 1936, 22, https://www.newspapers.com/image/182953465.

3. Daryl Bell, "The NHL's first black player, Willie O'Ree, had a short but pathbreaking stint with the Boston Bruins," *ESPN*, last modified February 14, 2017, https://theundefeated.com/features/nhl-first-black-player-willie-oree/.

4. Irvin Rudick, "Golden Glove Favorites Win," *Mpls Star Tribune*, (15 February 1939): 14, https://www.newspapers.com/image/180329249/?terms=%22Bobby%2BMarshall%22.

5. Irvin Rudick, "32 Survive in Terrific Glove Battling," *Mpls Star Tribune*, 16 February 1939, 15.

6. Frank Diamond, "N.W. Golden Glovers Outshine Twin Cities Entrants," *Mpls Star Tribune*, 13 February 1940, 13.

7. S. Hoffbeck, "Bobby Marshall: Pioneering African American Athlete," 170.

8. "Bob Marshall Defeats Rasley in Eagles Mix," *Mpls Star*, 7 November 1940, 25.

9. "Son of Famed Grid Player is Hurt in Crash," *Mpls Star*, 10 August 1939, 9.

10. "7 Kayoes Top City Ring Tourney," *Mpls Star Tribune*, 16 January 1941, 15.

11. Joe Hendrickson, "Bobby Marshall Gets Top Sports Thrill At 61," *Mpls Star*, 28 January 1941, 26.

12. "Bobby Marshall Swings with Wings," *Mpls Star*, 27 June 1941, 31; "Five Miscencik Brothers in Service," *Mpls Star Tribune*, 25 November 1943, 20; "Boxer's Mitts Get New Touch," *Mpls Star*, 13 April 1951, 40.

13. George A. Barton, "Zuke, Marshall, Wotzka Post Kayoes," *Mpls Star Tribune*, 25 February 1942, 13; Joe Hendrickson, "N.W. Glovers Become '42 Chicago Sensation," *Mpls Star*, 25 February 1942, 23.

14. George A. Barton, "Graves Gains Semis; 15 Win in 22 Bouts," *Mpls Star Tribune*, 26 February 1942, 13.

15. Bill Marshall, interviewed April 17, 2018.

16. "Marshall Ready for Long Hike to Ring Fame," *Mpls Star Tribune*, 27 January 1944, 11.

17. George A. Barton, "5,000 Hail Graves for Quick Knockout Of Law in Pro Bow," *Mpls Star Tribune*, 2 February 1944, 10.

18. "Golden Glove Vet Returns; May Turn Pro," *Mpls Star Tribune*, 14 August 1945, 15.

19. Frank Diamond, "Graves at Best in Torres Victory," *Mpls Star*, 15 June 1946, 6;

"Art Lambert, Marshall in Friday Bout," *Mpls Star*, 7 June 1946, 27.

20. Bill Marshall, interviewed April 17, 2018.
21. "Novice Crop biggest, Best," *Mpls Star*, 6 December 1946, 31.
22. Bill Marshall, interviewed April 17, 2018.
23. George A. Barton, "8 Champs Named in Night of Surprises," *Mpls Star Tribune*, 18 February 1947, 17, 19.
24. "National Golden Gloves: Rules, scoring, more," MLive.com, Last modified 4 April 2019, https://www.mlive.com/boxing/2008/05/national_golden_gloves_rules_s.html.
25. George A. Barton, "Donnelly Loses; Schaub Cops Pair," *Mpls Star Tribune*, 26 February 1947, 11; George A. Barton, "'Think I can Win Next Year,' Undismayed Vince Donnelly Says," *Mpls Star Tribune*, 27 February 1947, 17.
26. Charles Johnson, "Acevedo Outdoes Pep with Kayo," *Mpls Star*, 19 April 1947, 7.
27. Walter Bixby, "Brown, Flanagan Win by TK0's for Local Ring Sweep," *Mpls Star Tribune*, 18 October 1947, 12.
28. Frank Diamond, "Graves Fouls Way to Sierra Match," *Mpls Star*, 1 November 1947, 7.
29. Bill Marshall, interviewed April 17, 2018.
30. "Boxer's Mitts Get New Touch," *Mpls Star*, 13 April 1951, 40.
31. Ibid.
32. Bill Marshall, interviewed April 17, 2018.
33. Ibid.

Chapter 15

1. "'06 Grid Star Wins Divorce," *Mpls Star*, 28 June1939, 19.
2. George A. Barton, "Sport-O-Graphs," *Mpls Star Tribune*, 27 Feb 1942, 13, 14.
3. George A. Barton, "Sport-O-Graphs," *Mpls Star Tribune*, 5 August 1942, 13.
4. S. Hoffbeck (ed), *Swinging for the Fences* , 77, 78.
5. Todd Peterson, *Early Black Baseball in Minnesota*, 220.
6. S. Hoffbeck (ed), *Swinging for the Fences*, 77, 78.
7. Donald Wagner, "Great Negro End in 1906 at Last Forced to Head for the Sidelines," *The Brooklyn Citizen*, 19 February 1941, 7
8. Halsey Hall, "Vets Agree: Grissom's '47 Opener 'Best,'" *Mpls Star Tribune*, 30 April 1954, 21.
9. Charles Johnson, "The Lowdown on Sports," *Mpls Star*, 29 January 1947, 26
10 George A. Barton, "350 Honor Ex-Gopher Grid Greats," *Mpls Star Tribune*, 6 May 1947, 15.
11. Dick Gordon, "Gopher Grid Greats Oppose Paying College Football Players," *Mpls Star*, 30 December 1949, 13.
12. Michael Tarm, "Northwestern football team can unionize," *Mpls Star Tribune*, 27 March 2014, A1.
13. Dick Collum, "Cullum's Column," *Mpls Star Tribune*, 30 March 1950, 18.

14. S. Hoffbeck, "Bobby Marshall: Pioneering African American Athlete," 171.

15. Joe Hendrickson, "Bobby's Day of Memory," *Mpls Star Tribune*, 31 March 1950,19.

16.   Bill Marshall, interviewed May 9, 2018.

17. Dick Cullum, "Cullum's Column Typical Gopher Line Is Enough," *Mpls Star Tribune*, 3 April 1950, 23.

18. Bill Marshall, interviewed April 17, 2018.

19. Bill Marshall, interviewed October 3, 2018.

20. Bill Marshall, interviewed April 17, 2018 and November 16, 2018.

21. "McGovern Claims He Was Overrated," *Mpls Star*, 8 November 1952, 11; James Lileks, "Ghost of a grand hotel," *Mpls Star Tribune*, 29 November 2014.

22. "Famous Bronze Pig Gets Place in Trophy Case," *Mpls Star*, 4 June 1936, 26.

23. Halsey Hall, "Minnesota's Sig Harris, Sort of Little Brown Jug Himself," *Mpls Star*, 17 September 1941, 30.

24. "Gophers Ready To Try To Stop Michigan Wave," *Austin Daily Herald*, 23 October 1953.

25. "How Gopher Win Enthused '03 Players," *Mpls Star Tribune*, 25 October 1953, 36; Sid Hartman, "'Best Minnesota Ever Played for Me,' Says Fesler," *Mpls Star Tribune*, 25 October 1953, 36.

26. Dick Gordon, "Blakley, Martin Carry on Marshall Tradition," *Mpls Star*, 4 September 1957, 53.

27. "1957 Minnesota Golden Gophers Roster," Sports Reference LLC, 2020, https://www.sports-reference.com/cfb/schools/minnesota/1957-roster.html.

28. "University of Minnesota's first Black quarterback, Sandy Stephens," *African American Registry*, last modified 2018.

29. "Agony Instead of Roses in Columbus," *Sports Illustrated*, 11 December 1961, 22.

30. Dan Stoneking, "Sandy & Butch,: two viewpoints," *Mpls Star*, 21 August 1971, 14.

31. "The Golden Leader," BIG Big Ten Conference," 18 February 2008.

32. Paul Rovnak, Assistant Athletic Director, Communications, University of Minnesota, email, 4 April 2020.

Chapter 16

1. Marvin Quinn, "35 Years of Football Not Enough, Marshall Thinks of Comeback," *Mpls Star Tribune*, 14 June 1936, 20.

2. Bill Hengen, "Marshall Now Grid Immortal," *Mpls Star*, 22 March 1971, 24.

3. "The One and Only Bobby Marshall Enters Football's Hall of Fame," *Mpls Spokesman*, 28 October 1971.

4. Joe Hendrickson, "Bobby's Day of Memory," *Mpls Star Tribune*, 31 March 1950, 19.

5. Kathy Washington, Bobby's granddaughter, interviewed, May 30, 2018.

6. Robert Franklin, "A Forgotten Star on the Diamond Regains Luster," *Mpls Star Tribune*, 21 February 2005, B1.

7. Bill Marshall, interviewed July 17, 2018.

8. Bill Marshall, interviewed October 5, 2018.

9. Mark Craig, "Minnesota's forgotten stars," *Mpls Star Tribune*, 26 Jan 2018, C1.

10. Bill Marshall, interviewed April 15, 2018.

11. Ibid.

12. Ibid.

13. Ibid.

14. Ibid.

15. "Sig Harris Looks Back 31 Years; Says Football Better Game Today," *Mpls Star Tribune*, 12 September 1937, 40.

16. Joe Hendrickson, "Bobby Marshall Gets Top Sports Thrill At 61," *Mpls Star*, 28 January 1941, 26.

17. Bill Marshall, interviewed April 15, 2018.

18. Ibid.

19. Ibid.

20. Kathy Washington, interviewed May 30, 2018; Bill Marshall, interviewed November 16, 2018.

21. S. Hoffbeck, "Bobby Marshall: Pioneering African American Athlete," 170.

22. Joe Hendrickson, "Bobby Marshall Gets Top Sports Thrill At 61," *Mpls Star*, 28 January 1941, 26.

23. Bill Marshall, interviewed April 17, 2018.

24. Ibid.

25. Death Certificate of Robert Wells Marshall, Nicollet County, Minnesota, August 27, 1958.

26. Kathy Washington, interviewed May 30, 2018.

27. Todd Peterson, *Early Black Baseball in Minnesota*, 215.

28. Kathy Washington, interviewed May 30, 2018.

29. S. Hoffbeck (ed), *Swinging for the Fences*, 78, 79.

30. Bill Marshall, interviewed April 17, 2018.

31. Ibid.

32. Ibid.

33. Kathy Washington, interviewed May 30, 2018; Bill Marshall, interviewed April 17, 2018.

34. Marcella Mallett, former wife of Bill Marshall, interviewed May 3, 2018.

35. "The Magnificent Bobby Marshall," Vimeo, 2009, https://vimeo.com/4966354.

36. Shaun Hansen, grandson of Bobby Marshall, interviewed by author, December, 2020.

Epilogue

1. Steven Hoffbeck, "Bobby Marshall Pioneering African American Athlete." *Minnesota History* 59, no. 4 (Winter 2004/2005): 171, www.jstor.org/stable/20188454; "20 in Gopher Hall of Fame," *Minneapolis Star Tribune*, (10 September 1991): 3C, https://www.newspapers.com/image/192327698.

2. "FB 'Bronko' Bronko Nagurski," Pro Football Hall of Fame, 2020, https://www.profootballhof.com/players/bronko-nagurski/.

3. Steven Hoffbeck, "Bobby Marshall Pioneering African American Athlete."
   Minnesota History 59, no. 4 (Winter 2004/2005): 171, www.jstor.org/
   stable/20188454.

4. Loren Marshall, great granddaughter of Bobby Marshall, interviewed by the
   author, May 3, 2018.

5. Bill Marshall, grandson of Bobby Marshall, interviewed by the author, April 17,
   2018.

6. "Bob Marshall Is Perennial Star of the Gridiron; Plays at Age of 42," *Minneapolis
   Journal*, 19 December 19 1920, 3 Sports Section; Steven Hoffbeck, "Bobby
   Marshall Pioneering African American Athlete." *Minnesota History* 59, no. 4
   (Winter 2004/2005): 163, www.jstor.org/stable/20188454.

7. Dick Cullum, "Cullum's Column, *Minneapolis Star Tribune*, (12 February 1960):
   18, https://www.newspapers.com/image/183506933/?terms=%22Minneapolis
   %2BMarines%22%2B%22Jim%2BThorpe%22.

8. "Williams and Marshall Honored," *Minneapolis Tribune*, 4 August 1940, 36,
   https://www.newspapers.com/image/181675762.

9. Steven Hoffbeck, "Bobby Marshall Pioneering African American Athlete."
   Minnesota History 59, no. 4 (Winter 2004/2005): 171, www.jstor.org/
   stable/20188454.

10. "The One and Only Bobby Marshall Enters Football's Hall of Fame,"
    Minneapolis Spokesman, 28 October 1971.

11. Kathy Washington, granddaughter of Bobby Marshall, interviewed by the
    author, May 30, 2018; "The One and Only Bobby Marshall Enters Football's
    Hall of Fame," *Minneapolis Spokesman*, 28 October 1971.

12. Patrick Reusse, "Gophers: All Time Eleven," *Minneapolis Star Tribune*, 24 October
    1999, 4C.

13. Jay Weiner, "Millennium Top 100 Sports Figures; 51-100," *Minneapolis Star
    Tribune*, 25 December 1999, 7s.

14. Dick Cullum, "Cullum Picks All-Time Minnesota Grid Team," *Minneapolis
    Star Tribune*, (28 August 1949): 103, https://www.newspapers.com/
    image/181064218/.

15. Steven Hoffbeck, "Bobby Marshall Pioneering African American Athlete."
    Minnesota History 59, no. 4 (Winter 2004/2005): 171, www.jstor.org/
    stable/20188454.

16. "Robert W. Marshall Athlete, Minneapolis," *The Appeal*, (25 October 1913),
    http://chroniclingamerica.loc.gov/lccn/sn83016810/1913-10-25/ed-1/seq-
    10/#date1=1789&index=16&rows=20&words=Bobby+Marshall&searchType=
    basic&sequence=0&state=Illinois&date2=1922&proxtext=%22Bobby+Marsha
    ll%22&y=14&x=8&dateFilterType=yearRange&page=1.

17. Bill Marshall, grandson of Bobby Marshall, interviewed October 6, 2018.

18. Todd Peterson, *Early Black Baseball in Minnesota: The St. Paul Gophers,
    Minneapolis Keystones and other Barnstorming Teams of the Deadball Era*
    (Jefferson NC: McFarland, 2010), 214.

19. Steven Hoffbeck, "Bobby Marshall Pioneering African American Athlete." *Minnesota History* 59, no. 4 (Winter 2004/2005): 172, www.jstor.org/stable/20188454.

20. "Nicollet Ball Park, 3048 Nicollet Avenue, Minneapolis, Minnesota (1896-1955)," *Minnesota Historical Society*, last modified April 28, 2008, http://www.placeography.org/index.php/Nicollet_Ball_Park,_3048_Nicollet_Avenue,_Minneapolis,_Minnesota_%281896-1955%29.

21. Dick Cullum, "Cullum's Column," *Minneapolis Star Tribune*, (29 April 1954): 23,

22. Bill Marshall, interviewed April 17, 2018.

23. Peter Gorton, historian, interviewed by author, November 19, 2019.

Bibliography

NEWSPAPERS

The Appeal (St. Paul)
Atlanta Constitution
Argus-Leader (Sioux Falls, South Dakota)
Austin Daily Herald (Minnesota)
Bemidji Daily Pioneer, (Minnesota)
Boston Globe
Brooklyn Citizen (New York)
Chicago Broad Ax
Chicago Tribune
Daily Mail (United Kingdom)
Detroit Free Press
Daily Times (Davenport Iowa)
Duluth News Tribune (Minnesota)
Evening Times, (Grand Forks, ND)
Grand Forks Herald (North Dakota)
Hibbing Daily News (Minnesota)
Huffington Post
Hutchinson Leader (Minnesota)
Ironwood Daily Globe (Michigan)
Iron River Daily Globe (Michigan)
Minneapolis Journal
Minneapolis Spokesman
Minneapolis Star
Minneapolis Star Tribune
Minneapolis Tribune
Minnesota Daily (University of Minnesota, Minneapolis)
Minnesota Spokesman-Recorder
New Prague Times (Minnesota)
New York Times
Quad City Times (Davenport Iowa)
Rock Island Argus (Illinois)
Toronto Sun
USA Today
Virginia Enterprise (Minnesota)
Washington Post
Winnebago City Press-News (Minnesota)

BOOKS, JOURNALS, PERIODICALS

"Agony Instead of Roses in Columbus." Sports Illustrated. (11 December 1961): 22. https:// www.si.com/vault/1961/12/11/621635

agony-instead-of-roses-in-columbus.

Bergman, Jerry, PhD. "A Brief History of the Eugenics Movement." *Investigator 72*. Last modified May 2000. http://users.adam.com.au/bstett/ BEugenics72Bergman73Potter77.htm.

"Bobby Marshall." M Golden Gophers. 2018. Accessed February 23, 2018. http://www.gophersports.com/genrel/090607abq.html.

Carroll, John M. Fritz Pollard: pioneer in racial advancement. Urbana: U of Illinois Press, 1998.

"Charles Fremont Dight: An Inventory of His Papers at the Minnesota Historical Society." *Minnesota Historical Society*, Manuscripts Collection. Last modified 2015, http://www2.mnhs.org/library/findaids/P1628.xml.

"Current Returns to Foot Ball." *New Elm Review*, September 26, 1906. Accessed September 8, 2016. http://chroniclingamerica.loc.gov/lccn/ sn89081128/190609-26/ed-1/seq-1/.

"Eugenics in Minnesota: Charles Fremont Dight: Overview." Minnesota History Center Gale Family Library. July 14, 2016. Accessed July 26, 2016. http://libguides. mnhs.org/eugenics.

Fitzgerald, F. Scott. *The Great Gatsby*. New York, NY: Scribner, 1925.

Football at Minnesota. Minneapolis, MN: General Alumni Association of the University of Minnesota, 1914.

"Football at Minnesota The Story of Thirty Years' Contests on the Gridiron." *The Minnesota Alumni Weekly*, 11-9-1914, Vol. XIV, No. 9: 46. Historical Society Press (2002): 18.

Foster, Frank. *Breaking the Color Barrier: The Story of the First African American NFL Head Coach, Frederick "Fritz" Pollard*. Middletown, DE: Golgotha Press, INC, 2016.

Golden Gopher Football 1990 Media Guide. Minneapolis MN: University of Minnesota, 1990.

Hatle, Elizabeth Dorsey. *The Ku Klux Klan in Minnesota*. Charleston, SC: The History Press, 2013.

Hoffbeck, Steven. "Bobby Marshall Pioneering African American Athlete." *Minnesota History* 59, no. 4 (Winter 2004/2005): 158-74. www.jstor.org/ stable/20188454.

Hoffbeck, Steven R. *Swinging for the Fences: Black Baseball in Minnesota*. St. Paul: Minnesota Historical Society Press, 2018.

Murphy, Nora, and Mary Murphy-Gnatz. *African Americans in Minnesota: telling our own stories*. St. Paul: Minnesota Historical Society Press, 2000.

"Nicollet Ball Park, 3048 Nicollet Avenue, Minneapolis, Minnesota (1896-1955)." *Minnesota Historical Society*. Last modified April 28, 2008. http:// www.placeography.org/index.php/Nicollet Ball Park, 3048 Nicollet Avenue, Minneapolis, Minnesota %281896-1955%29.

Pappas, Al Jr., *Gophers illustrated: the incredible complete history of Minnesota football/ meticulously researched and drawn by Al Papas, Jr*. Minneapolis Minnesota: University of Minnesota Press, 2009.

Peterson, Robert W. *Pigskin: the Early Years of Pro Football.* New York: OUP USA, 1998.

Peterson, Todd. *Early Black Baseball in Minnesota: The St. Paul Colored Gophers, Minneapolis Keystones and other Barnstorming Teams of the Deadball Era.* Jefferson, N.C.: McFarland, 2010.

Phelps, Gary. "The Eugenics Crusade of Charles Fremont Dight." *Minnesota History* (Fall 1984): 99-108. http://collections.mnhs.org /MNHistoryMagazine/articles/49/v49i03p099-108.pdf.

Reed, Sheldon. "The Minnesota Human Genetics League." *Minnesota Medicine* 39, (November 1956): 748.

Rozendaal, Neal. *Duke Slater: pioneering black NFL player and judge.* Jefferson, NC: McFarland & Company, Inc., 2012.

Shepard, Grace. "Dight Institute to Serve Public." The Minnesota Alumni Weekly (May 16, 1942).

Taylor, David Vassar. *African Americans in Minnesota.* St. Paul, MN: Minnesota Historical Society Press, 2002.

Tischauser, Leslie V. Landmarks of the American Mosaic Jim Crow Laws. Santa Barbara CA: Greenwood, an imprint of ABC Clio LLC. 2012.

"University of Minnesota. Dight Institute of Human Genetics." *Social Networks and Archival Content, Andrew W. Mellon Foundation, Institute of Museum and Library Services, National Endowment for the Humanities.* http://snaccooperative.org/ark:/99166/w62c4cwz.

ELECTRONIC WEBSITES AND ARTICLES

"1905 Golden Gophers Schedule and Results." Sports Reference LLC. Last modified 2018. https://www.sports-reference.com/cfb/schools/minnesota/1905-schedule.html.

"1920 Akron Pros Schedule and Game Results," "1920 Rock Island Independents Schedule and Game Results." Pro Football Reference. Last modified 2017. http://www.pro-football-reference.com/teams/akr/1920_games.htm.

"1920 Rock Island Independents (APFA,)"." Pro Football Archives. Last modified 2018. http://www.profootballarchives.com/1920apfari.html.

"1920 Rock Island Independents Game Log." Pro Football Reference. Last modified 2018. https://www.pro-football-reference.com/teams/rii/1920/gamelog/.

"1920 Rock Island Independents Starters, Roster & Players." Pro Football Reference. Last modified 2018. https://www.pro-football-reference.com/teams/rii/1920_roster.htm.

"1957 Minnesota Golden Gophers." Sports Reference LLC. Last modified 2018. https://www.sports-reference.com/cfb/schools/minnesota/1957-roster.html.

"African-Americans in Big Ten Football- Minnesota." Ohio State Black Alumni Society. https://alumnigroups.osu.edu/blacksociety/wp-content/uploads/sites/155/2016/04/African-Americans-Big-Ten-Football-OSU.pdf.

Anastopoulo, Rossi. "Meet Fritz Pollard." Last modified November 25, 2012.http://

www.sportsinblackandwhite.com/2012/11/25/meet-fritz-pollard/.

Bell, Daryl. "The NHL's first black player, Willie O'Ree, had a short but pathbreaking stint with the Boston Bruins." ESPN. Last modified February 14, 2017. https://theundefeated.com/features/nhl-first-black-player-willie-oree/.

Bennett, Byron. "Chicago's West Side Grounds- Where the Cubs Last Won the World Series." deadballbaseball.com. Last modified 2016. http://deadballbaseball.com/?p=2358.

"Biggie Munn. Sports Reference. Last modified 2018. https://www.sports-reference.com/cfb/coaches/biggie-munn-1.html.

"Black Sporting Experience at Dartmouth." Last modified January 22, 2013. http://sites.dartmouth.edu/blacksportingexperience/matthew-bullock-04/.

"Bobby Marshall." Datab.us. Accessed February 25, 2018. http://datab.us/i/Bobby Marshall.

"Bobby Marshall." M Golden Gophers. Last modified 2018. http://www.gophersports.com/genrel/090607abq.html.

"Bobby Marshall, A Minnesota Icon." African American Registry. Last modified 2018. https://aaregistry.org/story/bobby-marshall-a-minnesota icon/.

"Cap's Great Shame." "The Lfe and Times of Adrian "Cap" Anson. Accessed April 22, 2016. http://www.capanson.com/chapter4.html.

"Curly Lambeau Athlete, Coach, Football Player (1898-1965.)" Biography. Last modified 2018. https://www.biography.com/people/curly-lambeau-21224337.

Dow, Bill. "Willie Who? Willie Heston, U. of M.'s First Football Star." Last modified September 25, 2010. https://www.detroitathletic.com/blog/2010/09/25/willie-who-willie-heston-u-of-m%E2%80%99s-first-football-star/.

"Drop It Like Its Hot." Pro Football Hall of Fame. Last modified December 6, 2015. https://www.profootballhof.com/the-last-dropkick/.

"Fleet Walker." Baseball Reference. Last modified 2000-2018. https://www.baseball-reference.com/players/w/walkefl01.shtml.

"Flutie converts first drop kick since 1941 championship." ESPN.com news services. Last modified Jan 2, 2006. http://www.espn.com/nfl/news/story?id=2277308.

Fouts, Chuck. "Chicago baseball legend Cap Anson should not be in the Hall Of Fame." ChicagoNow. Last modified March 19, 2014. http://www.chicagonow.com/chicago-sports-heroes-then-now/2014/03.

"Fritz Crisler." Sports Reference. Last modified 2018. https://www.sports-reference.com/cfb/coaches/fritz-crisler-1.html.

"Golden Gophers Year By Year Records." University of Minnesota Official Web Site. Last modified 2018. http://www.gophersports.com sports/m-footbl/specrel/yearly-records.html.

"The Golden Leader." Big Ten Conference. Last modified February 18, 2008.

http://www.bigten.org/genrel/021808aab.html.

Head, Tom. "The Klu Klux Klan: A Short Timeline History." Last modified 2016. http://civilliberty.about.com/od/hisabout news toryprofiles/tp/ History Ku-Klux-Klan-KKK.htm.

Herrera, Simon. Independents Use All Star Team to Get Back on Track." Last modified December 5, 2016. http://www.rockislandindependents.com.

"History of the Forward Pass." The Biletnikoff Award. Last modified 2012https://biletnikoffaward.com/.

Howard, Greg. "A Ban on Black Players Cost the NFL Its Most Exciting Quarterback." Deadspin. Last modified February 19, 2014. https://deadspin.com/the-big-book-of-black-quarterbac ks-1517763742/1526239170.

"Introduction to Genetics." Genetics Generation. Last modified 2015. http:// knowgenetics.org/history-of-eugenics/.

"Jack Johnson Biography." Biography. Last modified 2016. http://www. biography.com/people/jack-johnson-9355980#rise-to-champion.

"Jackie Robinson." United States History. Last modified 2018. https://www.u-s-history.com/pages/h2068.html.

"Jesse Owens A Lasting Legend." The Ohio State University. Last modified 2010. https://library.osu.edu/projects/jesse-owens/story_ohiostate.html.

"Harris, Sig," Jews in Sports, http://www.jewsinsports.org/profile. asp?sport=football&ID=9.

"History." Phyllis Wheatley Community Center. Last modified 2016. http:// phylliswheatley.org/history/.

Klein, Christopher. "The Birth of the National Football League." HISTORY IN THE HEADLINES (/NEWS). Last modified September 4, 2014. http:// www.history.com/news/the-birth-of-the-national-football league.

"Knockout." Unforgivable Blackness. Last modified 2005. http://www.pbs.org/ unforgivableblackness/knockout/.

Mancuso, Peter. "July 14, 1887: The color line is drawn." Society for American Baseball Research, Last modified 2013. http://sabr.org/gamesproj/game/ july-14-1887-color-line-drawn.

Matthews, Dylan. "Woodrow Wilson was extremely racist-even by the standards of his time." Vox. Last modified November 20, 2015. https://www.vox. com/policy-and politics/2015/11/20/9766896/woodrow-wilsonracist.

"Michigan Minnesota The Little Brown Jug Series." Last modified June 7, 2009. http://www.mgoblue.com/sports/m-footbl/spec-rel/061709aaa.html.

"Milwaukee, Wisconsin 1880s." Google Images. Accessed April 22, 2016.

"Mine Shafts of Michigan." Michigan Technology University. Last modified 2015. http://www.mg.mtu.edu/MINE_SHAFTS/shaft3.htm.

"Negro League Baseball." A&E Televison Networks, LLC. Last modified 2018. https://www.history.com/topics/negro-league-baseball.

"Oldest Living Pro Football Players." Pro Football's Online Encyclopedia.

Last modified January 20, 2016. http://www.oldestlivingfootball.com/
robertwbobbymarshall.htm.

"The Philippine-American War." Boundless.com. Last modified July 15,
2016. www.boundless.com/u-s-history/textbooks/boundless- u-s-history-
textbook/the-gilded-age-1870-1900-20/american-imperialism- 164/
the-philippine-american-war-903-3411/.

Quirk, Jim. "The Minneapolis Marines: Minnesota's Forgotten NFL Team."
The Coffin Corner 20, no. 1 (1998): 1-3. www.profootballresearchers.org/
archives/Website_Files/Coffin.../20-01-732.pdf.

Reed, Christopher R. "A century of civics and politics: the Afro Americans
of Chicago." Last modified July, 1987. http://www.lib.niu.edu/1987/
ii870732.html.

Rosengren, John. "A Football Martyr." SB Nation. Last modified November
25, 2014. https://www.sbnation.com/longform/2014/11/25/7275681/
jack-trice-iowa-state-football-profile

Rozendaal, Neal. "African-Americans in Big Ten Football, 1890-1963." Last
modified February 26, 2013. http://nealrozendaal.com/2013/02/26/
african-americans-in-big-ten-football-1890-1963/.

Rozendaal, Neal. "African-Americans in Pro Football, 1897-1946." NEAL
ROZENDAAL. Last modified February 15, 2013. http://nealrozendaal.
com/2013/02/15/african-americans-in-pro-football-1897-1946/.

Sandager, David. "When the NFL came to Duluth: the Story of the Eskimos."
the Growler, Last modified November 22, 2016. https://growlermag.com/
when-the-nfl-came-to-duluth-the-story-of-the-eskimos/.

"Segregated Student Housing and the Activists Who Defeated It," A Campus
Divided Essays, University of Minnesota, last modified 2017, http://
acampusdivided.umn.edu/index.php/essay/segregated-student-housing/.

"Sports Football: Rules." Ducksters Education Site. Last modified 2017. https://
www.ducksters.com/sports/footballrules.php.

"Sports Scholarships: A Look Back at History." Sportscholarship.
com. Last modified 2016. http://sportsscholarship.com/about/
history-of-sports-scholarships/.

"...Standings." Sports Reference LLC, Last modified 2018. www.pro-football-
reference.com/years/1924/index.htm.

"This Day in History: April 15"." A and E Networks. Last
modified 2017. http://www.history.com/this-day-in-history/
jackie-robinson-breaks-major-league-color-barrier.

"Thomas Dixon Jr., Segregationist and." African American Registry. Last
modified 2018. http://www.aaregistry.org/historic_events/view/thomas-
dixon-jr-segregationist-and author.

Thornley, Stew. "Nicollet Park." Last modified 2017. http://stewthornley.net/
nicollet_park.html.

"Top 10 Oldest NFL Stadiums Still in Use." TheRichest. Last modified 2018.

https://www.therichest.com/sports/football-sports/top-10-oldest-nfl stadiums still-in use/.

"Unforgivable Blackness." a film directed by Ken Burns. WETA. Last modified January 11, 2005. https://www.pbs.org/unforgivableblackness/knockout/women.html.

"University of Minnesota's first Black quarterback, Sandy Stephens." African American Registry. Last modified 2018. https://aaregistry.org/story/university-of-minnesotas-first-black-quarterback-sandy-stephens/.

Westhoff, Ben. "Eugenics & Me: How a Hitler fan paid my mother's college tuition and sent me down a rabbit hole." Last modified May 10, 2017. http://www.citypages.com/news eugenics-me-how-a-hitler-fan-paid-my-mothers- college-tuition-and-sent-me-down-a-rabbit-hole/421797153.

"'The White Man's Burden': Kipling's Hymn to U.S. Imperialism." American Social History Productions, Inc. Last modified August 8, 2016. http://historymatters.gmu.edu/d/5478/.

"Who Was 'Pudge?.'" Pro Football Hall of Fame. Last modified November 12, 2012. https://www.profootballhof.com/news/who-was-pudge/.

Williams, Chad. "African Americans and World War I." Africana Age. Last modified 2011. http://exhibitions.nypl.org/africanaage/essay-world-war-i.html.

"Year By Year Records, 1904." M Football. Last modified 2018. https://gophersports.com/schedule.aspx?path=football.

York, Randy. "The Legends of George Flippin Four More." Last modified 2016. http://www.huskers.com/ViewArticle.dbml?DB_OEM_ID=100&ATCLID=209377145.

INTERVIEWS

Bill Marshall. Interviewed by author, thirteen times between April 15, 2017 and March 4, 2019;

Marshall, Loren. Interview by author. May 3, 2018.

Marshall, Marcella. Interview by author. May 3, 2018.

Washington, Kathy. Interview by author. May 30, 2018.

PUBLIC RECORDS

Death Certificate of Robert Wells Marshall, Nicollet County, Minnesota, August 27, 1958. Microfilm Room, St. Paul. Minnesota History Center.

Hennepin County, Minnesota, Minnesota Official Marriage System (MOMS), Hennepin County Vital Records, Hennepin County, MN, v. 197:290, marriage of Robert W. Marshall and Irene B. Knott, 1916; SAM microfilm 447 microfilm reel 50, Minnesota Historical Society Hubbs Microfilm Room, St. Paul.

Index

ABOUT THE AUTHOR

Terry McConnell has been a secondary school educator for forty years, serving as a social studies teacher, school librarian, track and cross-country coach, tennis coach, video production teacher, and special education worker. He now serves as a breath instructor with his wife, Carol, teaching a course at Fitchburg State University in Fitchburg, MA, the nearby Greenfield YMCA, and in private practice. He is currently pursing a Masters Degree to become a certified clinical exercise physiologist at Springfield College in Springfield, MA. Terry and Carol have four children and eight grandchildren between them. Terry's grandfather, O.C. Olsen, was the general manager of the Minneapolis Deans pro football team from 1907 to 1909. Olsen gave Bobby Marshall his start in pro football.

Terry can be contacted at runnerwithasthma@gmail.com.

———————————

A percentage of the proceeds from this book will go to the Bobby Marshall Scholarship Fund for student athletes showing academic excellence and leadership skills at the University of Minnesota. To contribute to this tax-deductible fund, make check payable to the University of Minnesota Foundation, P.O. Box 860266, Minneapolis, MN 55486-0266 or at University of Minnesota Foundation website *give.umn.edu*. Search "Bobby Marshall" and then, under "Find a cause to support," select the first item, titled "Bobby Marshall Scholarship." The website will then direct you to make a gift to that fund.

Made in the USA
Middletown, DE
01 March 2022